GOSPEL

2004

Daily Gospel 2004

Copyright © 2003 by Claretian Publications. A division of Claretian Communications, Inc. U.P. P.O. Box 4 Diliman, 1101 Quezon City, Philippines
Tel.: (632) 921-3984 • Fax: (632) 921-7429
Email: cci@claret.org
Website: www.bible.claret.org

The **Daily Gospel**® is a pastoral endeavor of the Claretian Missionaries in the Philippines. It aims to promote a renewed spirituality rooted in the process of total liberation and solidarity in response to the needs, challenges and pastoral demands of the Church today.

Commentaries by: Fr. Donagh O'Shea, OP
Original Design: Juan Soler
Lay-out by: Fr. Fernando Torres, CMF
Artworks by: Maria Delia C. Zamora-Crosby

Biblical texts are taken from *Christian Community Bible, Catholic Pastoral Edition*.

Distributed in U.S.A. by **PBF International**
2500 Wilshire Blvd., Suite 910
Los Angeles, CA 90057
Tel.: 888-989-4528 • Fax: 213-387-7860
E-mail: pbf@claret.org
Website:www.wannagetaway.com

ISBN 971-501-302-3

PRESENTATION

There are countless new methods today for analyzing the self and searching for our deepest identity. Many of these have proved very fruitful, and it is by their fruits that we know them. A wise woman described them as "ways to the Way." While we Christians can learn from them all and be helped by them, the words of Jesus remain central for us: "I am the way and the truth and the life" (Jn 14:6).

For six years now the **Daily Gospel** has been putting the Word of God before us on a daily basis. This Word is "alive and active, sharper than any two-edged sword, piercing until it divides the soul from the spirit, the joint from the marrow. It is able to judge the thoughts and intentions of the heart" (Heb 4:12). These are terrifying words. But the Word of God is not a word that destroys; it is a word that builds up. It does not shine a pitiless light into our inner anguished world, our miseries and defeats; it is the hand of God's compassion reaching out to save us. It is "a lamp shining in a dark place" (2P 1:19). Jesus is himself the Word, and he is truly present to us when we read the Scriptures with an open mind and heart. We pray that this **Daily Gospel** will help you to live each day with Jesus.

Maria Delia C. Zamora-Crosby

DAILY
GOSPEL
2004

MARY, MOTHER OF GOD

World Day of Peace

Num 6:22-27   Gal 4:4-7   Lk 2:16-21

We begin this new year, as always, in the company of Mary, whose title, "Mother of God," affirms equally the humanity and the divinity of Christ (see September 8). Who else is with us? Shepherds, a carpenter, a baby put to sleep in an animal's feeding trough…. It's a humble beginning. There are no world leaders, no ambassadors, no retinue. There is no palace, nor ceremony, nor fancy dress. There is no cheering crowd, no press. There are no scholars to analyze its meaning. But far away and out of earshot of the powerful and the wise there is a rumor of angels. Only the shepherds, the simple of heart, can hear it.

The shepherds came hurriedly and found Mary and Joseph with the baby lying in the manger. On seeing this they related what they had been told about the child, and all were astonished on hearing the shepherds.

As for Mary, she treasured all these messages and continually pondered over them.

The shepherds then returned giving glory and praise to God for all they had heard and seen, just as the angels had told them.

On the eighth day the circumcision of the baby had to be performed; he was named Jesus, the name the angel had given him before he was conceived.

Friday

2

"Who are you?" "How do you see yourself?" These are questions we ask one another to this day. But today we ask these questions especially of ourselves. "Who am I?" "How do I see myself?" In our complex world these are not trivial questions. Many look at you and don't want to know who you are; they see only the identity they would like to impose on you. "Among you stands one whom you do not know." We do not know him because we cannot get away with imposing an identity on him—though we try all the time. Jesus the Catholic, Jesus the Protestant, Jesus the Baptist.... Yes, John, we too are unworthy to untie the strap of his sandals.

This was the testimony of John when the Jews sent priests and Levites to ask him, "Who are you?" John recognized the truth and did not deny it. He said, "I am not the Messiah."

And they asked him, "Then who are you? Elijah?" He answered, "I am not." They said, "Are you the Prophet?" And he answered, "No." Then they said to him, "Tell us who you are, so that we can give some answer to those who sent us. How do you see yourself?" And John said, quoting the prophet Isaiah, "I am the voice crying out in the wilderness: Make straight the way of the Lord."

Those who had been sent were Pharisees; so they put a further question to John: "Then why are you baptizing if you are not the Messiah, or Elijah, or the Prophet?" John answered, "I baptize you with water, but among you stands one whom you do not know; although he comes after me, I am not worthy to untie the strap of his sandal."

This happened in Bethabara beyond the Jordan, where John was baptizing.

The Holy Name of Jesus

1Jn 2:29–3:6   Jn 1:29-34

Jesus is called "lamb of God" more than thirty times in the New Testament. The title has overtones of the Jewish annual Passover feast, when a yearling lamb was killed and eaten. It is an enduring image of Jesus. A lamb is a figure of innocence. "Like a lamb that is led to the slaughter-house, like a sheep that is dumb before its shearers, never opening its mouth" (Is 53:7). Sheep, let alone lambs, have no real means of self-defense. Before they were domesticated they could defend themselves by climbing to inaccessible places in the mountains, but since they came among us they are particularly at our mercy. One could say the same about the Lamb of God....

When John saw Jesus coming towards him, he said, "There is the Lamb of God, who takes away the sin of the world. It is he of whom I said: A man comes after me who is already ahead of me, for he was before me. I myself did not know him, but I came baptizing to prepare for him, so that he might be revealed in Israel."

And John also gave this testimony, "I saw the Spirit coming down on him like a dove from heaven and resting on him. I myself did not know him but God who sent me to baptize told me: 'You will see the Spirit coming down and resting on the one who baptizes with the Holy Spirit.' Yes, I have seen! and I declare that this is the Chosen One of God."

Sunday

Notice one sentence of today's reading. "From you, Bethlehem, will come a leader, the one who is to shepherd my people Israel." Yesterday we saw Jesus as a lamb, today we see him as a shepherd. How can he be both? He is both. Like God whose throne he shares, he is "the Alpha and Omega, the beginning and the end " (Rev 1:8; 21:6; 22:13). The ecstatic poet Rumi wrote: "I am the candle and the moth that circles around it, / The rose and the rose-drunk nightingale." Jesus will continue forever to appear to us in new lights. He is not two-dimensional like our ideas, he is alive. It is forever the feast of Epiphany.

EPIPHANY OF THE LORD 4

Is 60:1-6

Arise, shine, for your light has come. The Glory of Yahweh rises upon you. Night still covers the earth and gloomy clouds veil the peoples, but Yahweh now rises and over you his glory appears. Nations will come to your light and kings to the brightness of your dawn. Lift up your eyes round about and see: they are all gathered and come to you, your sons from afar, your daughters tenderly carried. This sight will make your face radiant, your heart throbbing and full; the riches of the sea will be turned to you, the wealth of the nations will come to you. A flood of camels will cover you, caravans from Midian and Ephah. Those from Sheba will come, bringing with them gold and incense, all singing in praise of Yahweh.

Eph 3:2-3.5-6
Mt 2:1-12

When Jesus was born in Bethlehem, in Judea, during the days of King Herod, wise men from the east arrived in Jerusalem. They asked, "Where is the newborn king of the Jews? We saw the rising of his star in the east and have come to honor him." When Herod heard this he was greatly disturbed and with him all Jerusalem. He immediately called a meeting of all high-ranking priests and the scribes asked them where the Messiah was to be born. "In the town of Bethlehem in Judea," they told him, "for this is what the prophet wrote: And you, Bethlehem, in the land of Judah, you are by no means the least among the clans of Judah, for from you will come a leader, the one who is to shepherd my people Israel." Then Herod secretly called the wise men and asked them the precise time the star appeared. Then he sent them to Bethlehem with the instruction, "Go and get precise information about the child. As soon as you have found him, report to me, so that I too may go and honor him."

After the meeting with the king, they set out. The star that they had seen in the East went ahead of them and stopped over the place where the child was. The wise men were overjoyed on seeing the star again. They went into the house and when they saw the child with Mary his mother, they knelt and worshiped him. They opened their bags and offered him their gifts of gold, incense and myrrh. In a dream they were warned not to go back to Herod, so they returned to their home country by another way.

1Jn 3:22—4:6   Mt 4:12-17,23-25

Jesus leaves his hometown, never to live there again. That this decision was due to his experience of rejection at Nazareth (Lk 4:30,31). It is clear, however, that he was not embittered by this. Bitter people like to proclaim bad news. But he "went around all Galilee… proclaiming the good news of the Kingdom." It was their loss. There is no bitterness like small-town bitterness. But those townspeople could not infect him with their bitterness; it was they who remained bitter. Yet they were able to rob him of some of his power. "He could work no miracle there" (Mk 6:5). Not only Nazarenes but all of us have the power to poison the well of life and to stop miracles from happening perhaps even in our family.

When Jesus heard that John had been arrested, he withdrew into Galilee. He left Nazareth and went to settle down in Capernaum, a town by the lake of Galilee, at the border of Zebulun and Naphtali.

In this way the word of the prophet Isaiah was fulfilled: Land of Zebulun and land of Naphtali crossed by the Road of the Sea, and you who live by the Jordan, Galilee, land of pagans, listen: The people who lived in darkness have seen a great light; on those who live in the land of the shadow of death, a light has shone.

From that time on Jesus began to proclaim his message, "Change your ways: the kingdom of heaven is near."

Jesus went around all Galilee, teaching in their synagogues, proclaiming the good news of the Kingdom, and curing all kinds of sickness and disease among the people. The news about him spread through the whole of Syria, and the people brought all their sick to him, and all those who suffered: the possessed, the deranged, the paralyzed, and he healed them all. Large crowds followed him from Galilee and the Ten Cities, from Jerusalem, Judea, and from across the Jordan.

Bl. André Bessette

1Jn 4:7-10   Mk 6:34-44

As Jesus went ashore he saw a large crowd, and he had compassion on them for they were like sheep without a shepherd. And he began a long teaching session with them.

It was now getting late, so his disciples came to him and said, "This is a lonely place and it is now late. You should send the people away and let them go to the farms and villages around here to buy themselves something to eat."

Jesus replied, "You yourselves give them something to eat." They answered, "If we are to give them food, we must go and buy two hundred silver coins' worth of bread." But Jesus said, "You have some loaves: how many? Go and see." The disciples found out and said, "There are five loaves and two fish."

Then he told them to have the people sit down together in groups on the green grass. This they did in groups of hundreds and fifties. And Jesus took the five loaves and the two fish and, raising his eyes to heaven, he pronounced a blessing, broke the loaves and handed them to his disciples to distribute to the people. He also divided the two fish among them.

They all ate and everyone had enough. The disciples gathered up what was left and filled twelve baskets with broken pieces of bread and fish. Five thousand men had eaten there.

When someone is complaining, a friend of mine always says things like, "Why don't you fix it yourself?" The effect is like that of turning off a faucet: it stops all complaints instantly! His kind of language is real and practical, "Do it!" "Go and see the place yourself!" "Talk to him!" Jesus said, "You yourselves give them something to eat!" And when they began to do it, they found that it worked. Another time he said to a man who had been lying there for thirty-eight years, "Get up!" And when he went to get up he found he could! There are probably miracles everywhere just ready to pop, if only we would do the thing instead of talking about it.

AFTER EPIPHANY

St. Raymond of Peñafort

1Jn 4:11-18   Mk 6:45-52

All the details are so realistic, so workaday. Then suddenly the realism is shattered: he comes to them walking on the water. A strange irruption into the life of common sense. But it is no ghost, it is their familiar friend. Mark says, "their minds were closed." With this strong expression Mark likes to emphasize how little Jesus was understood. There is another symbolic meaning lost to us. The Jews at that time feared the sea, believing that at the bottom of it lurked Leviathan, the monster of chaos. The significance of Jesus' walking on the water then is that he has conquered evil.

Jesus obliged his disciples to get into the boat and go ahead of him to the other side, towards Bethsaida, while he himself sent the crowd away. And having sent the people off, he went by himself to the hillside to pray.

When evening came, the boat was far out on the lake while he was alone on the land. Jesus saw his disciples straining at the oars, for the wind was against them, and before daybreak he came to them walking on the lake; and he was going to pass them by.

When they saw him walking on the lake, they thought it was a ghost and cried out; for they all saw him and were terrified. But at once he called to them, "Courage! It's me; don't be afraid." Then Jesus got into the boat with them and the wind died down. They were completely aston-ished, for they had not really grasped the fact of the loaves; their minds were dull.

1Jn 4:19–5:4   Lk 4:14-22

Jesus acted with the power of the Spirit, and on his return to Galilee the news about him spread throughout all that territory. He began teaching in the synagogues of the Jews and everyone praised him.

When Jesus came to Nazareth where he had been brought up, he entered the synagogue on the Sabbath as he usually did. He stood up to read and they handed him the book of the prophet Isaiah.

Jesus then unrolled the scroll and found the place where it is written: "The Spirit of the Lord is upon me. He has anointed me to bring good news to the poor, to proclaim liberty to captives and new sight to the blind; to free the oppressed and announce the Lord's year of mercy."

Jesus then rolled up the scroll, gave it to the attendant and sat down, while the eyes of all in the synagogue were fixed on him. Then he said to them, "Today these prophetic words come true even as you listen."

All agreed with him and were lost in wonder, while he kept on speaking of the grace of God. Nevertheless they asked, "Who is this but Joseph's son?"

Jesus stood up in the synagogue and read from the book of Isaiah. There is silence as Jesus finishes. "The eyes of all in the synagogue were fixed on him." Into that dramatic moment he spoke the words, "Today these words come true even as you listen." Not some time in the future, not in eternity, but today. A zen master had spoken for an hour on the power of the present moment, the Now. At the end, someone said, "I like your concept of the Now!" The zen master reacted almost as if he had been struck. "It is not a concept!" 'Now' is reality." Good news to the poor and freedom to the oppressed is to be a reality today.

1Jn 5:5-13   Lk 5:12-16

"He doesn't have a single unpublished thought!" someone said about a writer. There is a kind of exhibitionism that is quickly recognized. An exhibitionist may seem very community-oriented, but he is just the opposite. He is contributing nothing, he just wants to see his own image reflected in people's eyes. Many people like "Jesus Christ Superstar," but it makes Jesus appear as just a media star who got out of his depth. Every passing age, I suppose, sees Jesus in its own terms, and ours is the age of media entertainment. It is striking then to read that Jesus said to the leper he had just healed, "Tell this to no one." And that "he would often withdraw to solitary places and pray."

One day in another town, a man came to Jesus covered with leprosy. On seeing him he bowed down to the ground, and said, "Lord, if you want to, you can make me clean."

Stretching out his hand, Jesus touched the man and said, "Yes, I want it. Be clean." In an instant the leprosy left him. Then Jesus instructed him, "Tell this to no one. But go and show yourself to the priest. Make an offering for your healing, as Moses prescribed; that should be a proof to the people."

But the news about Jesus spread all the more, and large crowds came to him to listen and be healed of their sickness. As for Jesus, he would often withdraw to solitary places and pray.

1Jn 5:14-21   Jn 3:22-30

When fifteen of us presented ourselves for entry into the Dominican order many years ago, naturally they asked us why we wanted to take such a step. One of my companions, slightly more naïve than the rest, replied that he didn't want to be a preacher. He hadn't realized then that OP stands for Order of Preachers! The humanity of it is that they only smiled and told him he was welcome. I remember it when I read today's gospel passage. "No one can take on anything except what has been given him from heaven." Our own agendas are mostly maps for a low horizon, for who can know the future? God has more in store for us than we dare imagine.

Jesus went into the territory of Judea with his disciples. He stayed there with them and baptized. John was also baptizing in Aenon near Salim where water was plentiful; people came to him and were baptized. This happened before John was put in prison.

Now John's disciples had been questioned by a Jew about spiritual cleansing, so they came to him and said, "Rabbi, the one who was with you across the Jordan, and about whom you spoke favorably, is now baptizing and all are going to him."

John answered, "No one can take on anything except what has been given him from heaven. You yourselves are my witnesses that I said: 'I am not the Christ but I have been sent before him.' Only the bridegroom has the bride; but the friend of the bridegroom stands by and listens, and rejoices to hear the bridegroom's voice. My joy is now full. It is necessary that he increase but that I decrease."

Sunday

How do you recognize John the Baptist in Christian art? He's the scruffy one—even though it's a scruffiness made genteel by generations of artists. He came from the desert, where "he wore a garment made of camel-hair...and his food was locusts and wild honey" (Mt 3:4). His message was equally rough: he didn't begin, "My dear brothers and sisters..."; he began, "Brood of vipers...!" (Lk 3:7). John's cousin too came from the desert, but his attitude was so different. Looking at the crowd "he felt sorry for them because they were like sheep without a shepherd" (Mt 9:36). It is because he believes in us that we are able to believe in him.

BAPTISM OF THE LORD   11

Is 40:1-5,9-11
Be comforted, my people, be strengthened, says your God. Speak to the heart of Jerusalem, proclaim to her that her time of bondage is at an end, that her guilt has been paid for, that from the hand of Yahweh she has received double punishment for all her iniquity. A voice cries, "In the wilderness prepare the way for Yahweh. Make straight in the desert a highway for our God. Every valley will be raised up; every mountain and hill will be laid low. The stumbling blocks shall become level and the rugged places smooth. The glory of Yahweh will be revealed, and all mortals together will see it; for the mouth of Yahweh has spoken." (...)

Tit 2:11-14;3:4-7
For the grace of God has appeared, bringing salvation to all, teaching us to reject an irreligious way of life and worldly greed, and to live in this world as responsible persons, upright and serving God, while we await our blessed hope-the glorious manifestation of our great God and Savior Christ Jesus. He gave himself for us, to redeem us from every evil and to purify a people he wanted to be his own and dedicated to what is good. But God our Savior revealed his eminent goodness and love for humankind and saved us, not because of good deeds we may have done but for the sake of his own mercy, to the water of rebirth and renewal by the Holy Spirit poured over us through Christ Jesus our Savior, so that having been justified by his grace we should become heirs in hope of eternal life.

Lk 3:15-16,21-22
The people were wondering about John's identity, "Could he be the Messiah?" Then John answered them, "I baptize you with water, but the one who is coming will do much more: he will baptize you with Holy Spirit and fire. As for me, I am not worthy to untie his sandal." Now, with all the people who came to be baptized, Jesus too was baptized. Then, while he was praying, the heavens opened: the Holy Spirit came down upon him in the bodily form of a dove and a voice from heaven was heard, "You are my Son, this day I have begotten you."

The gospels are not better described as booklets. Mark's is the shortest. That means that all the content is compressed. When he says in today's reading, "Jesus...saw Simon and his brother...and said to them, 'Follow me,' and at once they left their nets and followed him," this owes much to Mark's style of writing. Likewise when "he saw James and John...and immediately called them and they followed," this is more quickly said than done. But we have plenty of time, we can dwell on it and see everything with hindsight. When we are confused we can take time to sit down by the lake (or indeed anywhere) and enter into deep conversation with him, listening to his deep mind and great heart.

After John was arrested, Jesus went into Galilee and began preaching the Good News of God. He said, "The time has come; the kingdom of God is at hand. Change your ways and believe the Good News."

As Jesus was walking along the shore of Lake Galilee, he saw Simon and his brother Andrew casting a net in the lake, for they were fishermen. And Jesus said to them, "Follow me, and I will make you fish for people." At once, they abandoned their nets and followed him. Jesus went a little farther on and saw James and John, the sons of Zebedee; they were in their boat mending their nets. Immediately, Jesus called them and they followed him, leaving their father Zebedee in the boat with the hired men.

1S 1:9-20   **Mk 1:21-28**

I pity the man who had to preach in that synagogue on the following Saturday! I know how it feels: I have often had to speak after great people had finished. You feel about the size of a mouse, and very uninspired. In today's reading Mark says twice that Jesus spoke "with authority." "Not like their scribes," he added. These loved to quote; everything they said was second-hand, but Jesus was himself the source of what he said and did. Only once in the gospels did he give the expected reply: when the rich man asked him what he must do to gain eternal life, Jesus told him to keep the commandments. But immediately he drew him further on and challenged him to a new way of life.

Jesus and his disciples went into the town of Capernaum and began to teach in the synagogue during the Sabbath assemblies. The people were astonished at the way he taught, for he spoke as one having authority and not like the teachers of the Law.

It happened that a man with an evil spirit was in their synagogue and he shouted, "What do you want with us, Jesus of Nazareth? Have you come to destroy us? I know who you are: You are the Holy One of God." Then Jesus faced him and said with authority, "Be silent and come out of this man!" The evil spirit shook the man violently and, with a loud shriek, came out of him.

All the people were astonished and they wondered, "What is this? With what authority he preaches! He even orders evil spirits and they obey him!" And Jesus' fame spread throughout all the country of Galilee.

1S 3:1-10,19-20   Mk 1:29-39

When they told him everyone was looking for him he said, "Let's go somewhere else." There is a wrong kind of fame. Many people do everything they can to be famous, and some even resort to criminal acts. But on a smaller scale we all want to have our existence noted by at least a few people. Anyone who can live even for a while in a desert must have (or must develop) a powerful sense of their own existence. More profoundly they discover that their existence is not just a dull fact but a mysterious activity welling up from God moment by moment. All of us can discover it in a moment of solitude.

As soon as Jesus and his disciples left the synagogue, Jesus went to the home of Simon and Andrew with James and John. As Simon's mother-in-law was sick in bed with fever, they immediately told him about her. Jesus went to her and taking her by the hand, raised her up. The fever left her and she began to wait on them. That evening at sundown, people brought to Jesus all the sick and those who had evil spirits: the whole town was pressing around the door. Jesus healed many who had various diseases, and drove out many demons; but he did not let them speak, for they knew who he was.

Very early in the morning, before daylight, Jesus went off to a lonely place where he prayed. Simon and the others went out, too, searching for him; and when they found him they said, "Everyone is looking for you." Then Jesus answered, "Let's go to the nearby villages so that I may preach there too; for that is why I came."

So Jesus set out to preach in all the synagogues throughout Galilee; he also cast out demons.

1S 4:1-11   Mk 1:40-45

I've often heard people say, "I felt like a leper!" No need to look at their skin, though, or to count their fingers; what they are saying is that they felt isolated or completely discredited. In that sense the world is still full of lepers. There are lepers in every parish and there may even be a leper or two in one's own house. What can you do for someone who feels isolated but to reach out and touch them? You are more than just you when you do that: you are society, you are community, you are the Church, you are the human race. One may even say you are Jesus. "Moved with pity, Jesus stretched out his hand and touched him."

A leper came to Jesus and begged him, "If you so will, you can make me clean." Moved with pity, Jesus stretched out his hand and touched him, saying, "I will; be clean." The leprosy left the man at once and he was made clean. As Jesus sent the man away, he sternly warned him, "Don't tell anyone about this, but go and show yourself to the priest and for the cleansing bring the offering ordered by Moses; in this way you will make your declaration."

However, as soon as the man went out, he began spreading the news everywhere, so that Jesus could no longer openly enter any town. But even though he stayed in the rural areas, people came to him from everywhere.

1S 8:4-7,10-22   Mk 2:1-12

The Japanese zen master Deshimaru said that western culture had become weak and decadent. We have been weakened, he said, by excessive use of the mind and imagination, without action. Of course we are active, but it is nervous activism, which can be a flight from real action. We don't bring our deepest thoughts to fruition in action, we complicate them so much that we can scarcely even understand them ourselves. Jesus wasn't thinking about sin as a concept, he saw it as a crippling thing. "Is it easier to say to this paralyzed man: Your sins are forgiven, or to say: Rise, take up your mat and walk?" Then he said, "Stand up!" And the man stood up and walked.

Jesus returned to Capernaum. As the news spread that he was at home, so many people gathered that there was no longer room even outside the door. While Jesus was preaching the Word to them, some people brought a paralyzed man to him.

The four men who carried him couldn't get near Jesus because of the crowd, so they opened the roof above the room where Jesus was and, through the hole, lowered the man on his mat. When Jesus saw the faith of these people, he said to the paralytic, "My son, your sins are forgiven."

Now, some teachers of the Law who were sitting there wondered within themselves, "How can he speak like this insulting God? Who can forgive sins except God?"

At once Jesus knew through his spirit what they were thinking and asked, "Why do you wonder? Is it easier to say to this paralyzed man: 'Your sins are forgiven,' or to say: 'Rise, take up your mat and walk?' But now you shall know that the Son of Man has authority on earth to forgive sins."

And he said to the paralytic, "Stand up, take up your mat and go home." The man rose and, in the sight of all those people, he took up his mat and went out. All of them were astonished and praised God saying, "We have never seen anything like this!"

1S 9:1-4,17-19;10:1   Mk 2:13-17

Levi (also known as Bartholomew) was still working at his rotten job when Jesus called him. But Jesus didn't wait till he had turned his back on his old way of life. He called him while he was "sitting in his office," totting up his profits, it may be, for he was a tax collector. What do we see next? A whole crowd of tax collectors, having a meal—and Jesus in the middle of them! And for good measure there were some public sinners there too. In those days, to sit at table with someone was to express unrestricted friendship with them. What were they talking about? Try and imagine that!

When Jesus went out again beside the lake, a crowd came to him and he taught them. As he walked along, he saw a tax collector sitting in his office. This was Levi, the son of Alpheus. Jesus said to him, "Follow me." And Levi got up and followed him.

And it so happened that while Jesus was eating in Levi's house, tax collectors and sinners were sitting with him and his disciples for there were indeed many of them. But there were also teachers of the Law of the Pharisees' party, among those who followed Jesus, and when they saw him eating with sinners and tax collectors, they said to his disciples, "Why! He eats with tax collectors and sinners!"

Jesus heard them and answered, "Healthy people don't need a doctor, but sick people do. I did not come to call the righteous but sinners."

Sunday

We can see this scene as a sort of allegory of every marriage. Every marriage begins with joy and enthusiasm. Wine is a symbol of this joy. But everything human is transient: enthusiasm comes down to a lower register and sometimes disappears altogether, and love can die. It seems at times that there is nothing left but water. What's to be done? Invite Jesus to be present in your marriage. The water of routine can be changed little by little into wine—not a fizzy wine like the first, but a quieter and more mellow and longer-lasting wine. What happened at Cana in Galilee can happen here in your own home.

Is 60:1-6

For Zion's sake I will not hold my peace, for Jerusalem I will not keep silent, until her holiness shines like the dawn and her salvation flames like a burning torch. The nations will see your holiness and all the kings your glory. You will be called by a new name which the mouth of Yahweh will reveal. You will be a crown of glory in the hand of Yahweh, a royal diadem in the hand of your God. No longer will you be named Forsaken; no longer will your land be called *Abandoned*; but you will be called *My Delight* and your land *Espoused*. For Yahweh delights in you and will make your land his spouse.

1Cor 12:4-11

There is diversity of gifts, but the Spirit is the same. There is diversity of ministries, but the Lord is the same. There is diversity of works, but the same God works in all. The Spirit reveals his presence in each one with a gift that is also a service. (...) And all of this is the work of the one and only Spirit, who gives to each one as he so desires.

Jn 2:1-11

There was a wedding at Cana in Galilee and the mother of Jesus was there. Jesus was also invited to the wedding with his disciples. When all the wine provided for the celebration had been served and they had run out of wine, the mother of Jesus said to him, "They have no wine." Jesus replied, "Woman, what concern is that to you and me? My hour has not yet come." However his mother said to the servants, "Do whatever he tells you." Nearby were six stone water jars meant for the ritual washing as practiced by the Jews; each jar could hold twenty or thirty gallons. Jesus said to the servants, "Fill the jars with water." And they filled them to the brim. Then Jesus said, "Now draw some out and take it to the steward." So they did. The steward tasted the water that had become wine, without knowing from where it had come; for only the servants who had drawn the water knew. So, he called the bridegroom to tell him, "Everyone serves the best wine first and when people have drunk enough, that which is ordinary. Instead you have kept the best wine until the end."

This miraculous sign was the first, and Jesus performed it at Cana in this way he let his Glory appear and his disciples believed in him.

Monday 19

JANUARY

ORDINARY TIME
2nd Week

Martin Luther King's Birthday

1S 15:16-23   Mk 2:18-22

"How can the wedding guests fast while the bridegroom is with them?" Everything human is transient: joy doesn't last forever. A day will come, he said, when they will not be rejoicing; on that day they can fast. But while joy is here be filled with it! Then it will stay around you a little longer. And when you have to move into sadness there will still be some effect, some coloring of that joy in you; your sadness will not be miserable but quiet and deep. But if your joy is measured and miserable, your sadness will be an even greater misery. Our joy and our sorrow take the measure of each other.

One day, when the disciples of John the Baptist and the Pharisees were fasting, some people asked Jesus, "Why is it that both the disciples of John and of the Pharisees fast, but yours do not?" Jesus answered, "How can the wedding guests fast while the bridegroom is with them? As long as they have the bridegroom with them, they cannot fast. But the day will come when the bridegroom will be taken from them and on that day they will fast.

No one sews a piece of new cloth on an old coat, because the new patch will shrink and tear away from the old cloth, making a worse tear. And no one puts new wine into old wineskins, for the wine would burst the skins and then both the wine and the skins would be lost. But new wine, new skins!"

20 Tuesday

JANUARY

1S 16:1-13   Mk 2:23-28

I knew a canon lawyer who used to say, There are two kinds of canon lawyer: the one who studies the law in order to tie you down with it, and the one who studies it in order to set you free. Jesus never bound people up with the Law; in fact he accused the Pharisees of doing just this. In today's reading he made the most radical statement about law: it is for human beings, not human beings for it. He said this in relation to the Sabbath, which was a law of divine origin. The deepest intention of the Law is to set you free. When you think about it, this is not so surprising. Your freedom is God's gift. Jesus came "to set captives free" (Lk 4:18).

One Sabbath he was walking through grainfields. As his disciples walked along with him, they began to pick the heads of grain and crush them in their hands. Then the Pharisees said to Jesus, "Look! they are doing what is forbidden on the Sabbath!"

And he said to them, "Have you never read what David did in his time of need, when he and his men were very hungry? He went into the house of God when Abiathar was High Priest and ate the bread of offering, which only the priests are allowed to eat, and he also gave some to the men who were with him." Then Jesus said to them, "The Sabbath was made for man, not man for the Sabbath. So the Son of Man is master even of the Sabbath."

1S 17:32-33,37,40-51   Mk 3:1-6

Today's reading says that Jesus "looked around at them with anger." Many pictures of Jesus have him looking up at the sky with a sad sentimental look on his face. Have you ever seen a picture of him looking around with anger? I haven't. Such a picture would never become popular, but it would at least show that we weren't restricting Jesus to being merely "nice." (Incidentally, in Middle English the word "nice" meant "stupid.") Why was he so furious? "Because they had closed their minds," this translation says. Love is an opening, a kind of wound. Julian of Norwich prayed for "the wound of true compassion." God grant that we may never be healed of it!

Again Jesus entered the synagogue. A man who had a paralyzed hand was there and some people watched Jesus: Would he heal the man on the Sabbath? If he did they could accuse him.

Jesus said to the man with the paralyzed hand, "Stand here in the center." Then he asked them, "What does the Law allow us to do on the Sabbath? To do good or to do harm? To save life or to kill?" But they were silent.

Then Jesus looked around at them with anger and deep sadness because they had closed their minds. And he said to the man, "Stretch out your hand." He stretched it out and his hand was healed. But as soon as the Pharisees left, they met with Herod's supporters, looking for a way to destroy Jesus.

**ORDINARY TIME
2nd Week**

St. Vincent

22 Thursday

JANUARY

1S 18:6-9;19:1-7   Mk 3:7-12

Things were getting out of hand: this reading is crammed with people: "a large crowd," "a great number," "so many." Jesus hasn't room to stand, he has to sit in a little boat and speak from there. It seems to have been a turning point. After this he changed his method: he began to concentrate on teaching his disciples. This is a good reading for people who tend to over-stretch themselves and feel guilty if they are not always working frantically. More is not necessarily better. It doesn't flatter the ego to say so, but sometimes the best thing you can do for others is to rest! Even Jesus had to leave many things undone.

Jesus and his disciples withdrew to the lakeside and a large crowd from Galilee followed him. A great number of people also came from Judea, Jerusalem, Idumea, Transjordan and from the region of Tyre and Sidon, for they had heard of all that he was doing.

Because of the crowd, Jesus told his disciples to have a boat ready for him, to prevent the people from crushing him. He healed so many that all who had diseases kept pressing towards him to touch him. Even the people who had evil spirits, whenever they saw him, would fall down before him and cry out, "You are the Son of God." But he warned them sternly not to tell anyone who he was.

1S 24:3-21   Mk 3:13-19

Mark often uses this phrase "to be with (him)": 2:19; 4:36; 5:18; 14:14, 67; 15:41. Peter was Mark's source, and Peter wrote about the time "when we were with him on the holy mountain" (2Peter 1:18). In today's reading, too, it is a mountain (well… a hill). To be a disciple is to be with him on the holy mountain of prayer and meditation. But neither he nor they stayed forever on the mountain; they "went out" to the whole world. Every disciple is called not only to be with him but to go out to others. Prayer and action, said St. Catherine of Siena, are like our two feet: we need them both if we are to follow the Way.

Jesus went up into the hill country and called those he wanted and they came to him. So he appointed twelve to be with him; and he called them apostles. He wanted to send them out to preach, and he gave them authority to drive out demons.

These are the Twelve: Simon, to whom he gave the name Peter; James, son of Zebedee, and John his brother, to whom he gave the name Boanerges, which means "men of thunder"; Andrew, Philip, Bartholomew, Matthew, Thomas, James son of Alpheus, Thaddeus, Simon the Cananean and Judas Iscariot, the one who betrayed him.

24

Saturday

2S 1:1-4,11-12,19,23-27   Mk 3:20-21

Was Jesus mad? Or was the crowd mad? This reading could be taken either way. In Greek the word for "he" and the word "it" are the same; so it could read, "His relatives came to take charge of him because it (the crowd) was out of its mind." But what's the difference? If Jesus is described as mad and the crowd as sane, or if Jesus is described as sane and the crowd as mad, the contrast between them is the same. And who's calling Jesus mad? The crowd! So you have a choice: do you want to identify with the crowd calling Jesus mad, or with Jesus calling the crowd mad? Who do you believe in your heart of hearts?

Jesus and his disciples went home. The crowd began to gather again and they couldn't even have a meal. Knowing what was happening his relatives came to take charge of him: "He is out of his mind," they said.

Sunday

Scholars tell us that that first paragraph is the most polished Greek in the New Testament. Jesus arrives on the scene, "acting with the power of the Spirit." The Spirit has no form, and would therefore not appeal to Greeks. They appreciated order and harmony, not the formlessness and unpredictability of a Holy Spirit (symbolized in the New Testament as "wind" or "fire"). The Holy Spirit, through the guttural sounds of Hebrew, proclaimed new sight to the blind, freedom for the oppressed, good news for the poor. And Jesus did not say that it would come about in a timeless world of thought, but today and in this dusty and muddy world.

Ne 8:2-4.5-6.8-10

Ezra brought the Law before the assembly, both men and women and all the children who could understand what was being read. It was the first day of the seventh month. Ezra read the book before all of them from early morning until midday in the square facing the Water Gate; and all who heard were attentive to the Book of the Law.

Ezra, the teacher of the Law, stood on a wooden platform built for that occasion and to his right were Mattithiah, Shema, Anaiah, Uriah, Hilkiah and Maaseiah; and to his left were Pedaiah, Mishael, Malchijah, Hashum, Hasbaddanah, Zechariah and Meshullam.

Ezra opened the book in the sight of all the people, for he was in a higher place; and when he opened it, all the people stood. Ezra blessed Yahweh, the great God; and all the people lifted up their hands and answered, "Amen! Amen!" And they bowed their heads to the ground. They read from the Book of the Law of God, clarifying and interpreting the meaning, so that everyone might understand what they were hearing. (...)

1Cor 12,12-14.17
Lk 1:1-4;4:14-21

Several people have set themselves to relate the events that have taken place among us, as they were told by the first witnesses who later became ministers of the Word. After I myself had carefully gone over the whole story from the beginning, it seemed right for me to give you, Theophilus, an orderly account, so that your Excellency may know the truth of all you have been taught.

Jesus acted with the power of the Spirit, and on his return to Galilee the news about him spread throughout all that territory. He began teaching in the synagogues of the Jews and everyone praised him.

When Jesus came to Nazareth where he had been brought up, he entered the synagogue on the Sabbath as he usually did. He stood up to read and they handed him the book of the prophet Isaiah. Jesus then unrolled the scroll and found the place where it is written: "The Spirit of the Lord is upon me. He has anointed me to bring good news to the poor, to proclaim liberty to captives and new sight to the blind; to free the oppressed and announce the Lord's year of mercy." Jesus then rolled up the scroll, gave it to the attendant and sat down, while the eyes of all in the synagogue were fixed on him. Then he said to them, "Today these prophetic words come true even as you listen."

2Tim 1:1-8 or Tit 1:1-5   Lk 10:1-9

"Amen" (pronounced in every possible way) is a word in every language. A scholar says that "Amen I say to you" was an expression characteristic of Jesus, because it occurs nowhere else in literature. That is somehow interesting to know. Just as we have evidence that he had a country accent, we also know a speech habit of his. Just as the word Amen is in every language, it is (or was) marked on the landscape too. There is a place called Amen Corner in London, near St. Paul's Cathedral. It is at the end of Paternoster Row. All those places are still on the map of London.

The Lord appointed seventy-two other disciples and sent them two by two ahead of him to every town and place, where he himself was to go. And he said to them, "The harvest is rich, but the workers are few. So you must ask the Lord of the harvest to send workers to his harvest. Courage! I am sending you like lambs among wolves. Set off without purse or bag or sandals; and do not stop at the homes of those you know.

"Whatever house you enter, first bless them saying: 'Peace to this house.' If a friend of peace lives there, the peace shall rest upon that person. But if not, the blessing will return to you. Stay in that house eating and drinking at their table, for the worker deserves to be paid. Do not move from house to house.

"When they welcome you in any town, eat what they offer you. Heal the sick who are there and say to them: 'The kingdom of God has drawn near to you.'"

2S 6:12-15,17-19   Mk 3:31-35

Belonging to the same family or race as Jesus does not make one a disciple (see Mt 3:9). Not that, but doing the will of God. This was the passion of his life; anyone who was not part of that was not part of him. In the agony of Gethsemane he was able to say, "Not my will but yours be done." In him the passion to do the Father's will was deeper than death; it is not surprising then that it should also be deeper than birth and natural life. How many things are deeper than birth and death? Or more practically, how many things are deeper in me than birth and death? Or still more practically, what would I live and die for?

Jesus' mother and brothers came. As they stood outside, they sent someone to call him. The crowd sitting around Jesus told him, "Your mother and your brothers are outside asking for you." He replied, "Who are my mother and my brothers?"

And looking around at those who sat there he said, "Here are my mother and my brothers. Whoever does the will of God is brother and sister and mother to me."

Wednesday 28

2S 7:4-17   Mk 4:1-20

Again a reference to "those outside." But he will not reject those outsiders and shape his own followers into a narrow circle, a cult. No, he will teach them in parables: that is, with stories, images. Abstract statements you either understand there and then or you fail to understand. But a story stays with you even if you don't grasp its full meaning. It waits for you, it gives you time. It's part of courtesy to wait for people who cannot move fast. Think of parables as part of the courtesy of Jesus. He's waiting for your mind to open, your spirit to deepen. And that's the point of this particular parable: the readiness of the soil makes all the difference.

Again Jesus (...) said, "Listen! The sower went out to sow. As he sowed, some of the seed fell along a path and the birds came and ate it up. Some of the seed fell on rocky ground where it had little soil; it sprang up immediately because it had no depth; but when the sun rose and burned it, it withered because it had no roots. Other seed fell among thorn bushes and the thorns grew and choked it, so it didn't produce any grain. But some seed fell on good soil, grew and increased and yielded grain; some produced thirty times as much, others sixty and others one hundred times as much." And Jesus added, "Listen then, if you have ears."

When the crowd went away, some who were around him with the Twelve asked about the parables. (...) Jesus said to them, "Don't you understand this parable? How then will you understand any of the parables? What the sower is sowing is the word. Those along the path where the seed fell are people who hear the word, but as soon as they do, Satan comes and takes away the word that was sown in them. Other people receive the word like rocky ground. As soon as they hear the word, they accept it with joy, but they have no roots so it lasts only a little while. No sooner does trouble or persecution come because of the word, than they fall. Others receive the seed as among thorns. After they hear the word, they are caught up in the worries of this life, false hopes of riches and other desires. All these come in and choke the word so that finally it produces nothing. And there are others who receive the word as good soil. They hear the word, take it to heart and produce: some thirty, some sixty and some one hundred times as much."

Every language has its own homespun wisdom, and this is often best seen in its proverbs. In Irish, for example, "A friend's eye is a good mirror." "Don't break your shin on a stool that isn't in your way." "A wild goose never laid a tame egg." "The herb that can't be got is the one that brings relief." "The person who brings a story to you will take two away." And so on and on endlessly! Jesus quoted two proverbs from his own language in this passage, "No one lights a lamp to put it under a tub," and "The measure you give is the measure you get." Don't ask me to add a commentary to them: proverbs are well able to speak for themselves!

Jesus also said to them, "When the light comes, is it to be put under a tub or a bed? Surely it is put on a lampstand. Whatever is hidden will be disclosed, and whatever is kept secret will be brought to light. Listen then, if you have ears!"

And he also said to them, "Pay attention to what you hear. In the measure you give, so shall you receive and still more will be given to you. For to the one who produces something, more will be given, and from him who does not produce anything, even what he has will be taken away from him."

2S 11:1-4,5-10,13-17   Mk 4:26-34

For "kingdom" say "presence." Then read it again. The seeds of awareness of God are in us. They will not suddenly leap into the air, bypassing all stages of growth, and fill the grain loft to the door. Instead they will lie in the damp earth, lost and forgotten, seeming dead. But the miracle of life is happening there where no one can see and no one can understand or explain. Then the most vulnerable part appears just above the ground. It has no defenses, it doesn't find itself in a glasshouse; it is exposed to everything that could happen to it. That's life. Only love could take such risks. In this parable Jesus says that the presence of God is like that.

Jesus also said, "In the kingdom of God it is like this. A man scatters seed upon the soil. Whether he is asleep or awake, be it day or night, the seed sprouts and grows, he knows not how. The soil produces of itself; first the blade, then the ear, then the full grain in the ear. And when it is ripe for harvesting they take the sickle for the cutting: the time for harvest has come."

Jesus also said, "What is the kingdom of God like? To what shall we compare it? It is like a mustard seed which, when sown, is the smallest of all the seeds scattered upon the soil. But once sown, it grows up and becomes the largest of the plants in the garden and even grows branches so big that the birds of the air can take shelter in its shade."

Jesus used many such stories or parables, to proclaim the word to them in a way they would be able to understand. He would not teach them without parables; but privately to his disciples he explained everything.

2S 12:1-7,10-17   Mk 4:35-41

If you ask us today to say what the opposite of faith is, we would be inclined to say, Doubt. But in this passage it seems to be fear, or a certain kind of fear. See this contrast of fear and faith in the verse, "Why are you frightened? Do you still have no faith?" Our natural instincts are our friends; they are our equipment for survival. So this must be true of fear. But like all our instincts it can become neurotic and turn against us. Then it becomes a crippling force, preventing us from doing anything, good or bad. That little boat crossing a storm-tossed lake is a symbol of our life. Many things tell us to be afraid. But "do we still have no faith?"

One day when evening had come, Jesus said to his disciples, "Let's go across to the other side." So they left the crowd and took him away in the boat he had been sitting in, and other boats set out with him. Then a storm gathered and it began to blow a gale. The waves spilled over into the boat so that it was soon filled with water. And Jesus was in the stern, asleep on the cushion.

They woke him up and said, "Master, don't you care if we sink?" As Jesus awoke, he rebuked the wind and ordered the sea, "Quiet now! Be still!" The wind dropped and there was a great calm. Then Jesus said to them, "Why are you so frightened? Do you still have no faith?"

But they were terrified and they said to one another, "Who can this be? Even the wind and the sea obey him!"

Sunday

The rejection of Jesus in his hometown was no surprise. The whole world knows that familiarity breeds contempt! It's a bitter truth that the people closest to you are sometimes the least likely to support you. The people of Nazareth agreed with Jesus only just so long as he agreed with them! As soon as he began to say things they didn't like they tried to throw him over a cliff. They knew so many superficial things about him that they couldn't see anything new in him. Is there anything in you or me that makes our familiars want to throw us over a cliff?—or are we perfect villagers?

4TH SUNDAY IN ORDINARY TIME 1

Jer 1:4-5.17-19

A word of Yahweh came to me, "Even before I formed you in the womb I have known you; even before you were born I had set you apart, and appointed you a prophet to the nations. Get ready for action; stand up and say to them all that I command you. Be not scared of them or I will scare you in their presence. See, I will make you a fortified city, a pillar of iron with walls of bronze, against all the nations (...). They will fight against you but shall not overcome you, for I am with you to rescue you—it is Yahweh who speaks."

1Cor 12:31–13:13

(...) If I could speak all the human and angelic tongues, but had no love, I would only be sounding brass or a clanging cymbal. If I had the gift of prophecy, knowing secret things with all kinds of knowledge, and had faith great enough to remove mountains, but had no love, I would be nothing. If I gave everything I had to the poor, and even give up my body to be burned, if I am without love, it would be of no value to me. Love is patient, kind, without envy. It is not boastful or arrogant. It is not ill-mannered nor does it seek its own interest. Love overcomes anger and forgets offenses. It does not take delight in wrong, but rejoices in truth. Love excuses everything, believes all things, hopes all things, endures all things. Love will never end. (...)

Lk 4:21-30

Jesus began to speak in the synagogue, "Today these prophetic words come true even as you listen." All agreed with him and were lost in wonder, while he kept on speaking of the grace of God. Nevertheless they asked, "Who is this but Joseph's son?" So he said, "Doubtless you will quote me the saying: Doctor, heal yourself! Do here in your town what they say you did in Capernaum." Jesus added, "No prophet is honored in his own country. Truly, I say to you, there were many widows in Israel in the days of Elijah, when the heavens withheld rain for three years and six months and a great famine came over the whole land. Yet Elijah was not sent to any of them, but to a widow of Zarephath, in the country of Sidon. There were also many lepers in Israel in the time of Elisha, the prophet, and no one was healed except Naaman, the Syrian." On hearing these words, the whole assembly became indignant. They rose up and brought him out of the town, to the edge of the hill on which Nazareth is built, intending to throw him down the cliff. But he passed through their midst and went his way.

FEBRUARY

Monday

2

ORDINARY TIME
4th Week

The Presentation of the Lord

Mal 3:1-4   Heb 2:14-18   Lk 2:22-40

Jesus appears as fully within the Law; as a commentator with a lot of hindsight put it, "completely immersed in humanity." Very well, if there is to be hindsight, then let's see this child as a grown man put to death in accordance with the same Law. But can you still see the eight-day-old baby once you have mentioned his death? Sometimes it can be a good thing to try and set aside some of our hindsight. When hindsight gets in before sight itself, it can blind rather than illuminate. We have to give Jesus time to grow up!—not only in himself but in us.

When the day came for the purification according to the law of Moses, Joseph and Mary brought the baby up to Jerusalem to present him to the Lord, as it is written in the law of the Lord: Every firstborn male shall be consecrated to God. And they offered a sacrifice as ordered in the law of the Lord: a pair of turtledoves or two young pigeons.

There lived in Jerusalem at this time a very upright and devout man named Simeon; the Holy Spirit was in him. He looked forward to the time when the Lord would comfort Israel, and he had been assured by the Holy Spirit that he would not die before seeing the Messiah of the Lord. So he was led into the Temple by the Holy Spirit at the time the parents brought the child Jesus, to do for him according to the custom of the Law.

Simeon took the child in his arms and blessed God, saying: "Now, O Lord, you can dismiss your servant in peace, for you have fulfilled your word and my eyes have seen your salvation, which you display for all the people to see. Here is the light you will reveal to the nations and the glory of your people Israel."

His father and mother wondered at what was said about the child. Simeon blessed them and said to Mary, his mother, "See him; he will be for the rise or fall of the multitudes of Israel. He shall stand as a sign of contradiction, while a sword will pierce your own soul. Then the secret thoughts of many may be brought to light." (...)

2S 18:9-10,14,24-25,30–19:3   Mk 5:21-43

(...) Jairus, an official of the synagogue, came up and seeing Jesus, threw himself at his feet and asked him earnestly, "My little daughter is at the point of death. Come and lay your hands on her so that she may get well and live." (...) Among the crowd was a woman who had suffered from bleeding for twelve years. (...) Since she had heard about Jesus, this woman came up behind him and touched his cloak (...). Her flow of blood dried up at once, and she felt in her body that she was healed of her complaint. But Jesus was conscious that healing power had gone out from him, so he turned around in the crowd and asked, "Who touched my clothes?" (...) The woman, aware of what had happened, came forward trembling and afraid. She knelt before him and told him the whole truth. Then Jesus said to her, "Daughter, your faith has saved you; go in peace and be free of this illness." (...)

While Jesus was still speaking, some people arrived from the official's house to inform him, "Your daughter is dead. Why trouble the Master any further?" But Jesus ignored what they said and told the official, "Do not fear, just believe." And he allowed no one to follow him except Peter, James and John, the brother of James.

When they arrived at the house, Jesus saw a great commotion with people weeping and wailing loudly. Jesus entered and said to them, "Why all this commotion and weeping? The child is not dead but asleep." They laughed at him. But Jesus sent them outside and went with the child's father and mother and his companions into the room where the child lay. Taking her by the hand, he said to her, "Talitha kumi!" which means: "Little girl, get up!" The girl got up at once and began to walk around. (...)

There is nothing like a crisis to restore our humanity: not any kind of crisis but one of the heart. Any crisis that only challenges your mind is not deeply challenging; you are not really open till your heart is open. Your real inside is not your mind but your heart. Culture and travel and training can open your mind, but that isn't much. You are not open till your heart is exposed. As soon as the official had a sick child he ceased to be an official and became a father.

2S 24:2,9-17   Mk 6:1-6

The villagers wanted to keep Jesus within his limitations: he was a carpenter and the son of a carpenter. But he "broke through their midst and went his way" (Lk 4:30). We have to break through the midst of many things in order to become adult Christians. Childhood as a complete ideal doesn't work for most people. Yes, Jesus said we must be like children: we must have their qualities of simplicity, honesty, freshness…. "Like children," he said. Like my friend, who does wonderful things. We must be adults who are like children, not children who are like adults.

Jesus returned to his own country, and his disciples followed him. When the Sabbath came, he began teaching in the synagogue, and most of those who heard him were astonished. They commented, "How did this come to him? What kind of wisdom has been given to him that he also performs such miracles? Who is he but the carpenter, the son of Mary and the brother of James and Joset and Judas and Simon? His sisters, too, are they not here among us?" So they took offense at him.

And Jesus said to them, "Prophets are despised only in their own country, among their relatives and in their own family." And he could work no miracles there, but only healed a few sick people by laying his hands on them. Jesus himself was astounded at their unbelief. Jesus then went around the villages teaching.

1K 2:1-4,10-12   Mk 6:7-13

Jesus called the Twelve to him and began to send them out two by two, giving them authority over evil spirits. And he ordered them to take nothing for the journey except a staff; no food, no bag, no money in their belts. They were to wear sandals and were not to take an extra tunic.

And he added, "In whatever house you are welcomed, stay there until you leave the place. If any place doesn't receive you and the people refuse to listen to you, leave after shaking the dust off your feet. It will be a testimony against them."

So they set out to proclaim that this was the time to repent. They drove out many demons and healed many sick people by anointing them.

What's an extra tunic for? It is for tomorrow. What's a bag for? It is for carrying things that I will need tomorrow. What's money for? It is for tomorrow's food and shelter. We think of time as originating in the unimaginable past and flowing forward into the present and beyond us into the future. It occurred to me once that it would be better to reverse that image. Time originates now, it wells up into existence in the present moment and flows away into the past. Time flows backwards! This moment is the Big Bang! Take nothing for the journey—because you have already arrived!

February

Friday

6

ORDINARY TIME
4th Week

St. Paul Miki and Companions

Sir 47:2-11   Mk 6:14-29

"I had John beheaded, yet he has risen from the dead!" Don't be surprised; he has inevitably risen! If you want the truth to sprout, cut off its head! It will grow twenty heads. This was Herod's experience. However, because of his guilty conscience it was not a pleasant one for him. John was his evil conscience. John rose up again before him like a ghost, not like a resurrected being. He cannot be beheaded again; it is impossible to behead a ghost. That phantom pain will be with Herod for the rest of his life. But wasn't there forgiveness for him? Yes, but he was a tyrant and didn't know that word.

King Herod also heard about Jesus because his name had become well-known. Some people said, "John the Baptist has been raised from the dead and that is why miraculous powers are at work in him." (...) When Herod was told of this, he thought: "I had John beheaded, yet he has risen from the dead!"

For this is what had happened. Herod had ordered John to be arrested and had him bound and put in prison because of Herodias, the wife of his brother Philip. Herod had married her and John had told him, "It is not right for you to live with your brother's wife." (...)

Herodias had her chance on Herod's birthday, when he gave a dinner for all the senior government officials, military chiefs and the leaders of Galilee. On that occasion the daughter of Herodias came in and danced; and she delighted Herod and his guests. The king said to the girl, "Ask me for anything you want and I will give it to you." And he went so far as to say with many oaths, "I will give you anything you ask, even half my kingdom." She went out to consult her mother, "What shall I ask for?" The mother replied, "The head of John the Baptist." The girl hurried to the king and made her request: "I want you to give me the head of John the Baptist, here and now, on a dish." The king was very displeased, but he would not refuse in front of his guests because of his oaths. So he sent one of the bodyguards with orders to bring John's head. He went and beheaded John in prison; then he brought the head on a dish and gave it to the girl. And the girl gave it to her mother. When John's disciples heard of this, they came and took his body and buried it.

1K 3:4-13   Mk 6:30-34

"The apostles had no time even to eat." That sounds more like today! There are families that never sit together for a meal. Someone asked a meditation teacher how to meditate. "Taste your food!" replied the teacher. If you don't know how to stop and rest your busy mind, here's how: "rest" in the taste of a sip of coffee. Later you may learn how to rest each foot on the ground as you walk, rather than leaping over it. And if you have a moment with nothing to do, give yourself permission to rest. There!—you are meditating.

The apostles returned and reported to Jesus all they had done and taught. Then he said to them, "Go off by yourselves to a remote place and have some rest." For there were so many people coming and going that the apostles had no time even to eat. And they went away in the boat to a secluded area by themselves.

But people saw them leaving and many could guess where they were going. So, from all the towns they hurried there on foot, arriving ahead of them.

As Jesus went ashore he saw a large crowd, and he had compassion on them for they were like sheep without a shepherd. And he began a long teaching session with them.

Sunday

They had "worked hard all night and caught nothing." But next moment the boat was so full of fish that they were in danger of sinking. As usual, these opposites are not enemies. We have to be empty if we are to receive. What freedom would be ours if we could sit down sometimes with our emptiness (empty feelings especially) and see it not as something to be avoided at all costs, but as a purification and a clearing of space for something new to be born. In fact we will never come to anything new if we are afraid of emptiness; our whole lives will be only a rearrangement of what we already have.

Is 6:1-8
1Cor 15:1-11

Let me remind you, brothers and sisters, of the Good News that I preached to you and which you received and on which you stand firm. By that Gospel you are saved, provided that you hold to it as I preached it. Otherwise, you will have believed in vain. In the first place, I have passed on to you what I myself received: that Christ died for our sins, as Scripture says; that he was buried; that he was raised on the third day, according to the Scriptures; that he appeared to Cephas and then to the Twelve. Afterwards he appeared to more than five hundred brothers and sisters together; most of them are still alive, although some have already gone to rest. Then he appeared to James and after that to all the apostles. And last of all, he appeared to the most despicable of them, this is to me. For I am the last of the apostles, and I do not even deserve to be called an apostle, because I persecuted the Church of God. Nevertheless, by the grace of God, I am what I am, and his grace towards me has not been without fruit. Far from it, I have toiled more than all of them, although not I, rather the grace of God in me. Now, whether it was I or they, this we preach and this you have believed.

Lk 5:1-11

One day, as Jesus stood by the Lake of Gennesaret, with a crowd gathered around him listening to the word of God, he caught sight of two boats left at the water's edge by the fishermen now washing their nets. He got into one of the boats, the one belonging to Simon, and asked him to pull out a little from the shore. There he sat and continued to teach the crowd. When he had finished speaking he said to Simon, "Put out into deep water and lower your nets for a catch." Simon replied, "Master, we worked hard all night and caught nothing. But if you say so, I will lower the nets." This they did and caught such a large number of fish that their nets began to break. They signaled their partners in the other boat to come and help them. They came and filled both boats almost to the point of sinking. Upon seeing this, Simon Peter fell at Jesus' knees, saying, "Leave me, Lord, for I am a sinful man!" For he and his companions were amazed at the catch they had made and so were Simon's partners, James and John, Zebedee's sons. Jesus said to Simon, "Do not be afraid. You will catch people from now on." So they brought their boats to land and followed him, leaving everything.

1K 8:1-7,9-13   Mk 6:53-56

Popularity is a fickle goddess: the crowd that cheered "Hosanna!" to Jesus were crying "Crucify him!" a few days later. Jesus went through both; the rest of us, with few exceptions, would settle for just Hosanna! Popularity looks like glory, and it is a kind of glory: someone called it "glory's small change." There is the personality type described as "the pleaser." Such a person will never challenge you; they rely too much on your good opinion of them. But it backfires; most people would prefer that you said what you thought. "He more had pleased us had he pleased us less."

Having crossed the lake, Jesus and his disciples came ashore at Gennesaret where they tied up the boat. As soon as they landed, people recognized Jesus and ran to spread the news throughout the countryside. Wherever he was they brought to him the sick lying on their mats. And wherever he went, to villages, towns or farms, they laid the sick in the marketplace and begged him to let him touch just the fringe of his cloak. And all who touched him were cured.

1K 8:22-23,27-30   Mk 7:1-13

One day the Pharisees gathered around Jesus and with them were some teachers of the Law who had just come from Jerusalem. They noticed that some of his disciples were eating their meal with unclean hands, that is, without washing. Now the Pharisees, and in fact, all the Jews, never eat without washing their hands for they follow the tradition received from their ancestors. Nor do they eat anything when they come from the market without first washing themselves. And there are many other traditions they observe, for example, the ritual washing of cups, pots and plates.

So the Pharisees and the teachers of the Law asked him, "Why do your disciples not follow the tradition of the elders, but eat with unclean hands?" Jesus answered, "You, shallow people! How well Isaiah prophesied of you when he wrote: This people honors me with their lips, but their heart is far from me. The worship they offer me is worthless, for what they teach are only human rules. You even put aside the commandment of God to hold fast to human tradition."

And Jesus commented, "You have a fine way of disregarding the commandment of God in order to implant your own tradition. For example, Moses said: Do your duty to your father and your mother, and: Whoever curses his father or his mother is to be put to death. But according to you someone could say to his father or mother: 'I already declared Corban, which means "offered to God," what you could have expected from me.' In this case, you no longer let him do anything for a father or mother. So you nullify the word of God through the tradition you have handed on. And you do many other things like that."

Here they are: the scribes and Pharisees from Jerusalem. They are not bringing their sick, like the Galileans in yesterday's reading. So they are not vulnerable, they don't have to bother about love. That clarifies their minds so that they can think about the law. Immediately they find fault and go into the attack. "Shallow," Jesus called them: more concerned with law than with the heart (in the Scriptures the heart is a symbol of the whole inner life of a person). For all their talk about God, religious lawyers can't cope well with God. God seems too concerned with individuals, and is therefore unpredictable. Love just muddies the field for lawyers.

FEBRUARY

Wednesday 11

ORDINARY TIME
5th Week
Our Lady of Lourdes

Is 66:10-14   Jn 2:1-11

This was another "epiphany" of Jesus (Jan. 4), another manifestation, like the one to the Magi and the other at his Baptism (Jan. 11). He is becoming visible, or as John put it, "he let his Glory appear." He hadn't lived in hiding for thirty years; he was well known to his neighbors; they could see him any time they wanted. He was visible to them, and yet they could not see his true nature; he was too familiar to them. The ones to look out for are the most familiar people: they are often far more invisible to us than any stranger. In loving them we are entertaining the Lord unawares.

There was a wedding at Cana in Galilee and the mother of Jesus was there. Jesus was also invited to the wedding with his disciples. When all the wine provided for the celebration had been served and they had run out of wine, the mother of Jesus said to him, "They have no wine." Jesus replied, "Woman, what concern is that to you and me? My hour has not yet come."

However his mother said to the servants, "Do whatever he tells you."

Nearby were six stone water jars meant for the ritual washing as practiced by the Jews; each jar could hold twenty or thirty gallons. Jesus said to the servants, "Fill the jars with water." And they filled them to the brim. Then Jesus said, "Now draw some out and take it to the steward." So they did.

The steward tasted the water that had become wine, without knowing from where it had come; for only the servants who had drawn the water knew. So, he called the bridegroom to tell him, "Everyone serves the best wine first and when people have drunk enough, he serves that which is ordinary. Instead you have kept the best wine until the end."

This miraculous sign was the first, and Jesus performed it at Cana in Galilee. In this way he let his Glory appear and his disciples believed in him.

1K 11:4-13   Mk 7:24-30

Jesus went to the border of the Tyrian country. There he entered a house and did not want anyone to know he was there, but he could not remain hidden. A woman, whose small daughter had an evil spirit, heard of him and came and fell at his feet. Now this woman was a pagan, a Syrophoenician by birth, and she begged him to drive the demon out of her daughter.

Jesus told her, "Let the children be fed first, for it is not right to take the children's bread and throw it to the dogs." But she replied, "Sir, even the dogs under the table eat the crumbs from the children's bread." Then Jesus said to her, "You may go your way; because of such a reply the demon has gone out of your daughter." And when the woman went home, she found her child lying in bed and the demon gone.

Here we see Jesus away from his own country and culture; he is in the land of the Phoenicians, an ancient and gifted people whose greatest contributions to civilization were the alphabet and navigation by the stars; their industries (textiles, dyes, metalwork, glass-making, etc.) were famous in the ancient world. When Jesus arrives in this foreign place he seems reclusive; "he entered a house and did not want anyone to know he was there." What does all this mean? Don't we always expect Jesus to do the noblest, bravest, most loving thing? Don't we expect him to leap over all boundaries of race and even religion? Yes, that's the trouble: we expect him always to match our idea of him. Let's ponder this one and refuse any easy answers.

1K 11:29-32;12:19 **Mk 7:31-37**

Today's is a "hands-on" healing. They asked Jesus "to lay his hands on him." He did more than that; in fact he seemed to go to the opposite extreme! "Gestures and the use of a foreign word were commonplace among contemporary healers, and even suggest a sort of magical ritual," writes a scholar. We might add the use of spittle to that list. But what is missing is even more surprising: there is no mention of faith, nor of casting out a demon. Jesus appears to be measuring himself and searching for his style. Does it upset one's image of him? That might be a good thing. But it need not upset one's faith.

Again Jesus set out; from the country of Tyre, passed through Sidon and, skirting the sea of Galilee, he came to the territory of Decapolis. There a deaf man who also had difficulty in speaking was brought to him. They asked Jesus to lay his hand upon him.

Jesus took him apart from the crowd, put his fingers into the man's ears and touched his tongue with spittle. Then, looking up to heaven, he groaned and said to him, "Ephphetha," that is, "Be opened."

And his ears were opened, his tongue was loosened, and he began to speak clearly. Jesus ordered them not to tell anyone, but the more he insisted on this, the more they proclaimed it. The people were completely astonished and said, "He has done all things well; he makes the deaf hear and the dumb speak."

1K 12:26-32;13:33-34   Mk 8:1-10

Jesus was in the midst of another large crowd that obviously had nothing to eat. So he called his disciples and said to them, "I feel sorry for these people because they have been with me for three days and now have nothing to eat. If I send them to their homes hungry, they will faint on the way; some of them have come a long way."

His disciples replied, "Where in a deserted place like this could we get enough bread to feed these people?" He asked them, "How many loaves have you?" And they answered, "Seven."

Then he ordered the crowd to sit down on the ground. Taking the seven loaves and giving thanks, he broke them and handed them to his disciples to distribute. And they distributed them among the people. They also had some small fish, so Jesus said a blessing and asked that these be shared as well.

The people ate and were satisfied. The broken pieces were collected, seven wicker baskets full of leftovers. Now there had been about four thousand people. Jesus sent them away and immediately got into the boat with his disciples and went to the region of Dalmanutha.

Many say this is a second account of the miraculous feeding. But there are also differences: the first account shows the miracle performed for the benefit of Jews, the second for Gentiles. In the first, are twelve basketfuls of leftovers, in the second only seven. Scholars suggest that the twelve is a reference to the twelve Apostles, and the seven to the seven deacons. All these and other contrasts bear out the Jew/Gentile difference. The language is "eucharistic": he "took the loaves and giving thanks he broke them and handed them to his disciple to distribute." In the light of the readings for the last few days, this is a reassurance: we Gentiles are called to sit at the table as family members.

Sunday

The key to understanding the Beatitudes is this: Jesus does not accept the designations "rich" and "poor" and just reverse their positions; he transforms them. He reveals a new kind of richness and a new kind of poverty. He says: Blessed are you, the poor, because you have a kind of wealth that the rich don't have. How sad for you, the rich, because deep down you are poor. The opposition, then, is not between two groups of people, the rich and the poor, but between two kinds of poverty (and two kinds of wealth).

Jer 17:5-8

This is what Yahweh says, "Cursed is the man who trusts in human beings and depends on a mortal for his life, while his heart is drawn away from Yahweh! He is like a bunch of thistles in dry land, in parched desert places, in a salt land where no one lives and who never finds happiness. Blessed is the man who puts his trust in Yahweh and whose confidence is in him! He is like a tree planted by the water, sending out its roots towards the stream. He has no fear when the heat comes, his leaves are always green; the year of drought is no problem and he can always bear fruit."

1Cor 15:12,16-20

If Christ is preached as risen from the dead, how can some of you say that there is no resurrection of the dead? If the dead are not raised, neither has Christ been raised. And if Christ has not been raised, your faith gives you nothing, and you are still in sin. Also those who fall asleep in Christ are lost. If it is only for this life that we hope in Christ, we are the most unfortunate of all people. But no, Christ has been raised from the dead and he comes before all those who have fallen asleep.

Lk 6:17,20-26

Coming down the hill with them, Jesus stood on a level place. Many of his disciples were there and a large crowd of people who had come from all parts of Judea and Jerusalem and from the coastal cities of Tyre and Sidon. Then looking at his disciples, Jesus said,

"Fortunate are you who are poor, the kingdom of God is yours. Fortunate are you who are hungry now, for you will be filled. Fortunate are you who weep now, for you will laugh. Fortunate are you when people hate you, when they reject you and insult you and number you among criminals, because of the Son of Man. Rejoice in that day and leap for joy, for a great reward is kept for you in heaven. Remember that is how the ancestors of this people treated the prophets.

"But alas for you who have wealth, for you have been comforted now. Alas for you who are full, for you will go hungry. Alas for you who laugh now, for you will mourn and weep. Alas for you when people speak well of you, for that is how the ancestors of these people treated the false prophets."

February

Monday

16

ORDINARY TIME
6th Week
President's Day

Jas 1:1-11   Mk 8:11-13

"Hoping to embarrass him they asked for some heavenly sign." His miracles (which always appealed to faith) were not enough; they wanted a spectacle. A spectacle would amuse (or fail to amuse) the idle, not touch their hearts—because their hearts were untouchable. They wanted to make a trial of him, without being on trial themselves. They would taunt him from the sideline while remaining safely out of reach themselves. That's not fair play in any field. There are people whose whole life-game is that. Don't you just love them!

The Pharisess came and started to argue with Jesus. Hoping to embarrass him, they asked for some heavenly sign. Then his spirit was moved. He gave a deep sigh and said, "Why do the people of this present time ask for a sign? Truly, I say to you, no sign shall be given to this people." Then he left them, got into the boat again and went to the other side of the lake.

Jas 1:12-18   Mk 8:14-21

Luke speaks of the "leaven of the Pharisees," but he also tells us that Jesus used leaven as an image of the Kingdom of heaven (13:20). How can we hold these opposite meanings together? Every person has a capacity for good and evil; everything we use we can use for good or evil purposes. Consequently every object we touch takes on associations of human goodness or evil, and even comes to symbolize them. Leaven symbolizes rapid growth but it also symbolizes corruption. Life experiences illustrate the truth of this every day.

The disciples had forgotten to bring more bread and had only one loaf with them in the boat. Then Jesus warned them, "Keep your eyes open and beware of the yeast of the Pharisees and the yeast of Herod." And they said to one another, "He saw that we have no bread."

Aware of this, Jesus asked them, "Why are you talking about the loaves you are short of? Do you not see or understand? Are your minds closed? Have you eyes that don't see and ears that don't hear? And do you not remember when I broke the five loaves among five thousand? How many baskets full of leftovers did you collect?" They answered, "Twelve." "And having seven loaves for the four thousand, how many wicker baskets of leftovers did you collect?" They answered, "Seven." Then Jesus said to them, "Do you still not understand?"

Jas 1:19-27   Mk 8:22-26

Jesus took the blind man by the hand and led him outside the village; then when he had healed him he said, "Do not return to the village." A village identifies you in too great detail. It locks you into a narrow identity. (And you do the same to the others; village is something we do to one another. Spiritually the village may symbolize the ego. One's ego is seldom the independent thing it claims to be: it is supported (even imprisoned) by a rather small group of like-thinking people. When that ego is really isolated it is the village idiot. "Idiot" comes from the Greek word "idios", which means "peculiar, private." We may have to become a village idiot for a time. It's a long hard road to humanity.

When Jesus and his disciples came to Bethsaida, Jesus was asked to touch a blind man who was brought to him. He took the blind man by the hand and led him outside the village. When he had put spittle on his eyes and laid his hands upon him, he asked, "Can you see anything?" The man, who was beginning to see, replied, "I see people! They look like trees, but they move around." Then Jesus laid his hands on his eyes again and the man could see perfectly. His sight was restored and he could see everything clearly.

Then Jesus sent him home saying, "Do not return to the village."

Jas 2:1-9   Mk 8:27-33

Peter found it easy to say "You are the Messiah," but the reality was far from easy; it was unthinkable. Peter is a likeable figure, because he is so like all of us. He didn't want to hear about suffering. Much of our prayer is a plea to be spared suffering. How strange then to read Julian of Norwich, the 14th-century English mystic. She prayed for suffering and illness! It is challenging to hear this. If you have absorbed the book I'm OK, you're OK, how hard it is to pray for the wound of contrition, or compassion, or longing for God! Seeing these as wounds would challenge the popular axiom holiness = wholeness.

Jesus set out with his disciples for the villages around Caesarea Philippi; and on the way he asked them, "Who do people say I am?" And they told him, "Some say you are John the Baptist; others say you are Elijah or one of the prophets."

Then Jesus asked them, But you, who do you say I am?" Peter answered, "You are the Messiah." And he ordered them not to tell anyone about him.

Jesus then began to teach them that the Son of Man had to suffer many things and be rejected by the elders, the chief priests and the teachers of the Law. He would be killed and after three days rise again. Jesus said all this quite openly, so that Peter took him aside and began to protest strongly. But Jesus turning around, and looking at his disciples, rebuked Peter saying, "Get behind me Satan! You are thinking, not as God does, but as people do."

Jas 2:14-24,26   **Mk 8:34–9:1**

Saints are people who assure us that there is no such thing as a painless life, and so running from pain cannot be the answer: we only run into the arms of greater pain. Work with what is left—the inevitable pain of life. Rest at peace with this pain: it is your best teacher and friend; it opens the gate to life. It questions your understanding of who and what you are. It takes away your cushions so that you can feel reality. This is not horrible, it is a promise of life—because only reality can save us. If things go against you don't take it as a personal insult; it is God trusting you. The dream of endless comfort is an insult, not this. God loves you enough to take you out of yourself.

Jesus called the people and his disciples and said, "If you want to follow me, deny yourself, take up your cross and follow me. For if you choose to save your life, you will lose it; and if you lose your life for my sake and for the sake of the Gospel, you will save it.

"What good is it to gain the whole world but destroy yourself? There is nothing you can give to recover your life. I tell you: If anyone is ashamed of me and of my words among this adulterous and sinful people, the Son of Man will also be ashamed of him when he comes in the Glory of his Father with the holy angels."

And he went on to say, "Truly I tell you, there are some here who will not die before they see the kingdom of God coming with power."

Jas 3:1-10   Mk 9:2-13

Jesus took with him Peter and James and John, and led them up a high mountain. There his appearance was changed before their eyes. Even his clothes shone, becoming as white as no bleach of this world could make them. Elijah and Moses appeared to them; the two were talking with Jesus.

Then Peter spoke and said to Jesus, "Master, it is good that we are here; let us make three tents, one for you, one for Moses and one for Elijah." For he did not know what to say; they were overcome with awe. But a cloud formed, covering them in a shadow, and from the cloud came this word, "This is my Son, the Beloved; listen to him." And suddenly, as they looked around, they no longer saw anyone except Jesus with them.

As they came down the mountain, he ordered them to tell no one what they had seen, until the Son of Man be risen from the dead. So they kept this to themselves, although they discussed with one another what 'to rise from the dead' could mean.

Finally they asked him, "Why then do the teachers of the Law say that Elijah must come first?" Jesus answered them, "Of course, Elijah will come first so that everything may be as it should be… But, why do the Scriptures say that the Son of Man must suffer many things and be despised? I tell you that Elijah has already come and they have treated him as they pleased, as the Scriptures say of him."

The easiest thing to say about today's reading is that it comes directly in Mark's gospel, without a break, after yesterday's and the previous day's. Those readings were questions about the identity of Jesus. Today's reading then is the answer. He is "the Father's Son, the Beloved." We can say that as easily as we say our own name, but what does it mean? We could answer from the catechism, but again what do the words mean? We are in the presence of the profoundest mystery, and our words sound painfully inadequate. When we are faced with ultimate things we have to fall silent. If we could rest in that "don't know" we would be Christian contemplatives.

Sunday

Jesus tells us to give without expecting a reward. But then he goes on immediately to tell about the reward in store for us if we do! What is the reward that Jesus promises? "You will be sons and daughters of the Most High." You will be like your Father in heaven. What is the Father like? "He is kind towards the ungrateful and the wicked." Or as Matthew's gospel puts it, "He causes his sun to rise on the evil and the good, and sends rain on the just and the unjust" (5:45). The reward is something we will be, not something we will have. In other words, your reward for being generous is that you will be made capable of being endlessly generous! Anything less would be bribery.

1S 26:2,7-9,12-13,22-23
1Cor 15:45-49

Scripture says that Adam, the first man became a living being, was given natural life; but the last Adam has become a life-giving spirit. The spirit does not appear first, but the natural life, and afterwards comes the spirit. The first man comes from the earth and is earthly, while the second one comes from heaven. As it was with the earthly one, so is it with the earthly people. As it is with Christ, so with the heavenly. This is why, after bearing the image of the earthly one, we shall also bear the image of the heavenly one.

Lk 6:27-38

Jesus said to his disciples, "I say to you who hear me: Love your enemies, do good to those who hate you. Bless those who curse you and pray for those who treat you badly. To the one who strikes you on the cheek, turn the other cheek; from the one who takes your coat, do not keep back your shirt. Give to the one who asks and if anyone has taken something from you, do not demand it back.

"Do to others as you would have others do to you. If you love only those who love you, what kind of graciousness is yours? Even sinners love those who love them. If you do favors to those who are good to you, what kind of graciousness is yours? Even sinners do the same. If you lend only when you expect to receive, what kind of graciousness is yours? For sinners also lend to sinners, expecting to receive something in return.

"But love your enemies and do good to them, and lend when there is nothing to expect in return. Then will your reward be great and you will be sons and daughters of the Most High. For he is kind towards the ungrateful and the wicked. Be merciful, just as your Father is merciful.

"Don't be a judge of others and you will not be judged; do not condemn and you will not be condemned; forgive and you will be forgiven; give and it will be given to you, and you will receive in your sack good measure, pressed down, full and running over. For the measure you give will be the measure you receive back."

FEBRUARY

Monday

23

ORDINARY TIME
7th Week

St. Polycarp

Jas 3:13-18   Mk 9:14-29

Once we allow the word "if" a place in religion, all is lost. It is like allowing a hole in the bottom of a bucket; no matter how small the hole, everything leaks out. "I do believe, help my unbelief," said the man in today's reading. Is that a contradiction? Perhaps yes if you were to take belief as isolated from trust. There's a yes or no quality about pure belief, but there are many degrees of trust; in fact trust is all about degrees. By trusting you learn how to trust, and by trusting again you learn to trust more. Belief (or faith as we prefer to call it) doesn't just lie changeless in the mind; it grows out of itself. That's how every living thing grows.

When Jesus came to the place where they had left the disciples, they saw many people around and some teachers of the Law arguing with them. (...) He asked, "What are you arguing about with them?" A man answered him from the crowd, "Master, I brought my son to you for he has a dumb spirit. Whenever the spirit seizes him, it throws him down and he foams at the mouth, grinds his teeth and becomes stiff all over. I asked your disciples to drive the spirit out, but they could not." Jesus replied, "You faithless people. How long must I be with you? How long must I put up with you? Bring him to me." And they brought the boy to him.

(...) Then Jesus asked the father, "How long has this been happening to him?" He replied, "From childhood. And it has often thrown him into the fire and into the water to destroy him. If you can do anything, have pity on us and help us. Jesus said to him, "Why do you say: 'If you can?' All things are possible for one who believes." Immediately the father of the boy cried out, "I do believe, but help the little faith I have."

Jesus saw that the crowd was increasing rapidly, so he ordered the evil spirit, "Dumb and deaf spirit, I command you: Leave the boy and never enter him again." The evil spirit shook and convulsed the boy and with a terrible shriek came out. The boy lay like a corpse and people said, "He is dead." But Jesus took him by the hand and lifted him and the boy stood up. After Jesus had gone indoors, his disciples asked him privately, "Why couldn't we drive out the spirit?" And he answered, "Only prayer can drive out this kind, nothing else."

Jas 4:1-10   Mk 9:30-37

Jesus and his disciples made their way through Galilee; but Jesus did not want people to know where he was because he was teaching his disciples. And he told them, "The Son of Man will be delivered into human hands. They will kill him, but three days after he has been killed, he will rise." The disciples, however, did not understand these words and they were afraid to ask him what he meant.

They came to Capernaum and, once inside the house, Jesus asked them, "What were you discussing on the way?" But they did not answer because they had been arguing about who was the greatest.

Then he sat down, called the Twelve and said to them, "If someone wants to be first, let him be last of all and servant of all." Then he took a little child, placed it in their midst, and putting his arms around it he said to them, "Whoever welcomes a child such as this in my name, welcomes me; and whoever welcomes me, welcomes not me but the One who sent me."

When we are in the presence of death everything looks different from before. Jesus had just spoken about his imminent death. Then he asked the disciples, "What were you discussing?" But, "they did not answer because they had been arguing about who was the greatest." It's the ego that has to stake a claim to being the greatest. It's a false identity, so everything can threaten it; therefore it's always on high alert. Our true being makes no such claim; quite the opposite. Jesus patiently explained. "If someone wants to be first, let him be last of all." Our true being looks out at the world with wonder instead of criticism and competition, and it looks up at God with wordless trust.

Joel 2:12-18   2Cor 5:20–6:2   Mt 6:1-6,16-18

"O ye wha are sae guid yoursel, / Sae pious and sae holy, / Ye've nought to do but mark and tell / Your Neebour's fauts and folly!" Lent is not a time of depression—even though everything in the Liturgy is simplified and we try to simplify our own lives too. It is a time for returning to the heart. "Return to me with all your heart." Anyone with a heart has also a sense of humor. Sometimes it's the only way we can live with ourselves. It's painful work to strip away the ego's defenses and projections, and we have to do it with good grace if it's to stay done. Notice how often the word 'secret' occurs in today's reading. It is contrasted with "being seen." "Being seen" is about surfaces and appearances. the heart is about depth.

Jesus said to his disciples, "Be careful not to make a show of your righteousness before people. If you do so, you do not gain anything from your Father in heaven. When you give something to the poor, do not have it trumpeted before you, as do those who want to be seen in the synagogues and in the streets in order to be praised by the people. I assure you, they have been already paid in full.

"If you give something to the poor, do not let your left hand know what your right hand is doing, so that your gift remains really secret. Your Father who sees what is kept secret, will reward you.

"When you pray, do not be like those who want to be seen. They love to stand and pray in the synagogues or on street corners to be seen by everyone. I assure you, they have already been paid in full. When you pray, go into your room, close the door and pray to your Father who is with you in secret; and your Father who sees what is kept secret will reward you.

"When you fast, do not put on a miserable face as do the hypocrites. They put on a gloomy face, so people can see they are fasting. I tell you this: they have paid in full already. When you fast, wash your face and make yourself look cheerful, because you are not fasting for appearances or for people, but for your Father who sees beyond appearances. And your Father, who sees what is kept secret will reward you."

26 Thursday

Dt 30:15-20   Lk 9:22-25

Let me quote Joko Beck, a zen master, on this subject, "I notice that people who have been practicing [meditation] for some time begin to have a sense of humor about their burden. After all, the thought that life is a burden is only a concept. We're simply doing what we're doing. The measure of fruitful practice is that we feel life less as a burden and more as a joy. That does not mean there is no sadness, but the experience of sadness is exactly the joy. If we don't find such a shift happening over time, then we haven't yet understood what practice is; the shift is a reliable barometer."

Jesus said to his disciples, "The Son of Man must suffer many things. He will be rejected by the elders and chief priests and teachers of the Law, and put to death. Then after three days he will be raised to life."

He also said to all the people, "If you wish to be a follower of mine, deny yourself and take up your cross each day, and follow me. For if you choose to save your life, you will lose it, and if you lose your life for my sake, you will save it. What does it profit you to gain the whole world while you destroy or damage yourself?

Joyless religion may be the profoundest denial of God. If there is no joy in it, it's all your own work, so what need have you of God? If the Resurrection is not visible in you, then you are preaching death without resurrection. One of the fruits of the Spirit is joy, and it is mentioned next after love in St. Paul's list, "love, joy, peace, patience, kindness, goodness, faithfulness, gentleness and self-control" (Gal. 5:22). Joy does not come from avoiding pain and sorrow; on the contrary it is possible only when we have gone into the heart of our pain and sorrow.

The disciples of John came to Jesus with the question, "How is it that we and the Pharisees fast on many occasions, but not your disciples?"

Jesus answered them, "How can you expect wedding guests to mourn as long as the bridegroom is with them? Time will come when the bridegroom will be taken away from them, then they will fast."

Is 58:9-14   Lk 5:27-32

It would be strange if the Word became flesh, but stopped short of taking the final step: mingling with the common people, all of us, "the great unwashed." Jesus mixed with "the worst elements" in society. . There was not just one tax collector but "many".
It was inevitable that the "unco guid" would arrive too (see February 25). These Pharisees needed those tax collectors. It was essential for the Pharisees that there should be lots of tax collectors and sinners; it is essential for some 'good' (or 'guid') people that there should be great numbers of 'bad' people. But how disconcerting it always is to find Jesus among the bad!

After this Jesus went out, and as he noticed a tax collector named Levi sitting in the tax-office, he said to him, "Follow me." So Levi, leaving everything, got up and followed Jesus.

Levi gave a great feast for Jesus, and many tax collectors came to his house and took their place at table with the other people. Then the Pharisees and their fellow teachers complained to Jesus' disciples, "How is it that you eat and drink with tax collectors and other sinners?" But Jesus spoke up, "Healthy people don't need a doctor, but sick people do. I have come to call to repentance; I call sinners, not the righteous."

Sunday

"Tempted," in the Scriptures, means "put to the test." Jesus was led (in Mark, driven) into the desert to be put to the test. For a start, the desert itself put him to the test. A desert gives you nothing to eat, it makes you feel utterly powerless, and it seems totally indifferent to your fate. At any rate, temptations are never just disembodied ideas. The temptations of Jesus were not temptations to evil, but to limited kinds of goodness. How do you tempt a good person? With evil? No, he or she will not take that bait. You tempt them with goodness— but with some kind of short-term, self-defeating goodness.... On this first Sunday of Lent the Church encourages us to look with clear sight at our temptations.

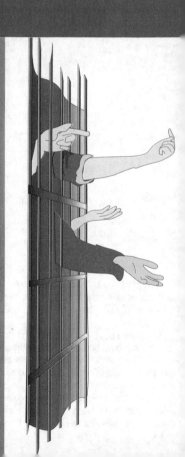

Dt 26:4-10

(...) You shall say these words before Yahweh, "My father was a wandering Aramean. He went down to Egypt to find refuge there, while still few in number, but in that country, he became a great and powerful nation. The Egyptians maltreated us, oppressed us and subjected us to harsh slavery. So we called to Yahweh, the God of our ancestors, and Yahweh listened to us. He saw our humiliation, our hard labor and the oppression to which we were subjected. He brought us out of Egypt with a firm hand, manifesting his power with signs and awesome wonders. And he brought us here to give us this land flowing with milk and honey. So now I bring and offer the firstfruits of the land which you, Yahweh, have given me."

Rom 10:8-13

Lk 4:1-13

Jesus was now full of Holy Spirit. As he returned from the Jordan, the Spirit led him into the desert where he was tempted by the devil for forty days. He did not eat anything during that time, and in the end he was hungry. The devil then said to him, "If you are son of God, tell this stone to turn into bread." But Jesus answered, "Scripture says: People cannot live on bread alone."

Then the devil took him up to a high place and showed him in a flash all the nations of the world. And he said to Jesus, "I can give you power over all the nations and their wealth will be yours, for power and wealth have been delivered to me and I give them to whom I wish. All this will be yours provided you worship me." But Jesus replied, "Scripture says: You shall worship the Lord your God and serve him alone."

Then the devil took him up to Jerusalem and set him on the highest wall of the Temple; and he said, "If you are son of God, throw yourself down from here, for it is written: God will order his angels to take care of you and again: They will hold you in their hands, lest you hurt your foot on the stones." But Jesus replied, "It is written: You shall not challenge the Lord your God."

When the devil had exhausted every way of tempting Jesus he left him, to return another time.

Lev 19:1-2,11-18   Mt 25:31-46

It's impossible to evade the question of ultimate judgment, however you think of it. In the sight of God what will my life amount to in the end? In the face of that ultimate question we all feel naked and uncertain. Human beings have imagined a scenario where they can start all over again: reincarnation. But the same question arises again and again. This is not how the Christian faith sees it. Christian teaching is more stark. Our ultimate destiny, the thing that seems farthest away, actually hangs on the things nearest to hand, the most proximate: on how we treat the Lord in "the hungry, the thirsty, the stranger, the naked, the sick, the imprisoned."

Jesus said to his disciples, "When the Son of Man comes in his glory with all his angels, he will sit on the throne of his Glory. (...) The King will say to those on his right: 'Come, blessed of my Father! Take possession of the kingdom prepared for you from the beginning of the world. For I was hungry and you fed me, I was thirsty and you gave me drink. I was a stranger and you welcomed me into your house. I was naked and you clothed me. I was sick and you visited me. I was in prison and you came to see me.'

"Then the good people will ask him: 'Lord, when did we see you hungry and give you food; thirsty and give you drink, or a stranger and welcome you, or naked and clothe you? When did we see you sick or in prison and go to see you?' The King will answer, 'Truly, I say to you: whenever you did this to these little ones who are my brothers and sisters, you did it to me.'

"Then he will say to those on his left: 'Go, cursed people, out of my sight into the eternal fire which has been prepared for the devil and his angels! For I was hungry and you did not give me anything to eat, I was thirsty and you gave me nothing to drink; I was a stranger and you did not welcome me into your house; I was naked and you did not clothe me; I was sick and in prison and you did not visit me.'

"They, too, will ask: 'Lord, when did we see you hungry, thirsty, naked or a stranger, sick or in prison, and did not help you?' The King will answer them: 'Truly, I say to you: whatever you did not do for one of these little ones, you did not do for me.' And these will go into eternal punishment, but the just to eternal life."

Is 55:10-11   Mt 6:7-15

Our Father... Our prayer is common; and when we pray we pray not for one but for the whole people, because we are one, not that we wish God to be sanctified by our prayers, but that we ask to keep his name holy in us.... We beg that God's Kingdom be revealed to us and pray that we may be able to fulfill his will in us....

"Give us this day our daily bread": We are in Christ, the Bread of Life and receive the Eucharist daily as the food of salvation.... we ask for forgiveness, so that we who are fed by God may be able to live in him. The enemy can do nothing against us without God's permission .... Praying [this petition] reminds us of our inconstancy and weakness. Who can fear this life, if God is his life-guardian?"

Jesus said to his disciples, "When you pray, do not use a lot of words, as the pagans do, for they hold that the more they say, the more chance they have of being heard. Do not be like them. Your Father knows what you need, even before you ask him.

This, then, is how you should pray:
Our Father in heaven,
holy be your name,
your kingdom come
and your will be done,
on earth as in heaven.
Give us today our daily bread.
Forgive us our debts
just as we have forgiven those who are in debt to us.
Do not bring us to the test
but deliver us from the evil one.

"If you forgive others their wrongs, your Father in heaven will also forgive yours. If you do not forgive others, then your Father will not forgive you either."

Jonah 3:1-10   Lk 11:29-32

The Book of Jonah is a delightful and amusing book, and short—about three pages. Broadminded, it rejects a too rigid interpretation of prophecy.... rejects, too, a narrow racialism....All the characters of this story are likeable; we are on the threshold of the Gospel. It's easy to imagine Jesus as a young man hearing it and laughing at the antics of Jonah, and the animals doing penance, and Jonah arguing heatedly with God (God, "Are you right to be angry?" Jonah, "I have every right to be angry!") In today's passage, Jesus uses Jonah as a headline for his own preaching. That's how close we are to the Gospel.

As the crowd increased, Jesus began to speak in this way, "People of the present time are evil people. They ask for a sign, but no sign will be given to them except the sign of Jonah. As Jonah became a sign for the people of Nineveh, so will the Son of Man be a sign for this generation. The Queen of the South will rise up on Judgment Day with the people of these times and accuse them, for she came from the ends of the earth to hear the wisdom of Solomon; and here there is greater than Solomon. The people of Nineveh will rise up on Judgment Day with the people of these times and accuse them, for Jonah's preaching made them turn from their sins, and here there is greater than Jonah."

LENT
1st Week
St. Casimir

Es C: 12,14-16, 23-25   Mt 7:7-12

4 Thursday

Julian of Norwich (14th century) wrote, "Often our trust is half-hearted, because we are not sure God hears us. This is because we think we are not good enough, and because we feel nothing at all—for often we are as barren and dry after praying as we were before. Such foolish thinking brings about our weakness in prayer. I know this feeling myself. Our Lord suddenly brought all this to my mind and revealed these words to me: 'I am the ground of your praying. First, it is my will that you have something, and then I make you want it too; then I make you beseech me for it—and you do beseech me. So how could you not have what you ask for?'"

Jesus said to his disciples, "Ask and you will receive; seek and you will find; knock and the door will be opened. For everyone who asks, receives; whoever seeks, finds; and the door will be opened to him who knocks. Would any of you give a stone to your son when he asks for bread? Or give him a snake, when he asks for a fish? As bad as you are, you know how to give good things to your children. How much more, then, will your Father in heaven give good things to those who ask him!

"So, do to others whatever you would that others do to you: there you have the Law and the Prophets."

Ezk 18:21-28   Mt 5:20-26

The Pharisees were "the Separated." They had retreated to a narrow place and taken refuge there. That narrow place was the Law and its rigorous application to the details of daily life. Against them, in today's reading, Jesus asserts the necessity of deep interiority: our actions ought to flow from the heart, the center of our being. It is hard for us to occupy the whole space of our religion. We are able to make interiority in turn a narrow place. Perhaps this is the most common temptation today: to take refuge in an inner private world, ignoring the outer.

Jesus said to his disciples, "I tell you, then, that if you are not righteous in a much broader way than the teachers of the Law and the Pharisees, you cannot enter the kingdom of heaven.

"You have heard that it was said to our people in the past: Do not commit murder; anyone who does kill will have to face trial. But now I tell you: whoever gets angry with a brother or sister will have to face trial. Whoever insults a brother or sister deserves to be brought before the council; whoever calls a brother or a sister "Fool" deserves to be thrown into the fire of hell. So, if you are about to offer your gift at the altar and you remember that your brother has something against you, leave your gift there in front of the altar, go at once and make peace with him, and then come back and offer your gift to God.

"Don't forget this: be reconciled with your opponent quickly when you are together on the way to court. Otherwise he will turn you over to the judge, who will hand you over to the police, who will put you in jail. There you will stay, until you have paid the last penny."

Dt 26:16-19   Mt 5:43-48

A real enemy is an alienated part of yourself, and if you refuse to make that alienation you have no real enemy. Even if the whole world hated you, you would have no enemies! Enmity grows by being reflected, and if you stopped reflecting it, in a while there would be less of it in the world. Usually we get into tangles of blaming and justifying and saying "who started it"; but all this is futile. The only way to stop it is to stop reflecting it. Gradually the tangle loosens and we are left with just ourselves, variously wounded and fearful. We are God's boisterous children. To know that is to know some kind of love.

Jesus said to his disciples, "You have heard that it was said: Love your neighbor and do not do good to your enemy. But this I tell you: Love your enemies, and pray for those who persecute you, so that you may be children of your Father in Heaven. For he makes his sun rise on both the wicked and the good, and he gives rain to both the just and the unjust.

"If you love those who love you, what is special about that? Do not even tax collectors do as much? And if you are friendly only to your friends, what is so exceptional about that? Do not even the pagans do as much? For your part you shall be righteous and perfect in the way your heavenly Father is righteous and perfect."

Sunday

For the gospels, usually so quick-paced, that is a strangely static scene on the mountain: Jesus, flanked by Moses and Elijah. This scene is like two other events in the life of Jesus: his baptism and his resurrection. The beginning and the end of the story are brought together in one luminous moment. In all three gospels this Transfiguration scene comes just after Jesus predicted his passion for the first time. Death, and even the thought of death, freezes the action and brings the whole of one's life into a point. But that point is not a fading into extinction; it is a moment of Transfiguration. In this lies the meaning of our own suffering too.

2ND SUNDAY OF LENT 7

Gen 15:5-12.17-18
Phil 3:17-4:1

Unite in imitating me, brothers and sisters, and look at those who walk in our way of life. For many live as enemies of the cross of Christ. I have said it to you many times, and now I repeat it with tears: they are heading for ruin; their belly is their god and they feel proud of what should be their shame. They only think of earthly things.

For us, our citizenship is in heaven, from where we await the coming of our Savior, Jesus Christ, the Lord. He will transfigure our lowly body, making it like his own body, radiant in Glory, through thr power which is his to submit everything to himself.

Therefore, my brothers and sisters, whom I love and long for, you my glory and crown, be steadfast in the Lord.

Lk 9:28-36

About eight days after Jesus had said all this, he took Peter, John and James and went up the mountain to pray. And while he was praying, the aspect of his face was changed and his clothing became dazzling white. Two men were talking with Jesus: Moses and Elijah. They had just appeared in heavenly glory and were telling him about his departure that had to take place in Jerusalem.

Peter and his companions had fallen asleep, but they awoke suddenly and saw Jesus' Glory and the two men standing with him. As Moses and Elijah were about to leave, Peter said to him, "Master, how good it is for us to be here for we can make three tents, one for you, one for Moses and one for Elijah." For Peter didn't know what to say. And no sooner had he spoken than a cloud appeared and covered them; and the disciples were afraid as they entered the cloud. Then these words came from the cloud, "This is my Son, my Chosen one, listen to him." And after the voice had spoken, Jesus was there alone.

The disciples kept this to themselves at the time, telling no one of anything they had seen.

Dan 9:4-10   Lk 6:36-38

If you cannot give you cannot receive either. The measure you give is the measure you are capable of receiving. A saint would give you his or her life, but a louse can only give you the itch. "With every creature, according to the nobility of its nature, the more it indwells in itself, the more it gives itself out," wrote Meister Eckhart. If I refuse to give (or forgive), this shows that I have not entered into the human and divine mystery of what we are. God does not limit his mercy; we do.

Jesus said to his disciples, "Be merciful, just as your Father is merciful.

"Don't be a judge of others and you will not be judged; do not condemn and you will not be condemned; forgive and you will be forgiven; give and it will be given to you, and you will receive in your sack good measure, pressed down, full and running over. For the measure you give will be the measure you receive back."

Is 1:10,16-20   Mt 23:1-12

Jesus said to the crowds and to his disciples, "The teachers of the Law and the Pharisees sat on the seat of Moses. So you shall do and observe all they say, but do not do as they do, for they do not do what they say. They tie up heavy burdens and load them on the shoulders of the people, but they do not even raise a finger to move them. They do everything in order to be seen by people; so they wear very wide bands of the Law around their foreheads, and robes with large tassels. They enjoy the first place at feasts and reserved seats in the synagogues, and being greeted in the marketplace and being called 'Master' by the people.

"But you, do not let yourselves be called Master because you have only one Master, and all of you are brothers and sisters. Neither should you call anyone on earth Father, because you have only one Father, he who is in heaven. Nor should you be called leader, because Christ is the only leader for you. Let the greatest among you be the servant of all. For whoever makes himself great shall be humbled, and whoever humbles himself shall be made great."

There are still many foolish rubrics and customs defacing the Church. We still cling to badges of distinction: titles, dress, rank, ceremonial…. These would be just harmless foibles if there wasn't a subtext: that others are in some way less significant beings. But "you are all brothers and sisters," Jesus said. Should we all be exactly the same then? Are wasting good time on appearances? In so doing, do we not assault in some way the dignity of others; and do not have any concern with serving our brothers and sisters.

Jer 18:18-20   Mt 20:17-28

Mark says that it was James and John who asked Jesus for important posts in his kingdom (10:37). But Matthew puts the blame on their mother! The anger of the others reveals something else. Why were they not just amused, or perhaps sorry for them? Anger reveals a personal stake in the matter. I think the others too saw themselves in the running for the top posts! Today's reading, has the same theme as yesterday's. Yesterday's was about the Pharisees, but today's is about the Apostles! Still, the Lord was able to love them to the end. Therein lies hope for us all.

When Jesus was going to Jerusalem, he took the Twelve aside and said to them on the way, "See, we are going to Jerusalem. There the Son of Man will be given over to the chief priests and the teachers of the Law who will condemn him to death. They will hand him over to the foreigners who will mock him, scourge him and crucify him. But he will be raised to life on the third day."

Then the mother of James and John came to Jesus with her sons, and she knelt down to ask a favor. Jesus said to her, "What do you want?" And she answered, "Here you have my two sons. Grant that they may sit, one at your right and one at your left, when you are in your kingdom."

Jesus said to the brothers, "You do not know what you are asking. Can you drink the cup that I am about to drink?" They answered, "We can." Jesus replied, "You will indeed drink my cup, but to sit at my right or at my left is not for me to grant. That will be for those for whom the Father has prepared it."

The other ten heard all this and were angry with the two brothers. Then Jesus called them to him and said, "You know that the rulers of the nations act as tyrants, and the powerful oppress them. It shall not be so among you; whoever wants to be more important in your group shall make himself your servant. And if you want to be first, make yourself the servant of all. Be like the Son of Man who has come, not to be served but to serve and to give his life to redeem many."

Jer 17:5-10   Lk 16:19-31

Jesus said to his disciples, "Once there was a rich man who dressed in purple and fine linen and feasted every day. At his gate lay Lazarus, a poor man covered with sores, who longed to eat just the scraps falling from the rich man's table. Even dogs used to come and lick his sores. It happened that the poor man died and angels carried him to take his place with Abraham. The rich man also died and was buried. From hell where he was in torment, he looked up and saw Abraham afar off, and with him Lazarus at rest.

"He called out: 'Father Abraham, have pity on me and send Lazarus with the tip of his finger dipped in water to cool my tongue, for I suffer so much in this fire.'

"Abraham replied: 'My son, remember that in your lifetime you were well-off while the lot of Lazarus was misfortune. Now he is in comfort and you are in agony. But that is not all. Between your place and ours a great chasm has been fixed, so that no one can cross over from here to you or from your side to us.'

"The rich man implored once more: 'Then I beg you, Father Abraham, to send Lazarus to my father's house where my five brothers live. Let him warn them so that they may not end up in this place of torment.' Abraham replied: 'They have Moses and the prophets. Let them listen to them.' But the rich man said: 'No, Father Abraham. But if someone from the dead goes to them, they will repent.'

"Abraham said: 'If they will not listen to Moses and the prophets, they will not be convinced even if someone rises from the grave.'"

This story is about the rich man, not about Lazarus. If it were about Lazarus, it would end with a recommendation to the poor to be patient in their poverty because a great reward was waiting for them. The story had even more punch in its original context: for many centuries in the Old Testament the belief was that riches were a sign of God's favor and poverty a sign of disfavor. The story is therefore one of the most revolutionary in the Bible. The rich man was not overtly cruel to Lazarus: he didn't have him chased away from his door. His sin was that he didn't see him at all: Lazarus was invisible to him. that's the problem: wealth is bad for your sight!

Gen 37:3-4,12-13,17-28   Mt 21:33-43,45-46

The vine was a symbol of Israel. When Jesus tells this story about the vineyard he is talking about his country and the people who ran it. It was a story that enraged them. It frightened them—lying just behind anger there is always fear. (This is a useful awareness: when you see an angry person you are looking at a fearful person.) This is not just a story about a comfortable "long ago"; it is for the Church of today. Many people, experiencing lack of community and spiritual support in their parishes, are looking to new religions and cults for support. But if we are sorry only because we are losing in a "numbers game," then we have to think more deeply.

Jesus said to the chief priests and elders, "Listen to another example: There was a landowner who planted a vineyard. He put a fence around it, dug a hole for the winepress, built a watchtower, leased the vineyard to tenants and then went to a distant country. When harvest time came, the landowner sent his servants to the tenants to collect his share of the harvest. But the tenants seized his servants, beat one, killed another and stoned another.

"Again the owner sent more servants, but they were treated in the same way.

"Finally, he sent his son, thinking: 'They will respect my son.' But when the tenants saw the son, they thought: 'This is the one who is to inherit the vineyard. Let us kill him and his inheritance will be ours.' So they seized him, threw him out of the vineyard and killed him.

"Now, what will the owner of the vineyard do with the tenants when he comes?" They said to him, "He will bring those evil to an evil end, and lease the vineyard to others who will pay him in due time."

And Jesus replied, "Have you never read what the Scriptures say? The stone which the builders rejected has become the keystone. This was the Lord's doing; and we marvel at it. Therefore I say to you: the kingdom of heaven will be taken from you and given to a people who will yield a harvest."

When the chief priests and the Pharisees heard these parables, they realized that Jesus was referring to them. They would have arrested him, but they were afraid of the crowd who regarded him as a prophet.

Mic 7:14-15,18-20   Lk 15:1-3,11-32

(...) Jesus told them this parable: "There was a man with two sons. The younger said to his father: 'Give me my share of the estate.' So the father divided his property between them.

"Some days later, the younger son gathered all his belongings and started off for a distant land where he squandered his wealth in loose living. Having spent everything, he was hard pressed when a severe famine broke out in that land. So he hired himself out to a well-to-do citizen of that place and was sent to work on a pig farm. (...) Finally coming to his senses, he said: 'How many of my father's hired men have food to spare, and here I am starving to death! I will get up and go back to my father and say to him: Father, I have sinned against God and before you. I no longer deserve to be called your son. Treat me then as one of your hired servants.' With that thought in mind he set off for his father's house.

"He was still a long way off when his father caught sight of him. His father was so deeply moved with compassion that he ran out to meet him, threw his arms around his neck and kissed him. The son said: 'Father, I have sinned against Heaven and before you. I no longer deserve to be called your son...' But the father turned to his servants: 'Quick! Bring out the finest robe and put it on him. Put a ring on his finger and sandals on his feet. Take the fattened calf and kill it. We shall celebrate and have a feast, for this son of mine was dead and has come back to life. He was lost and is found.' And the celebration began. (...)"

Long reading, short commentary! Let Julian of Norwich do it for us. "Our courteous Lord will show himself to the soul full joyfully and with glad countenance and friendly welcoming, as if he had been in pain and in prison, saying sweetly, 'My darling, I am glad that you are come to me: in all your woe I have always been with you, and now you see my love, and we will be united in bliss.' Thus are our sins forgiven by mercy and grace, and we are received with joy, just as it will be when we come to heaven."

Sunday

God revealed his name to Moses: it is Yahweh. "That will be my name forever, and by this name they shall call upon me for all generations to come." The Jews regarded this name as so holy that it should not be pronounced, It's somehow a wonderful thing to have a name for God that must never be pronounced. The 13th-century mystic, Bl. Angela of Foligno, had a deep experience of God, and she said, "Father, if you experienced what I experienced and then you had to stand in the pulpit to preach, you could only say to the people, 'My friends, go with God's blessing, because today I can say nothing to you about God.'"

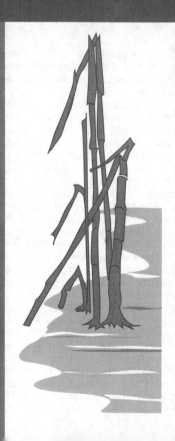

3RD SUNDAY OF LENT 14

Ex 3:1-8,13-15
1Cor 10:1-6,10-12

Let me remind you, brothers and sisters, about our ancestors. All of them were under the cloud and all crossed the sea. All underwent the baptism of the land and of the sea to join Moses and all of them ate from the same spiritual manna and all of them drank from the same spiritual drink. For you know that they drank from a spiritual rock following them, and the rock was Christ. However, most of them did not please God, and the desert was strewn with their bodies.

All of this happened as an example for us, so that we might not become people of evil desires, as they did. Nor grumble as some of them did and were cut down by the destroying angel.

These things happened to them as an example, and they were written as a warning for us, as the last times come upon us. Therefore, if you think you stand, beware, lest you fall.

Lk 13:1-9

One day some persons told Jesus what had occurred in the Temple: Pilate had Galileans killed and their blood mingled with the blood of their sacrifices. Jesus replied, "Do you think that these Galileans were worse sinners than all the other Galileans because they suffered this? I tell you: no. But unless you change your ways, you will all perish as they did.

And those eighteen persons in Siloah who were crushed when the tower fell, do you think they were more guilty than all the others in Jerusalem? I tell you: no. But unless you change your ways, you will all perish as they did."

And Jesus continued with this story, "A man had a fig tree growing in his vineyard and he came looking for fruit on it, but found none. Then he said to the gardener: 'Look here, for three years now I have been looking for figs on this tree and I have found none. Cut it down, why should it use up the ground?' The gardener replied: 'Leave it one more year, so that I may dig around it and add some fertilizer; and perhaps it will bear fruit from now on. But if it doesn't, you can cut it down."

2K 5:1-15   Lk 4:24-30

People have often used the expression "naked truth"; so it may be a good thing to be reminded that what conceals the truth from us is not something covering the truth, but something (or many things) covering the mind. It's rather easy to apply this to the contemporaries of Jesus: they liked him while he said things they liked to hear, but when he said things they didn't like to hear they wanted to throw him over a cliff. As always, it is far more difficult (and urgent) to apply it to oneself.

Jesus added, "No prophet is honored in his own country. Truly, I say to you, there were many widows in Israel in the days of Elijah, when the heavens withheld rain for three years and six months and a great famine came over the whole land. Yet Elijah was not sent to any of them, but to a widow of Zarephath, in the country of Sidon. There were also many lepers in Israel in the time of Elisha, the prophet, and no one was healed except Naaman, the Syrian."

On hearing these words, the whole assembly became indignant. They rose up and brought him out of the town, to the edge of the hill on which Nazareth is built, intending to throw him down the cliff. But he passed through their midst and went his way.

Dan 3:25,34-43   Mt 18:21-35

Peter asked Jesus, "Lord, how many times must I forgive the offenses of my brother or sister? Seven times?" Jesus answered, "No, not seven times, but seventy-seven times. This story throws light on the kingdom of heaven. A king decided to settle the accounts of his servants. Among the first was one who owed him ten thousand gold ingots. As the man could not repay the debt, the king commanded that he be sold as a slave with his wife, children and all his goods in payment.

"The official threw himself at the feet of the king and said, 'Give me time, and I will pay you back everything.' The king took pity on him and not only set him free but even canceled his debt.

"This official then left the king's presence and he met one of his companions who owed him a hundred pieces of silver. He grabbed him by the neck and almost strangled him, shouting, 'Pay me what you owe!' His companion threw himself at his feet and asked him, 'Give me time, and I will pay everything.' The other did not agree, but sent him to prison until he had paid all his debt. His companions saw what happened. They were indignant and so they went and reported everything to their lord. Then the lord summoned his official and said, 'Wicked servant, I forgave you all that you owed when you begged me to do so. Weren't you bound to have pity on your companion as I had pity on you?' The lord was now angry, so he handed his servant over to be punished, until he had paid his whole debt." Jesus added, "So will my heavenly Father do with you unless each of you sincerely forgive your brother or sister."

A very important list to compile: a list of the people I find it hard to forgive. (I must make sure that the list includes myself—often the hardest person to forgive.) Joko Beck wrote, "Failing to grasp the importance of forgiveness is always part of any failing relationship and a factor in our anxieties, depressions, and illnesses—in all our troubles. Our failure to know joy is a direct reflection of our inability to forgive...." I've been struck by the fact that the word "give" is part of the word "forgive." To give is to go beyond the care of the self-centered self; to forgive is to do the same, but in a way that is deeper and more personal.

Dt 4:1,5-9   Mt 5:17-19

"Not the smallest letter or stroke of the Law will change until all is fulfilled," said Jesus. But he himself often broke the Law—certainly as it was interpreted by his contemporaries. When is a law perfectly fulfilled? When it is observed to the letter? Hardly. Law is not the grip of someone's power over you, but guidance for your mind. It subverts neither your mind nor your will, but guides you along a path. It does not take away your freedom, but supports, enlightens and defends it. This is how there can be such a thing as the law of God. There is no real opposition between law and love.

Jesus said to his disciples, "Do not think that I have come to remove the Law and the Prophets. I have not come to remove but to fulfill them. I tell you this: as long as heaven and earth last, not the smallest letter or stroke of the Law will change until all is fulfilled.

"So then, whoever breaks the least important of these commandments and teaches others to do the same will be the least in the kingdom of heaven. On the other hand, whoever obeys them and teaches others to do the same will be great in the kingdom of heaven."

Jer 7:23-28   Lk 11:14-23

One day Jesus was driving out a dumb demon. When the demon had been driven out, the mute person could speak, and the people were amazed. Yet some of them said, "He drives out demons by the power of Beelzebul, the chief of the demons." So others wanted to put him to the test by asking him for a heavenly sign.

But Jesus knew their thoughts and said to them, "Every nation divided by civil war is on the road to ruin, and will fall. If Satan also is divided, his empire is coming to an end. How can you say that I drive out demons by calling upon Beelzebul? If I drive them out by Beelzebul, by whom do your fellow members drive out demons? They will be your judge, then.

"But suppose I drive out demons by the finger of God; would not this mean that the kingdom of God has come upon you? As long as the strong and armed man guards his house, his goods are safe. But when a stronger one attacks and overcomes him, the challenger takes away all the weapons he relied on and disposes of his spoils.

"Whoever is not with me is against me, and whoever does not gather with me, scatters."

Jesus was fully human, so it would not be a denial of his divinity to think that he did many things in that habitual, "ordinary" manner. But some people claimed that it was by the power of Beelzebul that Jesus cast out demons. This amounted to a claim that his life was split in two. Jesus is not divided against himself. It is by the unified power of God that he casts out demons, not by some schizoid self-destructive power. To be possessed by the Holy Spirit is not like other kinds of possession: it is to be enfolded in love, so that there is no difference between what he does and what God does.

2S 7:4-5,12-16   Rom 4:13-18,22   Lk 2:41-51

It may be a bit of a cliché to say that fathers are great when they can be strong silent types. It would have to be the silence of wisdom, though. "Your father and I," said Mary. To many children those words mean that they are being ganged-up on. But in the right atmosphere those same words can convey a sense that the world is not all rupture and discord and violence as on TV. To speak with one voice to their children, parents have to be at one with each other. Someone said that the best thing parents can do for their children is to love each other. Human life has to be 'modeled' rightly for children, because there are so many who model it wrong for them.

Every year the parents of Jesus went to Jerusalem for the Feast of the Passover, as was customary. And when Jesus was twelve years old, he went up with them according to the custom for this feast. After the festival was over, they returned, but the boy Jesus remained in Jerusalem and his parents did not know it.

They thought he was in the company and after walking the whole day they looked for him among their relatives and friends. As they did not find him, they went back to Jerusalem searching for him, and on the third day they found him in the Temple, sitting among the teachers, listening to them and asking questions. And all the people were amazed at his understanding and his answers.

His parents were very surprised when they saw him and his mother said to him, "Son, why have you done this to us? Your father and I were very worried while searching for you." Then he said to them, "Why were you looking for me? Do you not know that I must be in my Father's house?" But they did not understand this answer.

Jesus went down with them, returning to Nazareth, and he continued to be subject to them. As for his mother, she kept all these things in her heart.

Hos 6:1-6   Lk 18:9-14

A circle is complete: it marks out a small space and it divides it off; it needs nothing from the outside. The Pharisee was such a circle: he didn't come out of himself to God—nor of course to the tax-collector. But the tax-collector knew his own incompleteness. He was like a circle with a breach in the circumference. We are at our best when we are open: when we know our need of God and one another. Then something can flow in and out. Through our woundedness the mercy of God can flow through the world.

Jesus told another parable to some persons fully convinced of their own righteousness, who looked down on others, "Two men went up to the Temple to pray; one was a Pharisee and the other a tax collector. The Pharisee stood by himself and said: 'I thank you, God, that I am not like other people, grasping, crooked, adulterous, or even like this tax collector. I fast twice a week and give the tenth of all my income to the Temple.'

"In the meantime the tax collector, standing far off, would not even lift his eyes to heaven, but beat his breast saying: 'O God, be merciful to me, a sinner.'

"I tell you, when this man went down to his house, he had been set right with God, but not the other. For whoever makes himself out to be great will be humbled, and whoever humbles himself will be raised."

One of the meanings of the word "prodigal" is: lavish in the bestowal or disposal of things. If so, then this parable could equally well be called the parable of the Prodigal Father. The father lavished mercy and love on his son. Jesus told this story to illustrate what God is like. The younger son had the wisdom to throw himself on his father's mercy—much as he had thrown himself on the world some time before. They were a pair of Prodigals, with much in common! The older son couldn't throw himself at all, neither for better nor worse. He was a careful self-possessed man, and how poorly he understood his father!

Jos 5:9-12
2Cor 5:17-21
Lk 15:1-3,11-32

(...) Jesus told them this parable: "There was a man with two sons. The younger said to his father: 'Give me my share of the estate.' So the father divided his property between them. Some days later, the younger son gathered all his belongings and started off for a distant land where he squandered his wealth in loose living. Having spent everything, he was hard pressed when a severe famine broke out in that land. So he hired himself out to a well-to-do citizen of that place and was sent to work on a pig farm. So famished was he that he longed to fill his stomach even with the food given to the pigs, but no one offered him anything.

"Finally coming to his senses, he said: 'How many of my father's hired workers have food to spare, and here I am starving to death! I will get up and go back to my father and say to him: Father, I have sinned against God and before you. I no longer deserve to be called your son. Treat me then as one of your hired servants.' With that thought in mind he set off for his father's house. He was still a long way off when his father caught sight of him. His father was so deeply moved with compassion that he ran out to meet him, threw his arms around his neck and kissed him. The son said: 'Father, I have sinned against Heaven and before you. I no longer deserve to be called your son...' But the father turned to his servants: 'Quick! Bring out the finest robe and put it on him. Put a ring on his finger and sandals on his feet. Take the fattened calf and kill it. We shall celebrate and have a feast, for this son of mine was dead and has come back to life. He was lost and is found.' And the celebration began.

"Meanwhile, the elder son had been working in the fields. As he returned and was near the house, he heard the sound of music and dancing. (...) The elder son became angry and refused to go in. (...) The father said: 'My son, you are always with me, and everything I have is yours. But this brother of yours was dead, and has come back to life. He was lost and is found. And for that we had to rejoice and be glad.'"

Is 65:17-21   Jn 4:43-54

They had rejected him when he was at home, but when they saw him performing in the city they changed their attitude. At home they felt small beside him, but in the city they felt big because of him: he had put Nazareth on the map. The ego enters everywhere and leads wherever it will. It cares about nothing except its own need to feel big - or to feel at least that it exists. Is there any hope for us? Of course! How could there be no hope for a Christian? "Sir, come down before my child dies!" said the official. Love made that official think and feel beyond his ego.

When the two days were over, Jesus left for Galilee. Jesus himself said that no prophet is recognized in his own country. Yet the Galileans welcomed him when he arrived, because of all the things he had done in Jerusalem during the Festival and which they had seen. For they, too, had gone to the feast.

Jesus went back to Cana of Galilee where he had changed the water into wine. At Capernaum there was an official whose son was ill, and when he heard that Jesus had come from Judea to Galilee, he went and asked him to come and heal his son, for he was at the point of death. Jesus said, "Unless you see signs and wonders, you will not believe!" The official said, "Sir, come down before my child dies." And Jesus replied, "Go, your son is living."

The man had faith in the word that Jesus spoke to him and went his way. He was already going down the hilly road when his servants met him with this news, "Your son has recovered!" So he asked them at what hour the child had begun to recover and they said to him, "The fever left him yesterday in the afternoon about one o'clock." And the father realized that it was the time when Jesus told him, "Your son is living." And he became a believer, he and all his family.

Jesus performed this second miraculous sign when he returned from Judea to Galilee.

Ezk 47:1-9,12   Jn 5:1-16

There was a feast of the Jews and Jesus went up to Jerusalem. Now, by the Sheep Gate in Jerusalem, there is a pool (called Bethzatha in Hebrew) surrounded by five galleries. In these galleries lay a multitude of sick people-blind, lame and paralyzed. (All were waiting for the water to move, for at times an angel of the Lord would descend into the pool and stir up the water; and the first person to enter after this movement of the water would be healed of whatever disease that person had.)

There was a man who had been sick for thirty-eight years. Jesus saw him, and since he knew how long this man had been lying there, he said to him, "Do you want to be healed?" And the sick man answered, "Sir, I have no one to put me into the pool when the water is disturbed; so while I am still on my way, another steps down before me." Jesus then said to him, "Stand up, take your mat and walk." And at once the man was healed, and he took up his mat and walked. Now that day happened to be the Sabbath. So the Jews said to the man who had just been healed, "It is the Sabbath and the Law doesn't allow you to carry your mat." He answered them, "The one who healed me said to me: Take up your mat and walk." They asked him, "Who is the one who said to you: Take up your mat and walk?" But the sick man had no idea who it was who had cured him, for Jesus had slipped away among the crowd that filled the place. Afterwards Jesus met him in the Temple court and told him, "Now you are well; don't sin again, lest something worse happen to you." And the man went back and told the Jews that it was Jesus who had healed him. So the Jews persecuted Jesus because he performed healings like that on the Sabbath.

Then the miracle happened: the man made to stand up. He overcame the habits—physical and mental—of more than half a lifetime. His mind and will said, "Stand!" That was an amazing achievement. Then, when he made to stand up, he found that he could! The miracle was not worked "on" him, it was worked "with" him. This is not to say that it was just mind over matter. It was the presence of Jesus, but that presence in this case required the full conscious presence of the paralyzed man. What does it say to us? The very thing we can't do is sometimes the only thing worth doing.

Is 49:8-15   Jn 5:17-30

"As the Son lives by the Father, he who eats me will live by me." The three Persons are united by the possession of a secret. This secret is their relationship, their love. The how and why of this love will never be deciphered, never wholly uncovered. It is an incommunicable secret and fullness, which they communicate. What the three Persons give and communicate to one another is the depth of their being. This sharing makes a communion that no human sharing can achieve. This gift is the sharing of what each one has that is beautiful, true and luminous. Gasing at the three faces raises the question, "who are they? What are they saying" And we, our silence, can perceive something of this secret...."

Jesus said to the Jews, "My Father goes on working and so do I." And the Jews tried all the harder to kill him, for Jesus not only broke the Sabbath observance, but also made himself equal with God, calling him his own Father.

Jesus said to them, "Truly, I assure you, the Son cannot do anything by himself, but only what he sees the Father do. And whatever he does, the Son also does. The Father loves the Son and shows him everything he does; and he will show him even greater things than these, so that you will be amazed. As the Father raises the dead and gives them life, so the Son gives life to whom he wills. In the same way the Father judges no one, for he has entrusted all judgment to the Son, and he wants all to honor the Son as they honor the Father. Whoever ignores the Son, ignores as well the Father who sent him.

"Truly, I say to you, anyone who hears my word and believes him who sent me, has eternal life; and there is no judgment for him because he has passed from death to life. Truly, the hour is coming and has indeed come, when the dead will hear the voice of the Son of God and, on hearing it, will live. For the Father has life in himself and he has given to the Son also to have life in himself. And he has empowered him as well to carry out Judgment, for he is a son of man. Do not be surprised at this: the hour is coming when all those lying in tombs will hear my voice and come out; those who have done good shall rise to live, and those who have done evil will rise to be condemned. I can do nothing of myself, and I need to hear Another One to judge; and my judgment is just, because I seek not my own will, but the will of him who sent me."

25 Thursday

MARCH

Is 7:10-14;8:10   Heb 10:4-10   Lk 1:26-38

In the sixth month, the angel Gabriel was sent from God to a town of Galilee called Nazareth. He was sent to a young virgin who was betrothed to a man named Joseph, of the family of David; and the virgin's name was Mary.

The angel came to her and said, "Rejoice, full of grace, the Lord is with you." Mary was troubled at these words, wondering what this greeting could mean.

But the angel said, "Do not fear, Mary, for God has looked kindly on you. You shall conceive and bear a son and you shall call him Jesus. He will be great and shall rightly be called Son of the Most High. The Lord God will give him the kingdom of David, his ancestor; he will rule over the people of Jacob forever and his reign shall have no end."

Then Mary said to the angel, "How can this be if I am a virgin?" And the angel said to her, "The Holy Spirit will come upon you and the power of the Most High will over-shadow you; therefore, the holy child to be born shall be called Son of God. Even your relative Elizabeth is expecting a son in her old age, although she was unable to have a child, and she is now in her sixth month. With God nothing is impossible." Then Mary said, "I am the handmaid of the Lord, let it be done to me as you have said." And the angel left her.

We are at the origin of the human existence of the Word of God. The Word became flesh in Mary's womb. The Word came to Mary looking for far more than accommodation. He became flesh of her flesh. He was not human before he was conceived in her womb; he was not a divine "homunculus." He took flesh from Mary. That means: our flesh, human nature. Meister Eckhart said, "Whatever God the Father gave to his Only-Begotten Son in human nature, he gave all this to me." He means: to all of us. The Annunciation is not to Mary alone, but to you and me.

"We know where this man comes from," the people said. His identity was well pinned down. But, he said, "You say that you know me and know where I come from!" In fact, he told them, they didn't know. Nazareth was not his identity. They seemed to be equally sure of their own identity. But they came from nowhere, as the feast should have served to remind them. Certainty often conceals a vast amount of truth from us. I was sent by the One who is true, and you don't know him. I know him for I come from him and he sent me." This was his real identity. In our way, we too have to drop ~~superficial~~ identities and ~~... find~~ realization.

Jesus went around Galilee; he would not go about in Judea because the Jews wanted to kill him. Now the Jewish feast of the Tents was at hand.

But after his brothers had gone to the festival, he also went up, not publicly but in secret.

Some of the people of Jerusalem said, "Is this not the man they want to kill? And here he is speaking freely, and they don't say a word to him? Can it be that the rulers know that this is really the Christ? Yet we know where this man comes from; but when the Christ appears, no one will know where he comes from."

So Jesus announced in a loud voice in the Temple court where he was teaching, "You say that you know me and know where I come from! I have not come of myself; I was sent by the One who is true, and you don't know him. I know him for I come from him and he sent me."

They would have arrested him, but no one laid hands on him because his time had not yet come.

Jer 11:18-20   Jn 7:40-53

Jesus did not correspond to the expectations of the religious authorities. How could a prophet come from a backwater like Nazareth, a place never mentioned even once in their Scriptures? To despise someone, St. Thomas Aquinas said, is a great sin against charity. The strange thing is that a person of substance doesn't think little of anyone. It's only upstarts who do. "Whoever exalts himself will be humbled, and whoever humbles himself will be exalted," Jesus said (Mt 23:12). Whoever exalts himself will be humbled - not necessarily by someone else; he is already doing it to himself.

Many who had been listening to the words of Jesus began to say, "This is the Prophet." Others said, "This is the Christ." But some wondered, "Would the Christ come from Galilee? Doesn't Scripture say that the Christ is a descendant of David and from Bethlehem, the city of David?" The crowd was divided over him. Some wanted to arrest him, but no one laid hands on him.

The officers of the Temple went back to the chief priests who asked them, "Why didn't you bring him?" The officers answered, "No one ever spoke like this man." The Pharisees then said, "So you, too, have been led astray! Have any of the rulers or any of the Pharisees believed in him? Only these cursed people, who have no knowledge of the Law!"

Yet one of them, Nicodemus, who had gone to Jesus earlier, spoke out, "Does our law condemn people without first hearing them and knowing the facts?" They replied, "Do you, too, come from Galilee? Look it up and see for yourself that no prophet is to come from Galilee."

And they all went home.

Sunday

Everything was clear until Jesus started: the woman was a sinner, her accusers could remain just accusers. It was logic, and it was meant to trap him. If Jesus said, "No, she must not be put to death!" they could accuse him of breaking the Law; and if he said, "The Law has to be obeyed," his teaching about the mercy of God (for example, his story of the prodigal son) would only be fine words. It was a trap. The brilliant way in which he sprang their trap on themselves makes this one of the world's great stories. It shows that mercy isn't the sentimentality of soft-minded people, but a power that goes straight to the heart of the matter—and to the human heart.

Is 43:16-21

Thus says Yahweh, who opened a way through the sea and a path in the mighty waters, who brought down chariots and horses, a whole army of them, and there they lay, never to rise again, snuffed out like a wick. But do not dwell on the past, or remember the things of old. Look, I am doing a new thing: now it springs forth. Do you not see? I am opening up a way in the wilderness and rivers in the desert. The beasts of the land will honor me, jackals and ostriches, because I give water in the wilderness and rivers in the desert that my chosen people may drink. I have formed this people for myself; they will proclaim my praise.

Phil 3:8-14

Everything seems to me as nothing compared with the knowledge of Christ Jesus, my Lord. For his sake I have let everything fall away and I now consider all as garbage, if instead I may gain Christ. May I be found in him, not having a righteousness of my own that comes from the Law, but with the righteousness that God gives to those who believe. (...)

Jn 8:1-11

Jesus went to the Mount of Olives. At daybreak Jesus appeared in the Temple again. All the people came to him, and he sat down and began to teach them.

Then the teachers of the Law and the Pharisees brought in a woman who had been caught in the act of adultery. They made her stand in front of everyone. "Master," they said, "this woman has been caught in the act of adultery. Now the Law of Moses orders that such women be stoned to death; but you, what do you say?" They said this to test Jesus, in order to have some charge against him.

Jesus bent down and started writing on the ground with his finger. And as they continued to ask him, he straightened up and said to them, "Let anyone among you who has no sin be the first to throw a stone at her." And he bent down again, writing on the ground.

As a result of these words, they went away, one by one, starting with the elders, and Jesus was left alone with the woman standing before him. Then Jesus stood up and said to her, "Woman, where are they? Has no one condemned you?" She replied, "No one." And Jesus said, "Neither do I condemn you; go away and don't sin again."

Dn 13:41-62   Jn 8:12-20

Jesus said, "My testimony is true because I know where I have come from and where I am going." He is his own testimony, or rather he and his Father. He does not rely on other people agreeing with him. Jesus had not come to start another small movement of like-minded people, but to bring a new thing into existence. The old is evidence only for the old; the new thing is its own evidence. If you have something new to say, just say it and let it stand on its own feet (or fall!); or something new to do, just do it. The more you try to justify it, the more you destroy its newness.

Jesus said to the Jews, "I am the Light of the world; the one who follows me will not walk in darkness, but will have light and life." The Pharisees replied, "Now you are speaking on your own behalf, your testimony is worthless."

Then Jesus said, "Even though I bear witness to myself, my testimony is true, for I know where I have come from and where I am going. But you do not know where I came from or where I am going.

"You judge by human standards; as for me, I don't judge anyone. But if I had to judge, my judgment would be valid for I am not alone: the Father who sent me is with me. In your Law it is written that the testimony of two witnesses is valid; so I am bearing witness to myself, and the Father who sent me bears witness to me."

They asked him, "Where is your Father?" Jesus answered, "You don't know me or my Father; if you knew me, you would know my Father as well."

Jesus said these things when he was teaching in the Temple area, in the place where they received the offerings. No one arrested him, because his hour had not yet come.

Num 21:4-9   Jn 8:21-30

Jesus said to the Pharisees, "I am going away, and though you look for me, you will die in your sin. Where I am going you cannot come." The Jews wondered, "Why does he say that we can't come where he is going? Will he kill himself?"

But Jesus said, "You are from below and I am from above; you are of this world and I am not of this world. That is why I told you that you will die in your sins. And you shall die in your sins unless you believe that I am He."

They asked him, "Who are you?"; and Jesus said, "Just what I have told you from the beginning. I have much to say about you and much to condemn; but the One who sent me is truthful and everything I learned from him, I proclaim to the world."

They didn't understand that Jesus was speaking to them about the Father. So Jesus said, "When you have lifted up the Son of Man, then you will know that I am He and that I do nothing of myself, but I say just what the Father taught me. He who sent me is with me and has not left me alone; because I always do what pleases him." As Jesus spoke like this, many believed in him.

The "world" in John's gospel is not the physical world, but all the forces in human life that oppose the Kingdom of God. In that sense Jesus is not from here. To crucify someone was to say that he did not belong here, even as a memory. John loved to play on the double meaning of the words, "lifted up": Jesus would be lifted up in shame on the cross, but that lifting up in shame is also a lifting up in glory. God vindicated him by raising him up in glory. All the paradoxes of his life, as well as the paradoxes he spoke are expressed in this. But the gospel is written for us. These paradoxes are to be realized in our lives too—sooner or later, in one way or another.

Dn 3:14-20,91-92,95   Jn 8:31-42

"The truth will make you free" is hard medicine. We would all prefer to be free by an easier method: by escaping the harder realities. We have multiplied and varied the means of escape in the modern world: many of our technical advances are means of escaping not only from the past but also from the present. Here is a good rule: the answer is in the question, the solution is in the problem. It is not by escaping a question that we come to the answer, but by going deeply into it; it is not by escaping a problem that we solve it, but by staying with it. Then we will know for ourselves that it is only the truth that sets us free.

Jesus went on to say to the Jews who believed in him: "You will be my true disciples if you keep my word. Then you will know the truth and the truth will make you free." They answered him, "We are the descendants of Abraham and have never been slaves of anyone. What do you mean by saying: You will be free?"

Jesus answered them, "Truly, I say to you, whoever commits sin is a slave. But the slave doesn't stay in the house forever; the son stays forever. So, if the Son makes you free, you will be really free.

"I know that you are the descendants of Abraham; yet you want to kill me because my word finds no place in you. For my part I speak of what I have seen in the Father's presence, but you do what you have learned from your father."

They answered him, "Our father is Abraham." Then Jesus said, "If you were Abraham's children, you would do as Abraham did. But now you want to kill me, the one who tells you the truth—the truth that I have learned from God. That is not what Abraham did; what you are doing are the works of your father."

The Jews said to him, "We are not illegitimate children; we have one Father, God." Jesus replied, "If God were your Father you would love me, for I came forth from God, and I am here. And I didn't come by my own decision, but it was he himself who sent me."

Gen 17:3-9   Jn 8:51-59

Jesus said to the Jews, "Truly, I say to you, if anyone keeps my word, he will never experience death." The Jews replied, "Now we know that you have a demon. Abraham died and the prophets as well, but you say: 'Whoever keeps my word will never experience death.' Who do you claim to be? Do you claim to be greater than our father Abraham, who died? And the prophets also died."

Then Jesus said, "If I were to praise myself, it would count for nothing. But he who gives glory to me is the Father, the very one you claim as your God, although you don't know him. I know him and if I were to say that I don't know him, I would be a liar like you. But I know him and I keep his word.

"As for Abraham, your ancestor, he looked forward to the day when I would come; and he rejoiced when he saw it."

The Jews then said to him, "You are not yet fifty years old and you have seen Abraham?" And Jesus said "Truly, I say to you, before Abraham was, I am." They then picked up stones to throw at him, but Jesus hid himself and left the Temple.

"Before Abraham was, I am." This echoes God's revelation of his name to Moses, "God said to Moses, I AM WHO I AM. This is what you are to say to the Israelites: 'I AM has sent me to you'" (Exodus 3:14). This is Jesus' clearest claim to divinity in the gospel. It brings to a head all the questions about his identity. His statement was not lost on his hearers, who took up stones to kill him for blasphemy. Before Abraham was, "I am," not "I was." This was a moment "out of time", to use T.S. Eliot's phrase. Ordinary grammar buckles under the strain, past present and future tenses fuse into one. Many centuries later Julian of Norwich would say, mysteriously, "I saw God in a point."

Jer 20:10-13   Jn 10:31-42

Talking about God is not enough, even when it is a Jesus who is talking. This is the greatest challenge to every preacher and every professor of theology. Christians often talk about "the Christian message" as if it could be written on a piece of paper. The Word was made flesh, not ink. Our words have to become flesh too: to reach our fingertips, so to speak. "What good is it," wrote St. James, "if someone claims to have faith but has no deeds? Can such faith save him? St. Francis once said to his brothers, "Go and preach. Use words if you have to."

The Jews picked up stones to throw at Jesus so he said, "I have openly done many good works among you which the Father gave me to do. For which of these do you stone me?"

The Jews answered, "We are not stoning you for doing a good work but for insulting God; you are only a man and you make yourself God."

Then Jesus replied, "Is this not written in your Law: I said: you are gods? So those who received this word of God were called gods and the Scripture is always true. Then what should be said of the one anointed and sent into the world by the Father? Am I insulting God when I say: 'I am the Son of God'?

"If I am not doing the works of my Father, do not believe me. But if I do them, even if you have no faith in me, believe because of the works I do, and know that the Father is in me and I in the Father."

Again they tried to arrest him, but Jesus escaped from their hands. He went away again to the other side of the Jordan, to the place where John had baptized, and there he stayed.

Many people came to him and said, "John showed no miraculous signs, but he spoke of this man and everything he said was true." And many became believers in that place.

Ezk 37:21-28   Jn 11:45-57

Many of the Jews who had come with Mary believed in Jesus when they saw what he did; but some went to the Pharisees and told them what Jesus had done. So the chief priests and the Pharisees called the Sanhedrin Council.

They said, "What are we to do? For this man keeps on giving miraculous signs. If we let him go on like this, all the people will believe in him and, as a result of this, the Romans will come and sweep away our Holy Place and our nation."

Then one of them, Caiaphas, who was High Priest that year, spoke up, "You know nothing at all nor do you see clearly what you need. It is better to have one man die for the people than to let the whole nation be destroyed."

In saying this Caiaphas did not speak for himself, but being High Priest that year, he foretold as a prophet that Jesus would die for the nation, and not for the nation only, but also to gather into one the scattered children of God. So, from that day on, they were determined to kill him.

Because of this, Jesus no longer moved about freely among the Jews. He withdrew instead to the country near the wilderness and stayed with his disciples in a town called Ephraim.

The Passover of the Jews was at hand and people from everywhere were coming to Jerusalem to purify themselves before the Passover. They looked for Jesus and as they stood in the Temple, they talked with one another, "What do you think? Will he come to the festival?" Meanwhile the chief priests and the elders had given orders that anyone who knew where he was should let them know so that they could arrest him.

Sometimes words can be a substitute for action. But they don't always "survive in the valley of their saying," as Auden put it; sometimes they flood down from the mountaintops and shake an Empire. The Sanhedrin knew this. "The Romans will come and sweep away our Holy Place and our nation." So they were determined to kill him. "It is better to have one man die for the people than to let the whole nation be destroyed," said the High Priest. They were not the first, and they were not the last, to kill someone in order to silence him. Most of us don't go that far, but we go some of the way! An interesting list to compile: all the people I silence in subtle or unsubtle ways.

Sunday

"He changed sunset into sunrise," wrote Clement of Alexandria (about 200 AD). He changed the meaning of death. Ignatius of Antioch (martyred in 107 A.D.) wanted to be "a libation poured out to God." In a letter to the Christians in Rome, where he was being brought bound to be thrown to the beasts, he wrote, "There is an altar ready for me. You may form a loving choir around it and sing hymns… for permitting me, Syria's bishop, summoned from the realms of the morning [the East], to have reached the land of the setting sun [Italy, to the west of Syria]. How good it is to be sinking down below the world's horizon towards God, to rise again later into the dawn of his presence!"

PASSION / PALM SUNDAY 4

Is 50:4-7

The Lord Yahweh has taught me so I speak as his disciple and I know how to sustain the weary. Morning after morning he wakes me up to hear, to listen like a disciple. The Lord Yahweh has opened my ear. I have not rebelled, nor have I withdrawn. I offered my back to those who strike me, my cheeks to those who pulled my beard; neither did I shield my face from blows, spittle and disgrace. I have not despaired, for the Lord Yahweh comes to my help. So, like a flint I set my face, knowing that I will not be disgraced.

Phil 2:6-11

Though he was in the form of God, he did not regard equality with God as something to be gnashed but emptied himself, taking on the nature of a servant, made in human likeness, and in his appearance found as a man. He humbled himself by being obedient to death, death on the cross. That is why God exalted him and gave him the Name which outshines all names, so that at the Name of Jesus all knees should bend in heaven, on earth and among the dead, and all tongues proclaim that Christ Jesus is the Lord to the glory of God the Father.

Lk 23:1-49

(...) Along with Jesus, two criminals also were led out to be executed. There at the place called The Skull he was crucified together with the criminals—one on his right and another on his left. (Jesus said, "Father, forgive them for they do not know what they do.") And the guards cast lots to divide his clothes among themselves.

The people stood by watching. As for the rulers, they jeered at him, saying to one another, "Let the man who saved others now save himself, for he is the Messiah, the chosen one of God!"

The soldiers also mocked him and when they drew near to offer him bitter wine, they said, "So you are the king of the Jews? Free yourself!" For above him was an inscription which read, "This is the King of the Jews." (...) It was now about noon. The sun was hidden and darkness came over the whole land until mid-afternoon; and at that time the curtain of the Sanctuary was torn in two. Then Jesus gave a loud cry, "Father, into your hands I commend my spirit." And saying that, he gave up his spirit. (...)

Judas will be with us many times during Holy Week—almost every day. There must be significance in this. We cannot ignore him; we have to look at him. He comes to us already judged and condemned in John's gospel. He stands there, hopeless, expecting no mercy. "Do not judge, and you will not be judged," Jesus had said (Mt 7:1). Our judgment may be factually true: that's the bait on the trap. But it is not the whole truth: that's the trap. All our judgments are incomplete. We don't know the full truth about anyone. And we hardly begin to understand the mercy of God.

Six days before the Passover, Jesus came to Bethany where he had raised Lazarus, the dead man, to life. Now they gave a dinner for him, and while Martha waited on them, Lazarus sat at the table with Jesus.

Then Mary took a pound of costly perfume made from genuine nard and anointed the feet of Jesus, wiping them with her hair. And the whole house was filled with the fragrance of the perfume.

Judas, son of Simon Iscariot-the disciple who was to betray Jesus-remarked, "This perfume could have been sold for three hundred dinaríí and turned over to the poor." Judas, indeed, had no concern for the poor; he was a thief and as he held the common purse, he used to help himself to the funds.

But Jesus spoke up, "Leave her alone. Was she not keeping it for the day of my burial? (The poor you always have with you, but you will not always have me.)"

Many Jews heard that Jesus was there and they came, not only because of Jesus, but also to see Lazarus whom he had raised from the dead. So the chief priests thought about killing Lazarus as well, for many of the Jews were drifting away because of him and believing in Jesus.

6 Tuesday

APRIL

Is 49:1-6   Jn 13:21-33,36-38

Jesus was distressed in spirit and said plainly, "Truly, one of you will betray me." The disciples then looked at one another, wondering who he meant. One of the disciples, the one Jesus loved, was reclining near Jesus; so Simon Peter signaled him to ask Jesus whom he meant.

And the disciple who was reclining near Jesus asked him, "Lord, who is it?" Jesus answered, "I shall dip a piece of bread in the dish, and he to whom I give it, is the one."

So Jesus dipped the bread and gave it to Judas Iscariot, the son of Simon. And as Judas took the piece of bread, Satan entered into him. Jesus then said to him, "What you are going to do, do quickly." None of the others reclining at table understood why Jesus said this to Judas. As he had the common purse, they may have thought that Jesus was telling him, "Buy what we need for the feast," or, "Give something to the poor." Judas left as soon as he had eaten the bread. It was night.

When Judas had gone out, Jesus said, "Now is the Son of Man glorified and God is glorified in him. God will glorify him, and he will glorify him very soon. My children, I am with you for only a little while; you will look for me, but, as I already told the Jews, so now I tell you: where I am going you cannot come.

Simon Peter said to him, "Lord, where are you going?" Jesus answered, "Where I am going you cannot follow me now, but afterwards you will." Peter said, "Lord, why can't I follow you now? I am ready to give my life for you." Jesus answered, "To give your life for me! Truly, I tell you, the cock will not crow before you have denied me three times."

John (or rather the Johannine school) places himself as near to Jesus as he places Judas away. Such dualism is characteristic of John's gospel: light/darkness, above/below, etc. But notice that there are two betrayers in this reading; the other is Peter. But Peter had the courage (or perhaps the opposite) to wait for forgiveness; and he was forgiven (Jn 21). Tragically, Judas didn't wait; he too would have been forgiven. In a tragic twisted way he died for his Master. The writer of these commentaries in 1998, Fr. Fernando Torres, wrote, "Without doubt, God the Father, slow to anger and rich in mercy, had pity on him."

Everyone is capable of the worst. It has been said that one of the great tragedies of war is that we continue to brand the other side as "the enemy," even long after the war is over. That's why we fight another war and another: we never learn that we are all good and bad. Humanity reaches out to embrace the other because the other is a lost part of oneself. The fact that Judas is present to us nearly every day of Holy Week means that we are to try his shoes for size. Fr. Torres in 1998 made the perceptive remark that "Judas sold himself" for thirty pieces of silver. I found another writer of like mind: "Still as of old Men by themselves are priced—For thirty pieces Judas sold Himself, not Christ." (H.H. Cholmondeley)

One of the Twelve, who was called Judas Iscariot, went off to the chief priests and said, "How much will you give me if I hand him over to you?" They promised to give him thirty pieces of silver, and from then on he kept looking for the best way to hand him over to them.

On the first day of the Festival of the Unleavened Bread, the disciples came to Jesus and said to him, "Where do you want us to prepare the Passover meal for you?" Jesus answered, "Go into the city, to the house of a certain man, and tell him: 'The Master says: My hour is near, and I will celebrate the Passover with my disciples in your house." The disciples did as Jesus had ordered and prepared the Passover meal.

When it was evening, Jesus sat at table with the Twelve. While they were eating, Jesus said, "Truly, I say to you: one of you will betray me." They were deeply distressed and asked him in turn, "You do not mean me, do you, Lord?"

He answered, "He who will betray me is one of those who dips his bread in the dish with me. The Son of Man is going as the Scriptures say he will. But alas for that one who betrays the Son of Man; better for him not to have been born." Judas, who was betraying him, also asked, "You do not mean me, Master, do you?" Jesus replied, "You have said it."

8 Thursday

Ex 12:1-8,11-14   1Cor 11:23-26   Jn 13:1-15

It was before the feast of the Passover. Jesus realized that his hour had come to pass from this world to the Father, and as he had loved those who were his own in the world, he would love them with perfect love.

They were at supper and the devil had already put into the mind of Judas, son of Simon Iscariot, to betray. Jesus knew that the Father had entrusted all things to him, and as he had come from God, he was going to God. So he got up from table, removed his garment and taking a towel, wrapped it around his waist. Then he poured water into a basin and began to wash the disciples' feet and to wipe them with the towel he was wearing.

When he came to Simon Peter, Simon said to him, "Why, Lord, you want to wash my feet!" Jesus said, "What I am doing you cannot understand now, but afterwards you will understand it." Peter replied, "You shall never wash my feet." Jesus answered him, "If I do not wash you, you can have no part with me." Then Simon Peter said, "Lord, wash not only my feet, but also my hands and my head!" Jesus replied, "Whoever has taken a bath does not need to wash (except the feet), for he is clean all over. You are clean, though not all of you." Jesus knew who was to betray him; because of this he said, "Not all of you are clean."

When Jesus had finished washing their feet, he put on his garment again, went back to the table and said to them, "Do you understand what I have done to you? You call me Master and Lord, and you are right, for so I am. If I, then, your Lord and Master, have washed your feet, you also must wash one another's feet. I have just given you an example that as I have done, you also may do."

What we call Holy Week was once concentrated into a single night, preceded by a few days of fasting and followed by a long period of joy— Pentecost. At the heart of it was the Eucharist, celebrated at the end of the vigil. It signifies the moment of passage from sadness to joy. It was a vivid reliving of his death and resurrection. In the early centuries there were no other feasts; everything was concentrated into a point. It must have carried tremendous significance. To make sense to us, the Mass (any day of the year) has to be seen as part of this one concentrated event. It will help if we think of Holy Week as one single extended day in which we get time to attend to every detail of the mystery.

Language can only deal
with a small part of
reality; the rest—by far
the greater part—is
silence. Death is the
great silence ultimately
imposed on everyone. If
we are to hear the words
of Jesus, said an early
Christian writer, we must
hear his silence too.
Kneel by his cross, if you
will, but it is better to sit,
because we are going to
have to stay a long time:
all our life, in a way. We
have to sit with our own
pain and sorrow and
resist the temptation to
"solve" them or avoid
them. Only into silence
will they pour out their
meaning.

Christ became obedient for us even to death, dying
on the cross,
Therefore God raised him on high and gave him the
name above all other names.
The Passion of our Lord Jesus Christ according to
John.

Gen 1:1–2:2   Ex 14:15–15:1   Lk 24:1-12

On the sabbath the women rested according to the commandment, but the first day of the week, at dawn, they went to the tomb with the perfumes and ointments they had prepared. Seeing the stone rolled away from the opening of the tomb, they entered and were puzzled to find that the body of the Lord Jesus was not there.

Two men in dazzling garments appeared beside them. In fright the women bowed to the ground. But the men said, "Why look for the living among the dead? (You won't find him here. He is risen.) Remember what he told you in Galilee, that the Son of Man had to be given into the hands of sinners, be crucified, and rise on the third day." And they recalled Jesus' words.

Returning from the tomb, they informed the Eleven and their companions. Among the women who brought the news were Mary Magdalene, Joanna, and Mary the mother of James. But however much they insisted, those who heard did not believe the seemingly nonsensical story. Then Peter got up and ran to the tomb. All he saw there on bending down were the linen cloths. He went home wondering.

The following is from an ancient homily for Holy Saturday. "I command you: Awake, sleeper, I have not made you to be held a prisoner in the underworld. Arise from the dead; I am the life of the dead. Arise, O human being, work of my hands, arise, you who were fashioned in my image. Rise, let us go hence; for you in me and I in you, together we are one undivided person…. Arise, let us go hence. The enemy brought you out of the land of paradise; I will reinstate you, no longer in paradise, but on the throne of heaven. I denied you the tree of life, which was an image, but now I myself am united to you, I who am life…"

Sunday

The Resurrection of Jesus from the dead is the essential Christian proclamation. The gospels are unanimous in making Mary Magdalene and the other women the first to proclaim the distinctive Christian Good News. Tradition has called her "apostola apostolorum": the apostle of the apostles. She was the first Christian preacher. She is a patroness of the Dominican Order, which is called the Order of Preachers, and many Dominican houses are called "St. Magdalene's." She could also be seen as the patroness of all the women who have preached the Gospel in countless ways throughout the Christian centuries.

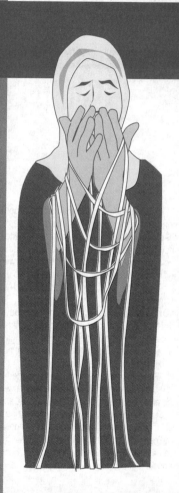

Peter then spoke to the people, "Truly, I realize that God does not show partiality. No doubt you have heard of the event that occurred throughout the whole country of the Jews, beginning from Galilee, after the baptism John preached. You know how God anointed Jesus the Nazarean with Holy Spirit and power. He went about doing good and healing all who were under the devil's power, because God was with him; we are witnesses of all that he did throughout the country of the Jews and in Jerusalem itself. Yet they put him to death by hanging him on a wooden cross. But God raised him to life on the third day and let him manifest himself, not to all the people, but to the witnesses that were chosen beforehand by God—to us who ate and drank with him after his resurrection from death. And he commanded us to preach to the people and to bear witness that he is the one appointed by God to judge the living and the dead. All the prophets say of him, that everyone who believes in him has forgiveness of sins through his Name."

Acts 10:34,37-43

If you are risen with Christ, seek the things that are above, where Christ is seated at the right hand of God. Set your mind on the things that are above, not on earthly things. For you have died and your life is now hidden with Christ in God. When Christ, who is your life, reveals himself, you also will be revealed with him in Glory.

Col 3:1-4

On the first day after the Sabbath, Mary of Magdala came to the tomb early in the morning, while it was still dark and she saw that the stone blocking the tomb had been moved away. She ran to Peter and the other disciple whom Jesus loved. And she said to them, "They have taken the Lord out of the tomb and we don't know where they have laid him." Peter then set out with the other disciple to go to the tomb. They ran together but the other disciple outran Peter and reached the tomb first. He bent down and saw the linen cloths lying flat, but he did not enter. Then Simon Peter came following him and entered the tomb; he, too, saw the linen cloths lying flat. The napkin, which had been around his head was not lying flat like the other linen cloths but lay rolled up in its place. Then the other disciple who had reached the tomb first also went in; he saw and believed. Scripture clearly said that he must rise from the dead, but they had not yet understood that.

Jn 20:1-9

Acts 2:14,22-32   Mt 28:8-15

In a culture that did not accept as valid the testimony of women, it is remarkable that the four gospels did not hesitate to make Mary Magdalene's first testimony of the resurrection of Jesus. It has much to say about the role of women as preachers today. The chief priests and the Jewish authorities were the first to give an explanation of the empty tomb. They would be followed by a cloud of theologians throughout the centuries who have tried to explain everything in the Faith. To "explain" means "to flatten out," and a mystery flattened out is only a theory at best. Perhaps it will be especially through the preaching of women that the mysteries will become mysteries again.

The women left the tomb at once in holy fear, yet with great joy, and they ran to tell the news to the disciples.

Suddenly, Jesus met them on the way and said, "Peace." The women approached him, embraced his feet and worshiped him. But Jesus said to them, "Do not be afraid. Go and tell my brothers to set out for Galilee; there they will see me."

While the women were on their way, the guards returned to the city and some of them reported to the chief priests all that had happened. The chief priests met with the Jewish authorities and decided to give the soldiers a good sum of money, with this instruction, "Say that his disciples came by night while you were asleep, and stole the body of Jesus. If Pilate comes to know of this, we will satisfy him and keep you out of trouble." The soldiers accepted the money and did as they were told. This story has circulated among the Jews until this day.

Acts 2:36-41   Jn 20:11-18

Mary stood weeping outside the tomb, and as she wept she bent down to look inside; she saw two angels in white sitting where the body of Jesus had been, one at the head, and the other at the feet. They said, "Woman, why are you weeping?" She answered, "Because they have taken my Lord and I don't know where they have put him."

As she said this, she turned around and saw Jesus standing there, but she did not recognize him. Jesus said to her, "Woman, why are you weeping? Who are you looking for?" She thought it was the gardener and answered him, "Lord, if you have taken him away, tell me where you have put him, and I will go and remove him."

Jesus said to her, "Mary." She turned and said to him, "Rabboni"—which means, Master. Jesus said to her, "Do not cling to me; you see I have not yet ascended to the Father. But go to my brothers and say to them: I am ascending to my Father, who is your Father, to my God, who is your God."

So Mary of Magdala went and announced to the disciples, "I have seen the Lord, and this is what he said to me."

Referring to himself, Jesus said, "The one who enters by the gate is the shepherd of his sheep.... The sheep listen to his voice. He calls his own sheep by name and leads them out" (Jn 10:2-3). A faith that does not go to the depth of one's personal existence is not faith but theory. Even theology is not faith: a person may know a great deal of theology but have no faith. I heard a woman describe her husband, "He's very interested in religion, but he has no faith." Conversely, a person may know little about religion but have profound faith. St. Thomas Aquinas said that one old lady (una vetera) may have more faith than a host of learned theologians.

Wednesday 14

Acts 3:1-10   Lk 24:13-35

Two men with heavy hearts, full of regrets and foreboding, going in the wrong direction…. Jesus walks beside them and talks with them but they are unable to recognize him. This story is an image of the life of the Church. "Why are you looking for him among the dead?" said the angels to the women at his tomb. Seek him among the living! Your life is unfolding in the present, not in the past; among the living, not among the dead; on the ground, not in the sky. Not in the tomb, not in the sky, but here on the ground; not in the past, not in future, but in the present.

Two disciples of Jesus were going to Emmaus, a village seven miles from Jerusalem, and they talked about what had happened. While they were talking and wondering, Jesus came up and walked with them, but their eyes were held and they did not recognize him.

He asked, "What is this you are talking about?" (…) "It is about Jesus of Nazareth. He was a prophet, you know, mighty in word and deed before God and the people. But the chief priests and our rulers sentenced him to death. They handed him over to be crucified. We had hoped that he would redeem Israel.

It is now the third day since all this took place. (…) He said to them, "How dull you are, how slow of understanding! You fail to believe the message of the prophets. Is it not written that the Christ should suffer all this and then enter his glory?" Then starting with Moses and going through the prophets, he explained to them everything in the Scripture concerning himself.

As they drew near the village they were heading for, Jesus made as if to go farther. But they prevailed upon him, "Stay with us, for night comes quickly. The day is now almost over." So he went in to stay with them. When they were at table, he took the bread, said a blessing, broke it and gave each a piece.

Then their eyes were opened, and they recognized him; but he vanished out of their sight. And they said to each other, "Were not our hearts filled with ardent yearning when he was talking to us on the road and explaining the Scriptures?" (…)

Acts 3:11-26   Lk 24:35-48

The two disciples told what had happened on the road and how Jesus made himself known when he broke bread with them.

As they went on talking about this, Jesus himself stood in their midst. (And he said to them, "Peace to you.") In their panic and fright they thought they were seeing a ghost, but he said to them, "Why are you upset and why do such ideas cross your mind? Look at my hands and feet and see that it is I myself. Touch me and see for yourselves that a ghost has no flesh and bones as I have." (As he said this, he showed his hands and feet.)

In their joy they didn't dare believe and were still astonished. So he said to them, "Have you anything to eat?" and they gave him a piece of broiled fish. He took it and ate it before them.

Then Jesus said to them, "Remember the words I spoke to you when I was still with you: Everything written about me in the Law of Moses, the Prophets and the Psalms had to be fulfilled." Then he opened their minds to understand the Scriptures.

And he went on, "You see what was written: the Messiah had to suffer and on the third day rise from the dead. Then repentance and forgiveness in his name would be proclaimed to all the nations, beginning from Jerusalem. Now you shall be witnesses to this."

The Vatican II document Lumen Gentium has these words, "Every lay person should be a witness before the world to the resurrection and the life of the Lord Jesus, and a sign of the living God" (n. 38). In the highly clericalised Church of the past the laity were cornered into passivity: they were hearers only, not preachers of the Word. Now is the time for them to come into their strength. They will preach what they have "seen and heard," and above all what they have experienced and lived. Preaching with words alone is like a pallid winter sun, giving light but no warmth. The warmth of their lived experienced will give life to their preaching.

APRIL

Friday

16

When we are in doubt we return to what we know: the past. Can I be said to "have" the faith at all if I think of it only as an old ideology battling for survival against new? What about that cataclysmic Now that those broken-down disciples had to enter in order to see the Lord? There is a way of appearing very Catholic, and it is to appear very concerned with the past. Can this be right? Our life doesn't often (or ever?) put us in a tight place like those first disciples. Then we can offer one another bland assurances about the faith, but they will convince no-one, not even ourselves. Unless we experience this "dying to oneself," our words will offer nothing but routes of escape into a reassuring past.

(...) Simon Peter, Thomas who was called the Twin, Nathanael of Cana in Galilee, the sons of Zebedee and two other disciples were together; and Simon Peter said to them, "I'm going fishing." They replied, "We will come with you" and they went out and got into the boat. But they caught nothing that night. When day had already broken, Jesus was standing on the shore, but the disciples did not know that it was Jesus. Jesus called them, "Children, have you anything to eat?" They answered, "Nothing." Then he said to them, "Throw the net on the right side of the boat and you will find some." When they had lowered the net, they were not able to pull it in because of the great number of fish. Then the disciple Jesus loved said to Peter, "It's the Lord!" At these words, "It's the Lord," Simon Peter put on his clothes, for he was stripped for work, and jumped into the water. The other disciples came in the boat dragging the net full of fish; they were not far from land, about a hundred meters. When they landed, they saw a charcoal fire with fish on it, and some bread. Jesus said to them, "Bring some of the fish you've just caught." So Simon Peter climbed into the boat and pulled the net to shore. It was full of big fish—one hundred and fifty-three—but, in spite of this, the net was not torn. Jesus said to them, "Come and have breakfast," and not one of the disciples dared ask him, "Who are you?" for they knew it was the Lord. Jesus then came and took the bread and gave it to them, and he did the same with the fish. This was the third time that Jesus revealed himself to his disciples after rising from the dead.

17 Saturday

APRIL

Acts 4:13-21   Mk 16:9-15

Is the faith something you "have," or something you "do"? The simplest words in the language are the most difficult to understand: God, faith, hope, love, soul, mind… and those real chestnuts: have, do, be. They don't appear to be difficult, because we use them so fluently and so often. But look at any one of them and tell me what it means. Our faith is a bottomless ocean. How could it be otherwise Our faith takes us beyond all our ready categories. Speak of it, if we will, as something we "have"; but it is safer to think of it as something we "do," and even something that we "are," by God's gift.

After Jesus rose early on the first day of the week, he appeared first to Mary of Magdala from whom he had driven out seven demons. She went and reported the news to his followers, who were now mourning and weeping. But when they heard that he lived and had been seen by her, they would not believe it.

After this he showed himself in another form to two of them, as they were walking into the country. These men too went back and told the others, but they did not believe them.

Later Jesus showed himself to the Eleven while they were at table. He reproached them for their unbelief and stubbornness in refusing to believe those who had seen him after he had risen.

Then he told them, "Go out to the whole world and proclaim the Good News to all creation."

Sunday

Timothy Radcliffe commented on this passage: "It is the sight of the wounded Christ that frees the disciples from fear and makes them glad. It is the wounded Christ that transforms them into preachers. One cannot be a preacher without getting wounded. The Word became flesh, and was hurt and killed. He was powerless in the face of the powers of this world....When we see the wounded Christ, then we can face the fact that we are already hurt. Every one of us is a wounded preacher. But the good news is that we are preachers because we are wounded."

Acts 5:12-16

Many miraculous signs and wonders were done among the people through the hands of the apostles. The believers, of one accord, used to meet in Solomon's Porch. None of the others dared to join them, but the people held them in high esteem. So an ever increasing number of men and women, believed in the Lord. The people carried the sick into the streets and laid them on cots and on mats, so that when Peter passed by, at least his shadow might fall on some of them. The people gathered from the towns around Jerusalem, bringing their sick and those who were troubled by unclean spirits, and all of them were healed.

Rev 1:9-13,17-19
Jn 20:19-31

On the evening of that day, the first day after the Sabbath, the doors were locked where the disciples were, because of their fear of the Jews, but Jesus came and stood in their midst. He said to them, "Peace be with you"; then he showed them his hands and his side. The disciples kept looking at the Lord and were full of joy.

Again Jesus said to them, "Peace be with you. As the Father has sent me, so I send you." After saying this he breathed on them and said to them, "Receive the Holy Spirit; for those whose sins you forgive, they are forgiven; for those whose sins you retain, they are retained." Thomas, the Twin, one of the Twelve, was not with them when Jesus came. The other disciples told him, "We have seen the Lord." But he replied, "Until I have seen in his hands the print of the nails, and put my finger in the mark of the nails and my hand in his side, I will not believe."

Eight days later, the disciples were inside again and Thomas was with them. Despite the locked doors Jesus came and stood in their midst and said, "Peace be with you." Then he said to Thomas, "Put your finger here and see my hands; stretch out your hand and put it into my side. Resist no longer and be a believer."

Thomas then said, "You are my Lord and my God." Jesus replied, "You believe because you see me, don't you? Happy are those who have not seen and believe."

There were many other signs that Jesus gave in the presence of his disciples, but they are not recorded in this book. These are recorded so that you may believe that Jesus is the Christ, the Son of God; believe and you will have life through his Name.

Acts 4:23-31   Jn 3:1-8

Julian of Norwich has this to say: "When our soul is breathed into our body, bringing our senses to life, then mercy and grace immediately begin to work, caring for us and protecting us with pity and love. At the same time the Holy Spirit takes our faith and in it forms the hope that when we have grown and become mature in the Holy Spirit, we shall return to our essential being above, to the powerful goodness of Christ. In this way I understood that our physical nature is grounded in God's nature, mercy, and grace—a grounding which enables us to receive gifts that lead us on to eternal life. I saw with absolute certainty that our being is in God…'"

Among the Pharisees there was a ruler of the Jews named Nicodemus. He came to Jesus by night and said, "Rabbi, we know that you have come from God to teach us, for no one can perform miraculous signs like yours unless God is with him."

Jesus replied, "Truly, I say to you, no one can see the kingdom of God unless he is born again from above."

Nicodemus said, "How can there be rebirth for a grown man? Who could go back to his mother's womb and be born again?" Jesus replied, "Truly, I say to you: No one can enter the kingdom of God without being born of water and Spirit. What is born of the flesh is flesh, and what is born of the Spirit is spirit. Because of this, don't be surprised when I say: 'You must be born again from above.'

"The wind blows where it pleases and you hear its sound, but you don't know where it comes from or where it is going. It is like that with everyone who is born of the Spirit."

Acts 4:32-37   Jn 3:7-15

In Hebrew and Aramaic the same word means "spirit," "breath," and "wind." These are well known and yet unknown realities. Of the four elements—fire, air, earth and water—only earth has fixed shapes; and in the long term even these shapes are not fixed. But the most volatile of the elements is air. The world is perpetually changing, and it's hard to "get a fix on it." But do we have to get a fix on it before we can live in it? Not at all. In fact there is no fixity anywhere, except as a thought in the mind. The words of Jesus in today's passage may be an echo of that verse. "The wind blows where it pleases.... It is like that with everyone who is born of the Spirit." It is the same then with the Holy Spirit as with wind, spirit, breath....

Jesus said to Nicodemus, "Because of this, don't be surprised when I say: 'You must be born again from above.'

"The wind blows where it pleases and you hear its sound, but you don't know where it comes from or where it is going. It is like that with everyone who is born of the Spirit."

Nicodemus asked again, "How can this be?" And Jesus answered, "You are a teacher in Israel, and you don't know these things!

"Truly, I say to you, we speak of what we know and we witness to the things we have seen, but you don't accept our testimony. If you don't believe when I speak of earthly things, what then, when I speak to you of heavenly things? No one has ever gone up to heaven except the one who came from heaven, the Son of Man.

"As Moses lifted up the serpent in the desert, so must the Son of Man be lifted up, so that whoever believes in him may have eternal life."

Acts 5:17-26   Jn 3:16-21

"The one who believes in the Son has eternal life" (3:36). To us this may sound equally premature. The key to it is the word "belief." John could not have imagined, I'm sure, that the day would come when believing could mean just a nominal adherence. He would not have been called a nominal Christian a believer. And conversely a nominal disbeliever is not beyond the reach of the Good Shepherd. That English word "belief".... The root of it is a now obsolete word "lief," which meant "love." Belief without love is not belief at all; it is only a mental game of noughts and crosses. If John were here today, and aware of our usage, he might say, "Don't tell me what you "believe"; tell me what you love."

Yes, God so loved the world that he gave his only Son that whoever believes in him may not be lost, but may have eternal life. God did not send the Son into the world to condemn the world; instead, through him the world is to be saved. Whoever believes in him will not be condemned. He who does not believe is already condemned, because he has not believed in the Name of the only Son of God.

This is how the Judgment is made: Light has come into the world and people loved darkness rather than light because their deeds were evil. For whoever does wrong hates the light and doesn't come to the light for fear that his deeds will be shown as evil. But whoever lives according to the truth comes into the light so that it can be clearly seen that his works have been done in God.

Acts 5:27-33   Jn 3:31-36

Jesus said to Nicodemus, "He who comes from above is above all; he who comes from the earth belongs to the earth and his words, too, are earthly. The One who comes from heaven speaks of the things he has seen and heard; he bears witness to this but no one accepts his testimony. Whoever does receive his testimony acknowledges the truthfulness of God.

"The one sent by God speaks God's words and gives the Spirit without measure. For the Father loves the Son and has entrusted everything into his hands. Whoever believes in the Son lives with eternal life, but he who will not believe in the Son will never know life and always faces the justice of God."

Jesus has given us everything, "I have made known to you everything I have learnt from my Father" (15:15). "The glory you have given me, I have given them" (17:22). The word "everything" seems to be God's kind of word; and the word "all." It was the fundamental command. "Love the Lord your God with all your heart and with all your soul and with all your strength" (Deut 6:5). He is not interested in how much it amounts to, so long as it is everything: the widow's mite was "all she had to live on" (Mk 12:44). We may not have much, but we have everything! When we give everything we have we are being drawn into the life of the Trinity.

APRIL

Monday

23

**EASTER
2nd Week**

Sts. Adalbert & George

Acts 5:34-42   Jn 6:1-15

Sitting on the ground is a symbol of poverty and powerlessness; it means we have no illusions of grandeur. We don't often sit on the ground nowadays, and almost never at Mass. But when we are at Mass we are spiritually those disciples in today's reading, sitting on the ground in humility and simplicity, sharing our poverty and (because of it) sharing the Lord's gift. Miracles seem to happen in situations of scarcity rather than plenty. Where there is plenty there is no need of miracles! The miracle is that some kind of abundance came from that poverty. Whatever divides us from one another (greed, self-sufficiency, illusions of grandeur) divides us also from God and God's gift.

Jesus went to the other side of the Sea of Galilee, near Tiberias, and large crowds followed him because of the miraculous signs they saw when he healed the sick. So he went up into the hills and sat down there with his disciples. Now the Passover, the feast of the Jews, was at hand. Then lifting up his eyes, Jesus saw the crowds that were coming to him and said to Philip, "Where shall we buy bread so that these people may eat?" He said this to test Philip, for he himself knew what he was going to do. Philip answered him, "Two hundred silver coins would not buy enough bread for each of them to have a piece."

Then one of Jesus' disciples, Andrew, Simon Peter's brother, said, "There is a boy here who has five barley loaves and two fish; but what good are these for so many?" Jesus said, "Make the people sit down." There was plenty of grass there so the people, about five thousand men, sat down to rest. Jesus then took the loaves, gave thanks and distributed them to those who were seated. He did the same with the fish and gave them as much as they wanted. And when they had eaten enough, he told his disciples, "Gather up the pieces left over, that nothing may be lost."

So they gathered them up and filled twelve baskets with bread, that is with pieces of the five barley loaves left by those who had eaten. When the people saw this sign that Jesus had just given, they said, "This is really the Prophet, he who is to come into the world." Jesus realized that they would come and take him by force to make him king; so he fled to the hills by himself.

Acts 6:1-7   Jn 6:16-21

As in other cultures, water had a double meaning for the Jews of old: it was both a benign and a destructive element. They especially feared the chaos of the sea, which brought remembrance of the Deluge. A constant theme in the Old Testament is the power of God over the sea. It was by such power that he delivered them from the Egyptians in the Exodus. Clearly John wants this association to be present to the reader. What meaning can this strange story have for us today? This occurs to me: the Lord can come to us in the least likely medium. We seat ourselves on the solid ground of common sense and logic, but he is well able to do without them!

When evening came, the disciples went down to the shore. After a while they got into a boat to make for Capernaum on the other side of the sea, for it was now dark and Jesus had not yet come to them. But the sea was getting rough because a strong wind was blowing.

They had rowed about three or four miles, when they saw Jesus walking on the sea, and he was drawing near to the boat. They were frightened, but he said to them, "It is Me; don't be afraid."

They wanted to take him into the boat, but immediately the boat was at the shore to which they were going.

Sunday

Three times Jesus asked Peter, "Do you love me?" People like to connect this with Peter's triple denial of Jesus: he was being given a chance to undo the damage. There is something touching about this. Peter wasn't yet able to love Jesus in that heroic way; he could love him only as the friend he had known for three years. But the third time around, Jesus steps down, as it were, to accept what Peter was able to offer at that time. Can we put it this way: all forms of love and friendship are capable of advancing gradually towards to 'agapè'. How do we go along that road? By doing the best we can.

Acts 5:27-32,40-41

The guards brought the disciples in the Temple and the Council and the High Priest began to questioned them, "We gave you strict orders not to preach such a Savior; but you have filled Jerusalem with your teaching and you intend charging us with the killing of this man." To this Peter and the apostles replied, "Better for us to obey God rather than any human authority! The God of our ancestors raised Jesus whom you killed by hanging him on a wooden post. God set him at his right hand as Leader and Savior, to grant repentance and forgiveness of sins to Israel. We are witnesses to all these things, as well as the Holy Spirit whom God has given to those who obey him. (...)"

Rev 5:11-14
Jn 21:1-19

(...) Simon Peter, Thomas who was called the Twin, Nathanael of Cana in Galilee, the sons of Zebedee and two other disciples were together; and Simon Peter said to them, "I'm going fishing." They replied, "We will come with you" and they went out and got into the boat. But they caught nothing that night. When day had already broken, Jesus was standing on the shore, but the disciples did not know that it was Jesus. (...) Jesus said to them, "Come and have breakfast," and not one of the disciples dared ask him, "Who are you?" for they knew it was the Lord. Jesus then came and took the bread and gave it to them, and he did the same with the fish. This was the third time that Jesus revealed himself to his disciples after rising from the dead. After they had finished breakfast, Jesus said to Simon Peter, "Simon, son of John, do you love me more than these?" He answered, "Yes, Lord, you know that I love you." And Jesus said, "Feed my lambs." A second time Jesus said to him, "Simon, son of John, do you love me?" And Peter answered, "Yes, Lord, you know that I love you." Jesus said to him, "Look after my sheep." And a third time he said to him, "Simon, son of John, do you love me?" Peter was saddened because Jesus asked him a third time, "Do you love me?" and he said, "Lord, you know everything; you know that I love you." Jesus then said, "Feed my sheep. Truly, I say to you, when you were young you put on your belt and walked where you liked. But when you grow old, you will stretch out your hands and another will put a belt around you and lead you where you do not wish to go." Jesus said this to make known the kind of death by which Peter was to glorify God. And he added, "Follow me."

Acts 6:8-15   Jn 6:22-29

A sign points away from itself, but people weren't interested in looking beyond, he said. This is a distinctive theme of John's gospel. Miracles, here, are not so much acts of compassion (as in the other gospels) as signs of the glory of Christ. John's gospel was written many years after the others, and his aim was not just to recount the deeds that Jesus did to try further to discern their meaning. The single incident has a meaning for all time. Jesus is forever feeding the hungry, illuminating the path, raising the dead. In the 4th century, St. Gregory of Nyssa wrote, "I believe Bethlehem, Golgotha, the Mount of Olives and the resurrection to be truly in the heart of the one who has found God."

Next day the people who had stayed on the other side realized that only one boat had been there and that Jesus had not entered it with his disciples; rather, the disciples had gone away alone. Bigger boats from Tiberias came near the place where all these people had eaten the bread. When they saw that neither Jesus nor his disciples were there, they got into the boats and went to Capernaum looking for Jesus.

When they found him on the other side of the lake, they asked him, "Master, when did you come here?"

Jesus answered, "Truly, I say to you, you look for me, not because you have seen through the signs, but because you ate bread and were satisfied. Work then, not for perishable food, but for the lasting food which gives eternal life. The Son of Man will give it to you, for he is the one the Father has marked."

Then the Jews asked him, "What shall we do? What are the works that God wants us to do?" And Jesus answered them, "The work God wants is this: that you believe in the One whom God has sent."

Acts 7:51–8:1   Jn 6:30–35

"Moses gave.... My Father gives." The meaning of the past is in the present. We are immersed once again in the endless puzzles about time. If the meaning of the past is in the present, did the past have any meaning when it was just the past? Now for a puzzle: the past was never the past! It is from the perspective of each succeeding present moment that the past is seen as past. So in a sense there never was a past! It is only our way of looking back at it that makes it past. We are more familiar with this when it regards the future. Tomorrow never comes, we say. No yesterday, no tomorrow. Then where are we? We are in an eternally renewed present moment.

They then said, "Show us miraculous signs, that we may see and believe you. What sign do you perform? Our ancestors ate manna in the desert; as Scripture says: They were given bread from heaven to eat."

Jesus then said to them, "Truly, I say to you, it was not Moses who gave you the bread from heaven. My Father gives you the true bread from heaven. The bread God gives is the One who comes from heaven and gives life to the world." And they said to him, "Give us this bread always."

Jesus said to them, "I am the bread of life; whoever comes to me shall never be hungry, and whoever believes in me shall never be thirsty."

Acts 8:1-8   Jn 6:35-40

In a bookshop recently I saw the old penny catechism. The last time I saw it, it was being beaten into me with a stick! The words were familiar, and somehow terrible. God was described as Creator of all things, who rewards the good and punishes the wicked. He was capable to do this, since he "sees our most secret thoughts and actions." There was no suggestion that God was love. I was suddenly aware of how damaged I had been by that catechism. "Whoever does not love does not know God, for God is love" (1 Jn 4:8). That catechism left me starving, and it is not surprising that many starved to death spiritually. Today's gospel reading merits long meditation.

Jesus said to the disciples, "I am the bread of life; whoever comes to me shall never be hungry, and whoever believes in me shall never be thirsty. Nevertheless, as I said, you refuse to believe, even when you have seen. Yet, all that the Father gives me will come to me, and whoever comes to me, I shall not turn away. For I have come from heaven, not to do my own will, but the will of the One who sent me.

"And the will of him who sent me is that I lose nothing of what he has given me, but instead that I raise it up on the last day. This is the will of the Father, that whoever sees the Son and believes in him shall live with eternal life; and I will raise him up on the last day."

Acts 8:26-40   Jn 6:44-51

Jesus said, "No one can come to me unless he is drawn by the Father who sent me; and I will raise him up on the last day. It has been written in the Prophets: They shall all be taught by God. So whoever listens and learns from the Father comes to me.

"For no one has seen the Father except the One who comes from God; he has seen the Father. Truly, I say to you, whoever believes has eternal life.

"I am the bread of life. Though your ancestors ate the manna in the desert, they died. But here you have the bread which comes from heaven so that you may eat of it and not die.

"I am the living bread which has come from heaven; whoever eats of this bread will live forever. The bread I shall give is my flesh and I will give it for the life of the world."

A few days after I found the catechism that I mentioned yesterday, I met the man who had it republished. I knew him, a good and forgiving man, and he was not at all aggrieved! He was disturbed, though, by the lack of knowledge of our religion among many people. In other times it was believed that we could be pushed into faith. Strange to say, being pushed makes a person resist. I often thought that if good were forbidden, more people would do it! The best way to move a person is to attract rather than push. Attraction is less clear and satisfactory than compulsion, but that's our life. Jesus rejected the way of compulsion and chose the way of love. It is the only one that has no trap built into it.

The phrase "eat my flesh and drink my blood" was wide open to misunderstanding. There was an expression "to eat someone's flesh", meaning to slander a person. Such texts were about vengeance, not about intimacy and communion. Christians tended to see the separate mention of flesh and blood as a sign of the death of Jesus, but the more common view among scholars now is that it means: the whole living Christ. The words of Jesus stand there, calling us to something deeper than the intellectual satisfaction that explanations give. We are hungry in deeper places than that.

The Jews were arguing among themselves, "How can this man give us flesh to eat?" So Jesus replied, "Truly, I say to you, if you do not eat the flesh of the Son of Man and drink his blood, you have no life in you. The one who eats my flesh and drinks my blood live with eternal life and I will raise him up on the last day.

"My flesh is really food and my blood is drink. Those who eat my flesh and drink my blood, live in me and I in them. Just as the Father, who is life, sent me and I have life from the Father, so whoever eats me will have life from me. This is the bread which came from heaven; unlike that of your ancestors, who ate and later died. Those who eat this bread will live forever."

Jesus spoke in this way in Capernaum when he taught them in the synagogue.

EASTER
3rd Week
St. Joseph the Worker

Gen 1:26–2:3   Mt 13:54-58

1   Saturday

M A Y

In the past we used to refer to manual work as "servile work". It was forbidden on Sundays. "Servile" comes from the Latin "servilis," meaning "of a slave." "Servile work" means "the work of slaves." This disdain of manual work is certainly not from the Gospel. It is from class-conscious societies that expected manual workers to be "servile" not only in their work but in their manners. It is tragic that this was ever allowed to infect Christian practice. We could honor St. Joseph today by consciously seeing our manual work as a way of meditation, and a way of sanctification.

Jesus went to his hometown and taught the people in their synagogue. They were amazed and said, "Where did he get this wisdom and these special powers? Isn't he the carpenter's son? Isn't Mary his mother and aren't James, Joseph, Simon and Judas his brothers? Aren't all his sisters living here? How did he get all this?" And so they took offense at him.

Jesus said to them, "The only place where prophets are not welcome is their hometown and in their own family." And he did not perform many miracles there because of their lack of faith.

Sunday

"I and the Father are one." This is one of "hard sayings" of Jesus. He is not saying it in a weak sense: that he and the Father are of like mind, etc. In Greek it says, literally, "I and the Father are one thing." The union of Jesus with the Father is the inexhaustible mystery of our Faith. It is not only about Jesus; it has to do with us too. In this age when so much emphasis is placed on the individual, we are inclined to see Jesus too just as an individual—a special one, to be sure, but still an individual. That could not be a full account of Jesus. He is "the first-born of many brothers and sisters," "He is the head, we are the body." He came into the world for us, not for himself.

Acts 13:14,43-52

Paul and Barnabas went on from Perga and came to Antioch in Pisidia. On the Sabbath day they entered the synagogue and sat down.

After that, when the assembly broke up, many Jews and devout God-fearing people followed them and to these they spoke, urging them to hold fast to the grace of God.

The following Sabbath almost the entire city gathered to listen to Paul, who spoke a fairly long time about the Lord. But the presence of such a crowd made the Jews jealous. So they began to oppose with insults whatever Paul said.

Then Paul and Barnabas spoke out firmly, saying, "It was necessary that God's word be first proclaimed to you, but since you now reject it and judge yourselves to be unworthy of eternal life, we turn to non-Jewish people. For thus we were commanded by the Lord: I have set you as a light to the pagan nations, so that you may bring my salvation to the ends of the earth." Those who were not Jews rejoiced when they heard this and praised the message of the Lord, and all those destined for everlasting life believed in it. Thus the Word spread throughout the whole region.

Some of the Jews, however, incited God-fearing women of the upper class and the leading men of the city, as well, and stirred up an intense persecution against Paul and Barnabas. Finally they had them expelled from their region. The apostles shook the dust from their feet in protest against this people and went to Iconium, leaving the disciples filled with joy and Holy Spirit.

Rev 7:9,14-17

Jn 10:27-30

Jesus said, "My sheep hear my voice and I know them; they follow me and I give them eternal life. They shall never perish and no one will ever steal them from me. What the Father has given me is above everything else and no one can snatch it from the Father's hand. I and the Father are one."

M A Y

Monday

3

EASTER
4th Week

Sts. Philip & James, Apostles

1Cor 15:1-8   Jn 14:6-14

Philip was the first person to whom Jesus said, "Follow me!" (Jn 1:45). James was "brother of the Lord," understood to mean cousin. From today's reading, four words to dwell on—spoken by Jesus to Philip—four words that are almost like icons, to come back to again and again:
1) "Whoever has seen me has seen the Father."
2) "I am in the Father and the Father is in me."
3) "The words that I say to you I do not speak on my own." 4) "The Father who dwells in me does his works." Don't forget that these words are not only about Jesus; they are about us too.

Jesus said, "I am the way, the truth and the life; no one comes to the Father but through me. If you know me, you will know the Father also; indeed you know him and you have seen him."

Philip asked him, "Lord, show us the Father and that is enough." Jesus said to him, "What! I have been with you so long and you still do not know me, Philip? Whoever sees me sees the Father; how can you say: 'Show us the Father'? Do you not believe that I am in the Father and the Father is in me?

"All that I say to you, I do not say of myself. The Father who dwells in me is doing his own work. Believe me when I say that I am in the Father and the Father is in me; at least believe it on the evidence of these works that I do.

"Truly, I say to you, the one who believes in me will do the same works that I do; and he will even do greater than these, for I am going to the Father. Everything you ask in my name, I will do, so that the Father may be glorified in the Son. And everything you ask in calling upon my Name, I will do."

Acts 11:19-26   Jn 10:22-30

"The works I do in my Father's name proclaim who I am." He is entirely transparent; he is hiding nothing; he is the revelation of what God is and what humanity is. Then we see him "walking back and forth in the portico of Solomon." This pacing back and forth is somehow deeply affecting. From our childhood we may retain some idea of him seated on a throne, or else doing only highly purposeful things—but pacing back and forth, alone…. "In him all the fullness of God was pleased to dwell" (Col 1:19), but here he is, in a kind of non-moment…. We should not interrupt. In a way it is in the non-moment that everything comes into being.

The time came for the feast of the Dedication. It was winter and Jesus walked back and forth in the portico of Solomon. The Jews then gathered around him and said to him, "How long will you keep us in doubt? If you are the Messiah, tell us plainly." Jesus answered, "I have already told you but you do not believe. The works I do in my Father's name proclaim who I am, but you don't believe because, as I said, you are not my sheep.

"My sheep hear my voice and I know them; they follow me and I give them eternal life. They shall never perish and no one will ever steal them from me. What the Father has given me is above everything else and no one can snatch it from the Father's hand. I and the Father are one."

"Honesty is the best policy," it is said. But if you are honest only as a policy, are you honest? If there arose a situation where honesty wasn't to your advantage, would you still want to be honest? If so, then honesty is much more to you than a policy. We could say the same about any virtue you mention. It has to be for its own sake, not for the sake of anything else. Jesus was entirely transparent. "Whoever sees me sees the One who sent me." Because he had moved beyond self-defense he was not in competition with anyone. He neither judged nor condemned. "I have come not to condemn the world but to save it."

Jesus had said, and even cried out, "Whoever believes in me, believes not in me but in him who sent me. And whoever sees me, sees him who sent me. I have come into the world as light, so that whoever believes in me may not remain in darkness.

"If anyone hears my words and does not keep them, I am not the one to condemn him; for I have come, not to condemn the world, but to save the world. The one who rejects me, and does not receive my word, already has a judge: the very word I have spoken will condemn him on the last day.

"For I have not spoken on my own authority; the Father who sent me has instructed me in what to say and how to speak. I know that his commandment is eternal life, and that is why the message I give, I give as the Father instructed me."

Acts 13:13-25   Jn 13:16-20

"I never saw, heard, nor read that the clergy were beloved in any nation where Christianity was the religion of the country. Nothing can render them popular but some degree of persecution," wrote Jonathan Swift, the author of Gulliver's Travels. Swift was himself a clergyman, and may be thought to speak from experience; but his temperament was more that of the persecutor. In Christian art and life why hasn't more been made of that Gospel's scene: Jesus washing the disciples' feet? The Church was too often distracted with other concerns: power, precedence, law.... Had it always remained faithful to the spirit of the Gospel—well, there should never be a world without a Swift!

[After Jesus had washed the feet of the disciples he said,] "Truly, I say to you, the servant is not greater than his master, nor is the messenger greater than he who sent him. Understand this, and blessed are you if you put it into practice.

"I am not speaking of you all, because I know the ones I have chosen and the Scripture has to be fulfilled that says, The one who shared my table has risen against me. I tell you this now before it happens, so that when it does happen, you may know that I am He.

"Truly, I say to you, whoever welcomes the one I send, welcomes me, and whoever welcomes me, welcomes the One who sent me."

Acts 13:26-33   Jn 14:1-6

One of the greatest tragedies of the Church is that it became, in many periods of history, a power-structure, a caste of insiders. It is in constant danger of defining itself in this way. "Outside the Church there is no salvation," was once a theological axiom. How did people of that time read today's passage, "In my Father's house there are many rooms"? No doubt it was put safely out of harm's way into the next world: as referring to heaven, not earth. (Scholars, ancient and modern, have much to add to that interpretation.) Even so, there still remains the saying of Jesus, "I am the way…". Jesus is the way: the Jesus who told a story about a lost sheep….

Jesus said to his disciples, "Do not be troubled; trust in God and trust in me. In my Father's house there are many rooms. Otherwise I would not have told you that I go to prepare a place for you. After I have gone and prepared a place for you, I shall come again and take you to me, so that where I am, you also may be. Yet you know the way where I am going."

Thomas said to him, "Lord, we don't know where you are going; how can we know the way?" Jesus said, "I am the way, the truth and the life; no one comes to the Father but through me."

Acts 13:44-52   Jn 14:7-14

Towards the end of the reading we see the words, "Everything you ask in my name I will do...." "In my name" means "in my presence." There are many things we could never ask for in the presence of Jesus; the words would die on our lips. Ultimately all our searching and seeking is a searching for God. Julian of Norwich, the 14th-century English mystic, wrote, "Seeking with faith, hope and love pleases our Lord and finding him pleases the soul, filling it full of joy... It is God's will for us to go on seeking until we see him, for it is because of this that he will show himself to us in his special grace, when he so wills." "Seeking with faith, hope and love."

Jesus said to his disciples, "If you know me, you will know the Father also; indeed you know him and you have seen him."

Philip asked him, "Lord, show us the Father and that is enough." Jesus said to him, "What! I have been with you so long and you still do not know me, Philip? Whoever sees me sees the Father; how can you say: 'Show us the Father'? Do you not believe that I am in the Father and the Father is in me?

"All that I say to you, I do not say of myself. The Father who dwells in me is doing his own work. Believe me when I say that I am in the Father and the Father is in me; at least believe it on the evidence of these works that I do.

"Truly, I say to you, the one who believes in me will do the same works that I do; and he will even do greater than these, for I am going to the Father. Everything you ask in my name, I will do, so that the Father may be glorified in the Son. And everything you ask in calling upon my Name, I will do."

Sunday

"I give you a new commandment: love one another." You can be commanded to obey, to behave this way or that, but how can you be commanded to love? External behavior is subject to external rules, but how can the inner movement of our spirit be commanded? Can you be commanded to remember, or to forget, to think, to feel…? How can you be commanded to love? In "commanding" us to love, Jesus is telling us to look, to see our true nature and to follow it. It is like the inner urgency to eat when you are hungry, to drink when you are thirsty.

5TH SUNDAY IN ORDINARY TIME

Mother's Day

9

Acts 14:21-27

After proclaiming the gospel in that town and making many disciples, they returned to Lystra and Iconium and on to Antioch. They were strengthening the disciples and encouraging them to remain firm in the faith, for they said, "We must go through many trials to enter the Kingdom of God." In each church they appointed elders and, after praying and fasting, they commended them to the Lord in whom they had placed their faith. Then they traveled through Pisidia, and came to Pamphylia. They preached the Word in Perga and went down to Attalia. From there they sailed back to Antioch, where they had first been commended to God's grace for the task they had now completed. On their arrival they gathered the Church together and told them all that God had done through them and how he had opened the door of faith to the non-Jews.

Rev 21:1-5

I, John, saw a new heaven and a new earth. The first heaven and the first earth had passed away and no longer was there any sea. I saw the new Jerusalem, the holy city coming down from God, out of heaven, adorned as a bride prepared for her husband. A loud voice came from the throne, "Here is the dwelling of God among mortals: He will pitch his tent among them and they will be his people; God will be with them and wipe every tear from their eyes. There shall be no more death or mourning, crying out or pain, for the world that was has passed away." The One seated on the throne said, "See, I make all things new." And then he said to me, "Write these words because they are sure and true."

Jn 13:31-35

When Judas had gone out, Jesus said, "Now is the Son of Man glorified and God is glorified in him. God will glorify him, and he will glorify him very soon.

My children, I am with you for only a little while; you will look for me, but, as I already told the Jews, so now I tell you: where I am going you cannot come. Now I give you a new commandment: love one another. Just as I have loved you, you also must love one another. By this everyone will know that you are my disciples, if you have love for one another."

Acts 14:5-18   Jn 14:21-26

"If anyone loves me," Jesus said, "...I shall show myself clearly to them." And if anyone just thinks about me (we could add) they may pass exams in theology but they will not know me at all. Ordinary seeing and understand are the view from the outside. Love is the view from the inside. It is less well able to compare and to see limits. For that reason it is sometimes imprudent and even mad. But it is a divine madness, deeper and larger-souled than all our reasoning. St. Catherine of Siena imagined God to be mad. "You are madly in love with the beauty of your creatures." (If love is mad, God is mad!)

Jesus said to his disciples, "Whoever keeps my commandments is the one who loves me. If he loves me, he will also be loved by my Father; I too shall love him and show myself clearly to him."

Judas—not the Iscariot—asked Jesus, "Lord, how can it be that you will show yourself clearly to us and not to the world?" Jesus answered him, "If anyone loves me, he will keep my word and my Father will love him; and we will come to him and make a room in his home. But if anyone does not love me, he will not keep my words, and these words that you hear are not mine but the Father's who sent me.

"I told you all this while I was still with you. From now on the Helper, the Holy Spirit whom the Father will send in my name, will teach you all things and remind you of all that I have told you."

Acts 14:19-28   Jn 14:27-31

The Jews say, "Shalom!", which means, "Peace!" This fine greeting too can become rather superficial unless we see some depth of God in it. It was a prayer for full harmony with God—for salvation. Here is the original text in which Jews were told to greet and bless one another with "Peace": "Thus you shall bless the Israelites: You shall say to them, 'The Lord bless you and keep you; the Lord make his face to shine upon you, and be gracious to you; the Lord lift up his countenance upon you, and give you peace" (Num 6:22-26). This is a wonderful blessing, worth learning by heart.. It is a prayer for "the peace that the world cannot give."

Jesus said to his disciples, "Peace be with you; I give you my peace. Not as the world gives peace do I give it to you. Do not be troubled; do not be afraid. You heard me say: 'I am going away, but I am coming to you.' If you loved me, you would be glad that I go to the Father, for the Father is greater than I.

"I have told you this now before it takes place, so that when it does happen you may believe. It is very little what I may still tell you, for the prince of this world is at hand, although there is nothing in me that he can claim. But see, the world must know that I love the Father and that I do what the Father has taught me to do. Come now, let us go."

M A Y

Wednesday

12

EASTER
5th Week
Sts. Nereus, Achilleus & Pancras

Acts 15:1-6   Jn 15:1-8

St. Paul said Jesus is the head of his body, the Church; he is the head, we the bodily members (see Col 1:18). We cannot be divided from the head and retain any life at all. Nor can a member separated from the body remain alive. A living body is an organism, not a collection of parts. We have to be careful about the images we use to describe the Church. False separations creep in subtly. The image in today's reading is even more striking than Paul's: a vine and its branches. Unlike a tree, where you can distinguish clearly between trunk and branches, the vine is just all branches! "I am the vine and you are the branches": the vine is the branches!

Jesus said to his disciples, "I am the true vine and my Father is the vinegrower. If any of my branches doesn't bear fruit, he breaks it off; and he prunes every branch that does bear fruit, that it may bear even more fruit.

"You are already made clean by the word I have spoken to you; live in me as I live in you. The branch cannot bear fruit by itself but has to remain part of the vine; so neither can you if you don't remain in me.

"I am the vine and you are the branches. As long as you remain in me and I in you, you bear much fruit; but apart from me you can do nothing. Whoever does not remain in me is thrown away as they do with branches and they wither. Then they are gathered and thrown into the fire and burned.

"If you remain in me and my words in you, you may ask whatever you want and it will be given to you. My Father is glorified when you bear much fruit: it is then that you become my disciples."

13 Thursday

MAY

Acts 15:7-21   Jn 15:9-11

What does love have to do with commandments? These two words feel and look like opponents. And for good measure there's the word "if" in the middle! "You will remain in my love if you keep my commandments." It calls for a fresh look. Likewise Jesus in this passage (and everywhere else) is showing us how to love. But the faith has mostly been presented to us in an authoritarian way. If someone gets the wrong idea, we call that misinterpretation. But there is another kind: it is when someone gets the wrong feeling. When it comes to our religion we have to be alert to this. We have to make a sustained effort to salvage the Scriptures and our faith from heretical feelings!

Jesus said to his disciples, "As the Father has loved me, so I have loved you; remain in my love. You will remain in my love if you keep my commandments, just as I have kept my Father's commandments and remain in his love.

"I have told you all this, that my own joy may be in you and your joy may be complete."

Acts 1:15-17,20-26   Jn 15:9-17

There is little you can say by way of commentary. If there is anything to be said, let Meister Eckhart say it: "God needs our friendship so much that He cannot wait for us to pray to Him: He approaches us and begs us to be His friends…. So much should your love be one, for love does not wish to be anywhere but where there is likeness and oneness. Where there is a master and servant there is no peace, for there is no likeness. A woman and a man are unlike, but in love they are alike. And so scripture rightly says that God took woman from the man's rib and side and not from the head or from the feet."

Jesus said to his disciples, "As the Father has loved me, so I have loved you; remain in my love. You will remain in my love if you keep my commandments, just as I have kept my Father's commandments and remain in his love.

"I have told you all this, that my own joy may be in you and your joy may be complete. This is my commandment: love one another as I have loved you. There is no greater love than this, to give one's life for one's friends; and you are my friends if you do what I command you.

"I shall not call you servants any more, because servants do not know what their master is about. Instead I have called you friends, since I have made known to you everything I learned from my Father.

"You did not choose me; it was I who chose you and sent you to go and bear fruit, fruit that will last. And everything you ask the Father in my name, he will give you.

"This is my command, that you love one another."

Acts 16:1-10   Jn 15:18-21

"The world loves its own." By "world," John does not mean those beautiful mountains, this sparkling stream, these trees...He meant something like the "idols." To be sure it loves its own; that is its nature. Or rather that it has become our nature, but not our true nature. Our true nature lies buried beneath piles of rubbish that we are sometimes painfully aware of, but also sometimes comfortably reconciled to. "The world loves its own" means "the world puts itself first." That's the nature of the ego. In the language of the Scriptures we say it is only "grace" that can lift us beyond that position. In other words, the leverage has to come from beyond: grace means "gift."

Jesus said to his disciples, "If the world hates you, remember that the world hated me before you. This would not be so if you belonged to the world, because the world loves its own. But you are not of the world since I have chosen you from the world; because of this the world hates you.

"Remember what I told you: the servant is not greater than his master; if they persecuted me, they will persecute you, too. If they kept my word, they keep yours as well. All this they will do to you for the sake of my name because they do not know the One who sent me."

Sunday

For the next several days the readings make reference to the Holy Spirit, the promised Helper or Comforter. This is because in two weeks' time there will be the great feast of Pentecost. The Spirit will come not just for a visit but to remain with us: to become ordinary. What kind of comfort can we expect from the Comforter? Comfort means strength! The Holy Spirit will make us robust. And what kind of peace can we expect? "I give you my peace. Not as the world gives peace do I give it to you." Not the ego's peace, which is like the peace after some private victory. He promises his peace. The readings these times are like Spring cleaning.

Acts 15:1-2,22-29
Rev 21:10-14,22-23

The angel took me up in a spiritual vision to a very high mountain and he showed me the holy city of Jerusalem, coming down out of heaven from God. It shines with the glory of God, like a precious jewel with the color of crystal-clear jasper.

Its wall, large and high, has twelve gates; stationed at them are twelve angels. Over the gates are written the names of the twelve tribes of the sons of Israel. Three gates face the east; three gates face the north; three gates face the south and three face the west. The city wall stands on twelve foundation stones on which are written the names of the twelve apostles of the Lamb.

I saw no temple in the city for the Lord God, Master of the universe, and the Lamb are themselves its temple. The city has no need of the light of the sun or the moon, since God's Glory is its light and the Lamb is its lamp.

Jn 14:23-29

Jesus said to his disciples, "If anyone loves me, he will keep my word and my Father will love him; and we will come to him and make a room in his home. But if anyone does not love me, he will not keep my words, and these words that you hear are not mine but the Father's who sent me.

"I told you all this while I was still with you. From now on the Helper, the Holy Spirit whom the Father will send in my name, will teach you all things and remind you of all that I have told you.

"Peace be with you; I give you my peace. Not as the world gives peace do I give it to you. Do not be troubled; do not be afraid. You heard me say: 'I am going away, but I am coming to you.' If you loved me, you would be glad that I go to the Father, for the Father is greater than I. I have told you this now before it takes place, so that when it does happen you may believe."

Acts 16:11-15   Jn 15:26–16:4

C.H. Spurgeon wrote, "This age is peculiarly the dispensation of the Holy Spirit, in which Jesus cheers us… by the indwelling and constant abiding of the Holy Ghost, who is evermore the Comforter of the Church. It is His office to console the hearts of God's people. He convinces of sin; He illuminates and instructs; but still the main part of His work lies in making glad the hearts of the renewed, in confirming the weak, and lifting up all those that be bowed down. He does this by revealing Jesus to them. The Holy Spirit consoles, but Christ is the consolation. If we may use the figure, the Holy Spirit is the Physician, but Jesus is the medicine."

Jesus said to his disciples, "From the Father, I will send you the Spirit of truth who comes from the Father. When this Helper comes, he will testify about me. And you, too, will be my witness for you have been with me from the beginning.

"I tell you all this to keep you from stumbling and falling away. They will put you out of the Jewish communities. Still more, the hour is coming when anyone who kills you will claim to be serving God; they will do this because they have not known the Father or me. I tell you all these things now so that when the time comes you may remember that I told you.

"I did not tell you about this in the beginning because I was with you."

Acts 16:22-34   Jn 16:5-11

"It is better for you that I go away," said Jesus. This is shocking. We are used to the idea of Jesus being killed, but what do we say when he himself freely decides to leave us? "Unless I go," he explained, the Paraclete cannot come." In John's gospel the "Paraclete" is the continued presence of Jesus. He is Jesus interiorized in us through the Holy Spirit. In other words, Jesus withdraws his visible presence in order to be more intimately present. He is the mind through which we look at the world and at the Father; he becomes 'subjective' in us. Now in the Spirit, he is present in all places and to all people and at all times.

Jesus said to his discipkes, "But now I am going to the One who sent me and none of you asks me where I am going; instead you are overcome with grief because of what I have said.

"Indeed believe me: It is better for you that I go away, because as long as I do not leave, the Helper will not come to you. But if I go away, it is to send him to you, and when he comes, he will vindicate the truth in face of the world with regard to sin, to the way of righteousness, and to the Judgment.

"What has been the sin? They did not believe in me. What is the way of righteousness? I am on the way to the Father, meanwhile you will not see me. What is Judgment? The Prince of this world has himself been condemned."

Acts 17:15,22–18:1   Jn 16:12-15

"He will take what is mine and make it known to you." "He will remind you of all that I have told you" (Jn 14:26). These verses suggest that we can know something and yet not know it at all. It is possible to know a great deal of theology and yet not to know Jesus or God at all. It can become just an abstract study. The Holy Spirit makes us capable of interiorizing what Jesus made visible to us. "The Holy Spirit has two workings in us," wrote Johann Tauler. "The first is that He empties. The other is that He fills the emptiness, as far and as much as He finds emptiness to fill."

Jesus said to his disciples, "I still have many things to tell you, but you cannot bear them now. When he, the Spirit of truth comes, he will guide you into the whole truth.

"He has nothing to say of himself but he will speak of what he hears, and he will tell you of the things to come. He will take what is mine and make it known to you; in doing this, he will glorify me. All that the Father has is mine; because of this I have just told you, that the Spirit will take what is mine and make it known to you."

EASTER
6th Week

St. Bernardine of Siena

20 Thursday

M A Y

Acts 18:1-8   Jn 16:16-20

"We don't understand!" That is real progress. Teachers know that the greatest obstacle to understanding is not ignorance but misunderstanding. A deep admission of ignorance is a wonderful and rather rare thing. It is the real foundation of learning. The kind of knowledge that becomes a "possession" is an obstacle. In moments of clarity we glimpse a humbling truth: that much of our knowledge is a protective layer for the ego. Pray God that we may be always lacking in that kind of knowledge that closes the mind and shields the ego (or becomes one of its weapons).

Jesus said to his disciples, "A little while and you will see me no more; and then a little while, and you will see me."

Some of the disciples wondered, "What does he mean by: 'A little while and you will not see me, and then a little while and you will see me'? And why did he say: 'I go to the Father'?" And they said to one another, "What does he mean by 'a little while'? We don't understand."

Jesus knew that they wanted to question him; so he said to them, "You are puzzled because I told you that in a little while you will see me no more, and then a little while later you will see me.

"Truly, I say to you, you will weep and mourn while the world rejoices. You will be sorrowful, but your sorrow will turn to joy."

M A Y

Friday

21

EASTER
6th Week

St. Christopher Magallanes

Acts 18:9-18   Jn 16:20-23

"Your sorrow will turn to joy." He did not say "Your sorrow will be replaced by joy." The joy will somehow be born out of the heart of the sorrow. Then it will be able to endure; it will not see sorrow as a threat and an enemy. It will not be at the mercy of sorrowful circumstances. Sorrow itself will give birth to a strange deep kind of joy. Jesus did not turn back from death; he went through the heart of it, and it was transformed into resurrection. "Your Son the royal path of suffering trod," says the hymn. Our faith does not hold us back from life or life's sorrows, but it enables them to be a royal path to God.

Jesus said to his disciples, "Truly, I say to you, you will weep and mourn while the world rejoices. You will be sorrowful, but your sorrow will turn to joy. A woman in childbirth is in distress because her time is at hand. But after the child is born, she no longer remembers her suffering because of such great joy: a human being is born into the world.

"You feel sorrowful now, but I will see you again, and your hearts will rejoice. And no one will take your joy from you. When that day comes you will not ask me anything. Truly, I say to you, whatever you ask the Father in my Name, he will give you."

EASTER
6th Week
St. Rita of Cascia

22 Saturday

M A Y

Acts 18:23-28   Jn 16:23-28

There is all the difference in the world between giving/receiving and buying/selling. We sometimes catch ourselves trying to buy our way with God: promising prayers and good works and pilgrimages, on condition that God will consent to give us something we want. We are not changed by it: we are conducting business rather than relating to God in a personal way. Giving and receiving, on the other hand, involve us in a personal way: there is a giver and a receiver. At the end of it we are changed, made more human. And the more human we are, the greater our capacity for joy. Moreover we are not promised a small portion, "ask and receive, that your joy may be full."

Jesus said to his disciples, "When that day comes you will not ask me anything. Truly, I say to you, whatever you ask the Father in my Name, he will give you. So far you have not asked in my Name; ask and receive that your joy may be full.

"I taught you all this in veiled language, but the time is coming when I shall no longer speak in veiled language, but will tell you plainly of the Father.

"When that day comes, you will ask in my Name and it will not be for me to ask the Father for you, for the Father himself loves you because you have loved me and you believe that I came from the Father. As I came from the Father and have come into the world, so I am leaving the world and going to the Father."

Sunday

"Remain in the city until you are invested with power from above." In other words, learn patience, learn how to wait; and unlearn the tendency to leap in, feet first. There is an urgency about the Gospel, but it is the part of wisdom to wait till the right time. Nowadays it's hard to wait. Within oneself too there is a need to learn how to wait and not jump in with ready answers. We pray today that the Holy Spirit, who so often drives people into very vocal prayer (see the end of today's reading), may also drive us sometimes, as Jesus was driven, into the desert—the place of silence and solitude.

Acts 1:1-11

In the first part of my work, Theophilus, I wrote of all that Jesus did and taught from the beginning until the day when he ascended to heaven.

But first he had instructed through the Holy Spirit the apostles he had chosen. After his passion, he presented himself to them, giving many signs that he was alive; over a period of forty days he appeared to them and taught them concerning the kingdom of God. Once when he had been eating with them, he told them, "Do not leave Jerusalem but wait for the fulfillment of the Father's promise about which I have spoken to you: John baptized with water, but you will be baptized with the Holy Spirit within a few days."

When they had come together, they asked him, "Is it now that you will restore the Kingdom of Israel?" And he answered, "It is not for you to know the time and the steps that the Father has fixed by his own authority. But you will receive power when the Holy Spirit comes upon you; and you will be my witnesses in Jerusalem, throughout Judea and Samaria, even to the ends of the earth."

After Jesus said this, he was taken up before their eyes and a cloud hid him from their sight. While they were still looking up to heaven where he went, suddenly, two men dressed in white stood beside them and said, "Men of Galilee, why do you stand here looking up at the sky? This Jesus who has been taken from you into heaven, will return in the same way as you have seen him go there."

Heb 9:24-28;10:19-23
Lk 24:46-53

Jesus said to the eleven, "You see what was written: the Messiah had to suffer and on the third day rise from the dead. Then repentance and forgiveness in his name would be proclaimed to all the nations, beginning from Jerusalem. Now you shall be witnesses to this. And this is why I will send you what my Father promised. So remain in the city until you are invested with power from above."

Jesus led them almost as far as Bethany; then he lifted up his hands and blessed them. And as he blessed them, he withdrew (and was taken to heaven. They worshiped him). They returned to Jerusalem full of joy and were continually in the Temple praising God.

The great threat for the Jews of old was that they would be scattered. "The Lord will scatter you among the peoples" (Dt 4:25. The New Testament reverses this. To be scattered is not a danger now but a challenge received with joy. "You will bear witness for me in Jerusalem... and away to the ends of the earth" (Acts 1:8). The time described in today's reading is a time between two Testaments. To be scattered is still a terrifying prospect, but Jesus is preparing them for it. Someone described our time as a time of exile between two worlds, "one dead, one powerless to be born." But our faith tells a positive story, "It is the Spirit that gives life" (Jn 6:63).

The disciples said to Jesus, "Now you are speaking plainly and not in veiled language! Now we see that you know all things, even before we question you. Because of this we believe that you came from God."

Jesus answered them, "You say that you believe! The hour is coming, indeed it has come, when you will be scattered, each one to his home, and you will leave me alone. Yet I am not alone, for the Father is with me.

I have told you all this, so that in me you may have peace. You will have trouble in the world; but, courage! I have overcome the world."

Acts 20:17-27   Jn 17:1-11

Jesus lifted up his eyes to heaven and said, "Father, the hour has come; give glory to your Son, that the Son may give glory to you. You have given him power over all mortals, and you want him to bring eternal life to all you have entrusted to him. For this is eternal life: to know you, the only true God, and the One you sent, Jesus Christ.

"I have glorified you on earth and finished the work that you gave me to do. Now, Father, give me in your presence the same Glory I had with you before the world began.

"I have made your name known to those you gave me from the world. They were yours and you gave them to me, and they kept your word. And now they know that all you have given me comes indeed from you. I have given them the teaching I received from you, and they received it and know in truth that I came from you; and they believe that you have sent me.

"I pray for them; I do not pray for the world but for those who belong to you and whom you have given to me—indeed all I have is yours and all you have is mine— and now they are my glory. I am no longer in the world, but they are in the world whereas I am going to you. Holy Father, keep them in your Name (that you have given me,) so that they may be one, just as we are."

Meister Eckhart comments on this, "It has been written that whenever our Lord raised up his eyes, he wished to perform a great work.... Thus he instructs us that when we would pray, we should first descend in true downcast humility beneath all creatures. Only then should we ascend before the throne of wisdom, and as far as we have descended, so far shall we be granted what we have prayed for John loved to play on the paradox of "raised up": Jesus would be lifted up in shame on the cross, but that lifting up in shame is also a lifting up in glory. Here, Eckhart uses it in another and a more general way. As he said, "The way down is the way up." It is a lesson that we all have to learn again and again.

Acts 20:28-38   Jn 17:11-19

What is there to believe in a name? A name is only a word. Is our faith just a belief in a set of words? Haven't we too often seen frenzied mobs, claiming to be defenders of their faith, "crying the catch-cries of the clown?" What are we defending when we defend our faith? Words? Could someone die for a few words? St. Thomas Aquinas said, "The act of faith is not directed to the formulation but to the reality." We don't believe in the Creed, we believe in God. In today's reading then, Jesus is saying, "I kept them safe in your Presence… Holy Father, keep them in your Presence."

Jesus looked up to heaven and prayed, "I am no longer in the world, but they are in the world whereas I am going to you. Holy Father, keep them in your Name (that you have given me,) so that they may be one, just as we are.

"When I was with them, I kept them safe in your Name, and not one was lost except the one who was already lost, and in this the Scripture was fulfilled. But now I am coming to you and I leave these my words in the world that my joy may be complete in them.

"I have given them your word and the world has hated them because they are not of the world; just as I am not of the world. I do not ask you to remove them from the world but to keep them from the evil one. They are not of the world, just as I am not of the world; consecrate them in the truth—your word is truth.

"I have sent them into the world as you sent me into the world, and for their sake, I go to the sacrifice by which I am consecrated, so that they too may be consecrated in truth."

Charles Spurgeon had the gift of extreme eloquence, and so let's listen to it: "If there were but one small loophole through which to talk with Jesus, it would be a high privilege to thrust a word of fellowship through the narrow door; how much we are blessed in having so large an entrance! Had the Lord Jesus been far away from us, with many a stormy sea between, we should have longed to send a messenger to Him to carry Him our love, and bring us tidings from His Father's house; but see His kindness, He has built His house next door to ours, nay, more, He takes lodging with us, and tabernacles in poor humble hearts, that so He may have perpetual conversation with us."

Jesus said, "I pray not only for these but also for those who through their word will believe in me. May they all be one as you Father are in me and I am in you. May they be one in us; so the world may believe that you have sent me.

"I have given them the Glory you have given me, that they may be one as we are one: I in them and you in me. Thus they shall reach perfection in unity and the world shall know that you have sent me and that I have loved them just as you loved me.

"Father, since you have given them to me, I want them to be with me where I am and see the Glory you gave me, for you loved me before the foundation of the world.

"Righteous Father, the world has not known you but I have known you, and these have known that you have sent me. As I revealed your Name to them, so will I continue to reveal it, so that the love with which you loved me may be in them and I also may be in them."

Peter was not able to rise to heroic love, agapè, on that occasion (see April 25). But he understood friendship. Friendship is the best rehearsal for agapè. It is a deep mystery in itself. "I have called you friends," Jesus said (Jn 15:15). Perhaps it comes to this: I must be aware how subtly and quickly the ego begins to deny the independent existence of the other person, turning him or her into a function of myself. I must realize: it is the other person's difference from me that will teach me and challenge me and drive me out of my ego-trance. But at that point, friendship is already becoming agapè.

After Jesus and his disciples had finished breakfast, Jesus said to Simon Peter, "Simon, son of John, do you love me more than these?" He answered, "Yes, Lord, you know that I love you." And Jesus said, "Feed my lambs."

A second time Jesus said to him, "Simon, son of John, do you love me?" And Peter answered, "Yes, Lord, you know that I love you." Jesus said to him, "Look after my sheep." And a third time he said to him, "Simon, son of John, do you love me?"

Peter was saddened because Jesus asked him a third time, "Do you love me?" and he said, "Lord, you know everything; you know that I love you."

Jesus then said, "Feed my sheep. Truly, I say to you, when you were young you put on your belt and walked where you liked. But when you grow old, you will stretch out your hands and another will put a belt around you and lead you where you do not wish to go." Jesus said this to make known the kind of death by which Peter was to glorify God. And he added, "Follow me."

Acts 28:16-20,30-31   Jn 21:20-25

Rumor, gossip, tittle-tattle, tell-tale, hearsay, prattle…. The very number and expressiveness of the words show how much we live with it! Even in the presence of the Risen Lord the disciples were marking one another's cards. There's a gossipy atmosphere about today's reading. There are things we don't need to know. Julian of Norwich (14th century) wrote, "In the same Revelation I saw that many things are hidden which we shall never know until God in his goodness has made us fit to see them. And I am quite content to wait for our Lord to reveal his will in this wonderful mystery."

Peter looked back and saw that the disciple Jesus loved was following as well, the one who had reclined close to Jesus at the supper and had asked him, "Lord, who is to betray you?" On seeing him Peter asked Jesus, "Lord, what about him?" Jesus answered, "If I want him to remain until I come, does that concern you? Follow me."

Because of this the rumor spread in the community that this disciple would not die. Yet Jesus had not said to Peter, "He will not die," but "suppose I want him to remain until I come."

It is this disciple who testifies about the things he has recorded here and we know that his testimony is true. But Jesus did many other things; if all were written down, the world itself would not hold the books recording them.

Sunday

James and John once asked Jesus to send fire from heaven to burn up the Samaritans, who had offered no hospitality. He told them, more or less, to grow up (Lk 9:55). But a year or two later, fire of a different kind did come down on the Samaritans, at the hands of Peter and John. Jessica Powers wrote about today's feast of Pentecost: "That was the day when Fire came down from heaven, inaugurating the first spring of love. Blood melted in the frozen veins, and even the least bird sang in the mind's inmost grove."

Acts 2:1-11

When the day of Pentecost came, they were all together in one place. And suddenly out of the sky came a sound like a strong rushing wind and it filled the whole house where they were sitting. There appeared tongues as if of fire which parted and came to rest upon each one of them. All were filled with Holy Spirit and began to speak other languages, as the Spirit enabled them to speak. Staying in Jerusalem were religious Jews from every nation under heaven. When they heard this sound, a crowd gathered, all excited because each heard them speaking in his own language. Full of amazement and wonder, they asked, "Are not all these who are speaking Galileans? How is it that we hear them in our own native language? Here are Parthians, Medes and Elamites (...); and all of us hear them proclaiming in our own language what God, the Savior, does.

Rom 8:8-17

(...) Christ is within you; though the body is branded by death as a consequence of sin, the spirit is life and holiness. And if the Spirit of Him who raised Jesus from the dead is within you, He who raised Jesus Christ from among the dead will also give life to your mortal bodies. Yes, he will do it through his Spirit who dwells within you. Then, brothers, let us leave the flesh and no longer live according to it. If not, we will die. Rather, walking in the Spirit, let us put to death the body's deeds so that we may live.

All those who walk in the Spirit of God are sons and daughters of God. Then, no more fear: you did not receive a spirit of slavery, but the Spirit that makes you sons and daughters and every time we cry, "Abba! (this is Dad!) Father!" the Spirit assures our spirit that we are sons and daughters of God. (...)

Jn 14:15-16,23-26

Jesus said to his disciples, "If you love me, you will keep my commandments; and I will ask the Father and he will give you another Helper to be with you forever, Jesus answered him, "If anyone loves me, he will keep my word and my Father will love him; and we will come to him and make a room in his home. But if anyone does not love me, he will not keep my words, and these words that you hear are not mine but the Father's who sent me. I told you all this while I was still with you. From now on the Helper, the Holy Spirit whom the Father will send in my name, will teach you all things and remind you of all that I have told you."

M A Y

Monday

31

ORDINARY TIME
9th Week
Feast of the Visitation

Zep 3:14-18   Lk 1:39-56

The Canticle of Hannah (1Sam 2:1-10), mother of Samuel, is the source on which Mary's Magnificat is based. Mary is shaped, you might say, by the best of the Old Testament. But she is also a figure looking to the future. She is an image of the new community, the Church. That is a community where the topsy-turvy logic of the Gospel is intended to hold sway: the first is the last, the weak is the strong, the greatest is the least, the poorest is the richest, the lowest is the highest.... But when we look at the Church—at ourselves—sadly, we see that we live mostly by straightforward logic: power and privilege, palaces, badges and titles of honor....

Mary then set out for a town in the Hills of Judah. She entered the house of Zechariah and greeted Elizabeth. When Elizabeth heard Mary's greeting, the baby leapt in her womb. Elizabeth was filled with holy spirit, and giving a loud cry, said, "You are most blessed among women and blessed is the fruit of your womb! How is it that the mother of my Lord comes to me? The moment your greeting sounded in my ears, the baby within me suddenly leapt for joy. Blessed are you who believed that the Lord's word would come true!" And Mary said:

"My soul proclaims the greatness of the Lord, my spirit exults in God my savior! He has looked upon his servant in her lowliness, and people forever will call me blessed. The Mighty One has done great things for me, Holy is his Name! From age to age his mercy extends to those who live in his presence. He has acted with power and done wonders, and scattered the proud with their plans. He has put down the mighty from their thrones and lifted up those who are downtrodden. He has filled the hungry with good things but has sent the rich away empty. He held out his hand to Israel, his servant, for he remembered his mercy, even as he promised our fathers, Abraham and his descendants forever."

Mary remained with Elizabeth about three months and then returned home.

2P 3:12-15,17-18   Mk 12:13-17

In the ancient world, coinage was considered the property of the ruler, since it had his image on it. Jesus asked them to show him a coin. This was clever, because by possessing a Roman coin they were already showing themselves to be collaborators with the Romans. This was a sore point, especially for Pharisees. He only had to say, "Give back to Caesar this worthless thing that belongs to him in any case." Then he added, "Give back to God what belongs to God," as if to say, "You were made in God's image: you have his image stamped on you, just as this coin has Caesar's image stamped on it. You don't owe your souls to Caesar." This principle has served societies well, when it has been observed.

Jewish leaders sent to Jesus some Pharisees with members of Herod's party, with the purpose of trapping him in his own words. They came and said to Jesus, "Master, we know that you are true; you are not influenced by anyone, and your answers do not vary according to who is listening to you but you truly teach God's way. Tell us, is it against the Law to pay taxes to Caesar? Should we pay them or not?"

But Jesus saw through their trick and answered, "Why are you testing me? Bring me a silver coin and let me see it." They brought him one and Jesus asked, "Whose head is this, and whose name?" They answered, "Caesar's." Then Jesus said, "Return to Caesar what is Caesar's, and to God what is God's."

And they were greatly astonished.

JUNE

Wednesday 2

ORDINARY TIME
9th Week

Sts. Marcellinus & Peter

2Tim 1:1-3,6-12   Mk 12:18-27

No rabbi had ever produced evidence of a next life from the first five books of the Scriptures. But Jesus managed to do so! In this way: Abraham, Isaac and Jacob are the most prominent figures in those first books. In the second of those books God had proclaimed himself "the God of Abraham, the God of Isaac and the God of Jacob" (Ex 3:6). If these men are just dead, said Jesus, then God is reigning over a kingdom of death, not a kingdom of life! If you believe only in death you see only death everywhere. Jesus, who is "the way, the truth and the life," calls us to believe in life. Like diet, it is important to pay attention to your beliefs, because you are what you believe.

The Sadducees came to Jesus. Since they claim that there is no resurrection, they questioned him in this way, "Master, in the Scriptures Moses gave us this law: 'If anyone dies and leaves a wife but no children, his brother must take the wife and give her a child who will be considered the child of his deceased brother.' Now, there were seven brothers. The first married a wife, but he died without leaving any children. The second took the wife and he, too, died leaving no children. The same thing happened to the third. Finally the seven died leaving no children. Last of all the woman died. Now, in the resurrection, to which of them will she be wife? For the seven had her as wife."

Jesus replied, "You could be wrong in this regard because you understand neither the Scriptures nor the power of God. When they rise from the dead, men and women do not marry but are like the angels in heaven.

"Now, about the resurrection of the dead, have you never reflected on the chapter of the burning bush in the book of Moses? God said to him: I am the God of Abraham, the God of Isaac and the God of Jacob. Now, he is the God, not of the dead but of the living. You are totally wrong."

ORDINARY TIME
9th Week

St. Charles Lwanga & Companions

3 Thursday

JUNE

2Tim 2:8-15   Mk 12:28-34

I know a woman who treasures a scrawled note from her wayward son. The father of the Prodigal Son would have done the same. Love is like that. In fiction, said Oscar Wilde, good people do good things and bad people do bad: that's why it is called fiction! In real life bad people can do good things and good people can do bad things. That is what makes it an astonishing adventure rather than a project.

The wonder, as Kavanagh put it, is "to get a true note from a dead flat string."

A teacher of the Law had been listening to this discussion and admired how Jesus answered them. So he came up and asked him, "Which commandment is the first of all?"

Jesus answered, "The first is: Hear, Israel! The Lord, our God, is One Lord; and you shall love the Lord, your God, with all your heart, with all your soul, with all your mind and with all your strength. And after this comes another one: You shall love your neighbor as yourself. There is no commandment greater than these two."

The teacher of the Law said to him, "Well spoken, Master; you are right when you say that he is one and there is no other. To love him with all our heart, with all our understanding and with all our strength, and to love our neighbor as ourselves is more important than any burnt offering or sacrifice."

Jesus approved this answer and said, "You are not far from the kingdom of God." But after that, no one dared to ask him any more questions.

2Tim 3:10-17   Mk 12:35-37

There are people who insist on clarity above all else, thinking that clarity is a proof of truth. But there are many things that are clear and false. When we think we have understood something we say "I have it!" We use the words "having," "grasping," "holding," and the like. Even the word "concept" (from Latin capio) means "to seize." These words should make us pause, because fundamentally it is not we who seize the truth, it is the truth that should seize us. As Chesterton put it, we are not here to get the skies into our heads, but to get our heads into the skies. To promote false clarity is to be an enemy of the truth.

As Jesus was teaching in the Temple, he said, "The teachers of the Law say that the Messiah is the son of David. How can that be? For David himself, inspired by the Holy Spirit declared: The Lord said to my Lord: sit at my right until I put your enemies under your feet. If David himself calls him Lord, in what way can he be his son?" Many people came to Jesus and listened to him gladly.

2Tim 4:1-8   Mk 12:38-44

Clothes are for warmth and protection, but the layers accumulate— layers of meaning! Clothes become an assertion of one's self-image, one's identity. Clothes are a language. Uniforms assert membership of a particular class: the army, the police, the clergy…. In today's passage Jesus pointed out a casualty of the Temple system: the poor. A widow at that time was a very symbol of poverty and helplessness. In that world, to lose one's husband was to lose one's identity. This poor widow of no identity was being exploited by people who clung desperately to a false identity. It's the tragic story of the world.

As Jesus was teaching, he also said to them, "Beware of those teachers of the Law who enjoy walking around in long robes and being greeted in the marketplace, and who like to occupy reserved seats in the synagogues and the first places at feasts. They even devour the widow's and the orphan's goods while making a show of long prayers. How severe a sentence they will receive!"

Jesus sat down opposite the Temple treasury and watched the people dropping money into the treasury box; and many rich people put in large offerings. But a poor widow also came and dropped in two small coins.

Then Jesus called his disciples and said to them, "Truly I say to you, this poor widow put in more than all those who gave offerings. For all of them gave from their plenty, but she gave from her poverty and put in every-thing she had, her very living."

Here is another of Evdokimov's meditations on Roublev's famous icon of the trinity: "Gazing at the three faces raises the question, 'Who are they? What are they saying?' and we, in our silence, can perceive something of this secret…. The heads leaning towards one another can be seen from a distance—it looks as if they cannot abide being apart at all—each one is there only for the other…. Each one of them is giving himself to the others, defenseless before the other. That is why their faces are full of an infinite tenderness, the tenderness that is without resistance before what the other offers or asks.

Pro 8:22-31

Yahweh created me first, at the beginning of his works. He formed me from of old, from eternity, even before the earth. The abyss did not exist when I was born, the springs of the sea had not gushed forth, the mountains were still not set in their place nor the hills, when I was born before he made the earth or countryside, or the first grains of the world's dust. I was there when he made the skies and drew the earth's compass on the abyss, when he formed the clouds above and when the springs of the ocean emerged; when he made the sea with its limits, that it might not overflow. When he laid the foundations of the earth, I was close beside him, the designer of his works, and I was his daily delight, forever playing in his presence, playing throughout the world and delighting to be with the sons of men.

Rom 5:1-5

By faith we have received true righteousness, and we are at peace with God, through Jesus Christ, our Lord. Through him we obtain this favor in which we remain and we even boast to expect the Glory of God.

Not only that, we also boast even in trials, knowing that trials produce patience, from patience comes merit, merit is the source of hope, and hope does not disappoint us because the Holy Spirit has been given to us, pouring into our hearts the love of God.

Jn 16:12-15

Jesus said to his disciples, "I still have many things to tell you, but you cannot bear them now. When he, the Spirit of truth comes, he will guide you into the whole truth.

"He has nothing to say of himself but he will speak of what he hears, and he will tell you of the things to come. He will take what is mine and make it known to you; in doing this, he will glorify me. All that the Father has is mine; because of this I have just told you, that the Spirit will take what is mine and make it known to you."

If the sermon on the mount is a summary of all Christian doctrine, the beatitudes are a summary of the sermon on the mount. Here, then, if anywhere, we have the essence of the Gospel. The beatitudes are a measure of how far beyond this the Gospel calls us. The morality of the beatitudes is harder to quantify: how poor in spirit are you? How meek, gentle, merciful…? You can never say: I've reached it! You can never be self-righteous. And you can never even begin to think that you are better than another—because you can't compare. As Simon Tugwell wrote, "There is something about God which is better expressed in weakness than in strength, in foolishness than in wisdom, in poverty than in richness."

When Jesus saw the crowds, he went up the mountain. He sat down and his disciples gathered around him. Then he spoke and began to teach them:

"Fortunate are those who are poor in spirit, for theirs is the kingdom of heaven.

"Fortunate are those who mourn, they shall be comforted.

"Fortunate are the gentle, they shall possess the land.

"Fortunate are those who hunger and thirst for justice, for they shall be satisfied.

"Fortunate are the merciful, for they shall find mercy.

"Fortunate are those with a pure heart, for they shall see God.

"Fortunate are those who work for peace, they shall be called children of God.

"Fortunate are those who are persecuted for the cause of justice, for theirs is the kingdom of heaven.

"Fortunate are you, when people insult you and persecute you and speak all kinds of evil against you because you are my followers. Be glad and joyful, for a great reward is kept for you in God. This is how this people persecuted the prophets who lived before you."

1K 17:7-16   Mt 5:13-16

If we are ever at rights with God it is not because of anything we have done, but because of God's goodness and mercy. Success stories are nearly always riddled with ambiguity and hidden compromise; they are the ego's work. The only success story that holds any interest for us is that of Jesus—and he was a failure! On the level of ordinary wisdom, yes, he failed. "He saved others but he cannot save himself," the onlookers said as he died. This tremendous failure is the revelation of God in human terms. It is fatal to have the wrong kind of strength. Such people will never be the "salt of the earth"; they may well set the world on fire, but they will never be "the light of the world."

Jesus said to his disciples, "You are the salt of the earth. But if salt has lost its strength, how can it be made salty again? It has become useless. It can only be thrown away and people will trample on it.

"You are the light of the world. A city built on a mountain cannot be hidden. No one lights a lamp and covers it; instead it is put on a lampstand, where it gives light to everyone in the house. In the same way your light must shine before others, so that they may see the good you do and praise your Father in heaven."

JUNE

Wednesday 9

ORDINARY TIME
10th Week
St. Ephrem

1K 18:20-39   Mt 5:17-19

By fulfilling the law Jesus meant fulfilling the purpose for which it was made: that is, justice (or "righteousness," as the Scriptures calls it: that includes a just relationship with God). But why then does he say that "not the smallest letter or stroke of the law will change until all is fulfilled"? It is not the law that is wrong, but its separation from justice. What justifies the existence of a law, if not that it should be in the service of justice? Clever people can even make the law an enemy of justice. This happens daily in the wide world, and sadly, also in the Church.

Jesus said to his disciples, "Do not think that I have come to remove the Law and the Prophets. I have not come to remove but to fulfill them. I tell you this: as long as heaven and earth last, not the smallest letter or stroke of the Law will change until all is fulfilled.

"So then, whoever breaks the least important of these commandments and teaches others to do the same will be the least in the kingdom of heaven. On the other hand, whoever obeys them and teaches others to do the same will be great in the kingdom of heaven."

1K 18:41-46   Mt 5:20-26

Jesus said to the crowds, "I tell you, then, that if you are not righteous in a much broader way than the teachers of the Law and the Pharisees, you cannot enter the kingdom of heaven.

"You have heard that it was said to our people in the past: Do not commit murder; anyone who does kill will have to face trial. But now I tell you: whoever gets angry with a brother or sister will have to face trial. Whoever insults a brother or sister deserves to be brought before the council; whoever calls a brother or a sister "Fool" deserves to be thrown into the fire of hell. So, if you are about to offer your gift at the altar and you remember that your brother has something against you, leave your gift there in front of the altar, go at once and make peace with him, and then come back and offer your gift to God.

"Don't forget this: be reconciled with your opponent quickly when you are together on the way to court. Otherwise he will turn you over to the judge, who will hand you over to the police, who will put you in jail. There you will stay, until you have paid the last penny."

Today's reading follows yesterday's. Law without justice is superficial; it is only about words and appearances of justice. We use all kinds of substitutes for wisdom. If a court doesn't know how to decide, it consults precedent. But that precedent was either based on another precedent, or it was someone's guess at justice in a particular case in the past. Yesterday's guess, then, becomes today's justice. The law doesn't go down to the roots of things: to the mind and heart. It is in the mind and heart that all our actions are conceived and born. If we never look into those sometimes dark places, we could find later that we have been breeding monsters there.

Acts 11:21-26;13:1-3   Mt 10:7-13

It's a severe criticism to be told that you are living in the past. But strangely we think it's the highest praise to be told that you are living in the future. It's hard to see why we make such a difference between them, for one is just as unreal as the other. Some of us cheat ourselves of life by living in the past; the rest of us do it by living in the future! (I exaggerate, I know!) Many people almost kill themselves amassing wealth; even in their old age they still want to be turning a profit. It's an endless deferral of life. But the Gospel challenges us to face it now or never.

Jesus said to his disciples, "Go and proclaim this message: The kingdom of heaven is near. Heal the sick, bring the dead back to life, cleanse the lepers, and drive out demons. You received this as a gift, so give it as a gift. Do not carry any gold, silver or copper in your purses. Do not carry a traveler's bag, or an extra shirt, or sandals, or walking-stick: workers deserve their living.

"When you come to a town or a village, look for a worthy person and stay there until you leave.

"As you enter the house, wish it peace. If the people in the house deserve it, your peace will be on them; if they do not deserve it, your blessing will come back to you."

1K 19:19-21   Mt 5:33-37

Shakespeare mentioned "a good mouth-filling oath." Perhaps this is just the point: swearing is language pretending to do more than language can do. But something said with the emphasis of an oath isn't more true than it would have been without the oath. The oath doesn't change anything, it doesn't fill the horizon—it only fills the mouth. Far from bolstering the truth, it weakens it. It has often been remarked that the more swearing of oaths, the more lying. Let your yes be yes and your no be no, said Jesus. If the truth cannot stand by itself, nothing can. In fact other things are meant to stand only by virtue of the truth that is in them.

Jesus said to his disiciples, "You have also heard that people were told in the past: Do not break your oath; an oath sworn to the Lord must be kept. But I tell you this: do not take oaths. Do not swear by the heavens, for they are God's throne, nor by the earth, because it is his footstool, nor by Jerusalem because it is the city of the great king. Do not even swear by your head, because you cannot make a single hair white or black. Say yes when you mean yes and say no when you mean no. Anything else you say comes from the devil."

Sunday

The Eucharist is an assembly of the faithful. It brings us together, expressing our union in Christ and our eternal union with God. How can we say these things and still go on sitting far apart? I often think that the farther from the mouth, the more truthful our language. We tell lies with our mouth, we tell the truth with our feet. The Eucharist is bodily: the truth stands out in it more clearly and powerfully than anywhere else - so powerfully that it is expected to affect our whole subsequent life. But what if it doesn't affect us even while we are present at it? The feast of the Body and Blood of Christ is a day for meditating on the bodily truth—our own, and that of the Eucharist.

Gen 14:18-20 Then Melchizedek, king of Salem, brought bread and wine; he was a priest of God Most High, and he blessed Abram saying, "Blessed be Abram by God Most High, maker of heaven and earth! And blessed be God Most High who has delivered your enemies into your hands!" And Abram gave him a tenth part of everything.

1Cor 11:23-26 This is the tradition of the Lord that I received and that in my turn I have handed on to you; the Lord Jesus, on the night that he was delivered up, took bread and, after giving thanks, broke it, saying, "This is my body which is broken for you; do this in memory of me." In the same manner, taking the cup after the supper, he said, "This cup is the new Covenant in my blood. Whenever you drink it, do it in memory of me." So, then, whenever you eat of this bread and drink from this cup, you are proclaiming the death of the Lord until he comes.

Lk 9:11-17 When the crowd caught up with Jesus in Bethsaida, he welcomed them and began speaking about the kingdom of God, curing those who needed healing.

The day was drawing to a close and the Twelve drew near to tell him, "Send the crowd away and let them go into the villages and farms around, to find lodging and food, for we are here in a lonely place." But Jesus replied, "You yourselves give them something to eat." They answered, "We have only five loaves and two fish; do you want us to go and buy food enough for all this crowd?" For there were about five thousand men. Then Jesus said to his disciples, "Make people sit down in groups of fifties."

So they made all of them settle down. Jesus then took the five loaves and two fish, and raising his eyes to heaven, pronounced a blessing over them; he broke them and gave them to the disciples to distribute to the crowd. They ate and everyone had enough; and when they gathered up what was left, twelve baskets were filled with broken pieces.

If today's reading were put into practice, all war would cease immediately; and not only war but every kind of conflict, even minor domestic squabbles. It is highly improbable, to say the least, that that will ever happen. Society will never be improved by everyone telling everyone else to improve. A wise friend said to me once, "Let's not waste our energy criticizing what is wrong; let's just do our own work to the very best of our ability. If it's any good it will displace what is bad." This must be true not only of work but of everything!

Jesus said to his disciples, "You have heard that it was said: An eye for an eye and a tooth for a tooth. But I tell you this: do not oppose evil with evil; if someone slaps you on your right cheek, turn and offer the other. If someone sues you in court for your shirt, give your coat as well. If someone forces you to go one mile, go also the second mile. Give when asked and do not turn your back on anyone who wants to borrow from you."

1K 21:17-29   Mt 5:43-48

A book to recommend: C.S. Lewis, The Four Loves. His lucid writing clears up the mess that is the word "love." This word has come to mean just anything, and therefore nothing. Lewis expounds the classic fourfold distinction of love: The Greek names are storge (family love), philia (friendship), eros (passionate love), and agapè (Christian love). Today's reading is the most perfect formulation of Christian love. "Love your enemies" is the summit of love. But ideally all other forms of love are on their way towards it. Friendship is often very close.

Jesus said to his disciples, "You have heard that it was said: Love your neighbor and do not do good to your enemy. But this I tell you: Love your enemies, and pray for those who persecute you, so that you may be children of your Father in Heaven. For he makes his sun rise on both the wicked and the good, and he gives rain to both the just and the unjust.

"If you love those who love you, what is special about that? Do not even tax collectors do as much? And if you are friendly only to your friends, what is so exceptional about that? Do not even the pagans do as much? For your part you shall be righteous and perfect in the way your heavenly Father is righteous and perfect."

J U N E

Wednesday

16

ORDINARY TIME
11th Week

2K 2:1,6-14   Mt 6:1-6,16-18

Some ancient rabbis used to say that the most perfect form of almsgiving is when you do not know to whom you are giving, and the receiver does not know from whom he or she is receiving. Such an act would have no anchor in the ego; it would be like a pure sound, with no echo. If you do something good and another gets the credit, enjoy the pure sound (it may take a little getting used to)! You have an opportunity to experience and study the pure essence of an act in itself, without the fog that usually surrounds it. This is what goodness feels like in itself when it is separated from the ego's demands (gratitude, recognition, looking good, etc.).

Jesus said to his disciples, "Be careful not to make a show of your righteousness before people. If you do so, you do not gain anything from your Father in heaven. When you give something to the poor, do not have it trumpeted before you, as do those who want to be seen in the synagogues and in the streets in order to be praised by the people. I assure you, they have been already paid in full.

"If you give something to the poor, do not let your left hand know what your right hand is doing, so that your gift remains really secret. Your Father who sees what is kept secret, will reward you.

"When you pray, do not be like those who want to be seen. They love to stand and pray in the synagogues or on street corners to be seen by everyone. I assure you, they have already been paid in full. When you pray, go into your room, close the door and pray to your Father who is with you in secret; and your Father who sees what is kept secret will reward you.

"When you fast, do not put on a miserable face as do the hypocrites. They put on a gloomy face, so people can see they are fasting. I tell you this: they have been paid in full already. When you fast, wash your face and make yourself look cheerful, because you are not fasting for appearance or for people, but for your Father who sees beyond appearances. And your Father, who sees what is kept secret will reward you."

Jesus said to his disciples, "When you pray, do not use a lot of words, as the pagans do, for they hold that the more they say, the more chance they have of being heard. Do not be like them. Your Father knows what you need, even before you ask him.

This, then, is how you should pray:
Our Father in heaven,
holy be your name,
your kingdom come
and your will be done,
on earth as in heaven.
Give us today our daily bread.
Forgive us our debts
just as we have forgiven those who are in debt to us.
Do not bring us to the test
but deliver us from the evil one.

"If you forgive others their wrongs, your Father in heaven will also forgive yours. If you do not forgive others, then your Father will not forgive you either."

In services of Church unity, the Our Father is the safe ground on which everyone begins. But it's not only a beginning; it's a path that goes all the way. It is the distinctive prayer of a disciple of Jesus, who reached out to "the weak, the sick, the wounded, the strayed, the lost" (Ezechiel 34), without enquiring what their faith credentials were. He even praised the faith of pagans! (e.g., Mt 15:28; Lk 7:9). Sometimes when Christians talk about unity they mean only sameness. And what is sameness but "same as me!" Sameness is built on exclusion. But unity is unity in diversity.

JUNE

Friday

18

**ORDINARY TIME
11th Week**

Sacred Heart of Jesus

Ezk 34:11-16   Rom 5:5-11   Lk 15:3-7

The head makes distinctions and oppositions; it thinks in numbers and percentages; it would mince everything down to a featureless sameness like chipboard. The shepherd in today's Gospel passage, had he been working only with his head, would have found 99% quite satisfactory. But he was working from his heart, which knows nothing about percentages, and he went searching for the one that was lost. That's the nature of the heart. How do we see the outsider, the marginal person, the failure…? That is the surest way of checking whether we live out of our head or out of our heart.

Jesus told them this parable, "Who among you, having a hundred sheep and losing one of them, will not leave the ninety-nine in the wilderness and seek out the lost one till he finds it? And finding it, will he not joyfully carry it home on his shoulders? Then he will call his friends and neighbors together and say: 'Celebrate with me for I have found my lost sheep.' I tell you, just so, there will be more rejoicing in heaven over one repentant sinner than over ninety-nine upright who do not need to repent."

19 Saturday

JUNE

Jdt 13:17-20;15:9   Lk 2:41-51

Mary's "pondering in her heart" is surely the headline for Christian contemplation. It may be appropriate to let Meister Eckhart interpret today's gospel for us in his distinctive way. "And so in truth, if you would find this noble birth [of God in the soul] you must leave the crowd and return to the source and round whence you came. All must well up from within, out of God, if this birth is to shine forth truly and clearly, and all your activity must cease, and all your powers must serve His ends, not your own. If this work is to be done, God alone must do it, and you must just allow it to be. Where you truly go out from your will and your knowledge, God with His knowledge surely and willingly goes in and shines there clearly."

Every year the parents of Jesus went to Jerusalem for the Feast of the Passover, as was customary. And when Jesus was twelve years old, he went up with them according to the custom for this feast. After the festival was over, they returned, but the boy Jesus remained in Jerusalem and his parents did not know it.

They thought he was in the company and after walking the whole day they looked for him among their relatives and friends. As they did not find him, they went back to Jerusalem searching for him, and on the third day they found him in the Temple, sitting among the teachers, listening to them and asking questions. And all the people were amazed at his understanding and his answers.

His parents were very surprised when they saw him and his mother said to him, "Son, why have you done this to us? Your father and I were very worried while searching for you." Then he said to them, "Why were you looking for me? Do you not know that I must be in my Father's house?" But they did not understand this answer.

Jesus went down with them, returning to Nazareth, and he continued to be subject to them. As for his mother, she kept all these things in her heart.

Sunday

For a commentary on today's
gospel see September 24.
Today is Father's Day. Let's
think about fathers. In the New
Testament the image of father
is far removed both from the
stern Victorian father and the
absentee father of today whose
place in the lives of his children
is becoming less and less. It is
full of tenderness and affection.
In the story of the Prodigal Son
(Lk 15), for example, the father
rushed out to greed his
wayward son, clasped him in
his arms and kissed him. Jesus
knew himself totally loved by
his Father, "As the Father has
loved me, so I have loved you"
(Jn 15:9). The fact that we can
even imagine what this was like
means that the image of father
is not dead in us.

Zec 12:10—13:1

I will pour out on the family of David and the inhabitants of Jerusalem a spirit of love and supplication. They will look at the one who was pierced and mourn for him as for an only child, weeping bitterly as for a firstborn. The mourning in Jerusalem will be as great as the mourning of Haddadrimmon in the plain of Megiddo.

Gal 3:26-29

Now, in Christ Jesus, all of you are sons and daughters of God through faith. All of you who were given to Christ through baptism, have put on Christ. Here there is no longer any difference between Jew or Greek, or between slave or freed, or between man and woman: but all of you are one in Christ Jesus. And because you belong to Christ, you are of Abraham's race and you are to inherit God's promise.

Lk 9:18-24

One day when Jesus was praying alone, not far from his disciples, he asked them, "What do people say about me?" And they answered, "Some say that you are John the Baptist; others say that you are Elijah, and still others that you are one of the former prophets risen from the dead." Again Jesus asked them, "Who then do you say I am?" Peter answered, "The Messiah of God." Then Jesus spoke to them, giving them strict orders not to tell this to anyone.

And he added, "The Son of Man must suffer many things. He will be rejected by the elders and chief priests and teachers of the Law, and put to death. Then after three days he will be raised to life."

Jesus also said to all the people, "If you wish to be a follower of mine, deny yourself and take up your cross each day, and follow me. For if you choose to save your life, you will lose it, and if you lose your life for my sake, you will save it.

JUNE

Monday

21

**ORDINARY TIME
12th Week**

St. Aloysius Gonzaga

2K 17:5-8,13-15,18   Mt 7:1-5

"Do not judge and you will not be judged," said Jesus. "The measure you give is the measure you get." This already puts the spotlight on the judge in each of us, suggesting like Rumi that our judging has more to do with ourselves than with the truth of things. What or whom do you hate? Look again now. This time don't look at the object or the person you hate, but at the hate itself. What is it about? And what are the things and who are the people you approve of? What are you really approving of? What is it about?

Jesus said to his disciples, "Do not judge and you will not be judged. In the same way you judge others, you will be judged, and the measure you use for others will be used for you. Why do you look at the speck in your brother's eye and not see the plank in your own eye? How can you say to your brother: 'Come, let me take the speck from your eye,' as long as that plank is in your own? Hypocrite, take first the plank out of your own eye, then you will see clear enough to take the speck out of your brother's eye."

2K 19:9-11,14-21,31-35,36   Mt 7:6,12-14

"Do to others whatever you would that others do to you." This rule is considered a summary of the Christian's duty to others. But I often wonder if this "golden rule" should be considered the peak of Christian perfection. It makes the self the measure, and therefore cannot carry very far. Jesus said "Love one another as I have loved you" (Jn 15:12). There is a wide world of difference between the way Jesus loves you and the way that you would wish others to love you.

Jesus said to his disciples, "Do not give what is holy to the dogs, or throw your pearls to the pigs: they might trample on them and even turn on you and tear you to pieces.

"So, do to others whatever you would that others do to you: there you have the Law and the Prophets.

"Enter through the narrow gate; for wide is the gate and broad is the road that leads to destruction, and many go that way. How narrow is the gate that leads to life and how rough the road; few there are who find it."

JUNE

Wednesday **23**

ORDINARY TIME
12thª Week

2K 22:8-13,23:1-3   Mt 7:15-20

"There is nothing hidden but it must be disclosed, nothing kept secret except to be brought to light" (Mk 4:22). Today's reading is saying the same thing. The fruit is the plain truth about the tree, and everyone can not only see it but test it and taste it for themselves. Likewise human action. Everything becomes visible sooner or later. I feel that the word "depth" can hold us too much in thrall. When we talk too much about depth we give ourselves the impression that it's a whole inner separate world, sufficient unto itself.

Jesus said to his disciples, "Beware of false prophets: they come to you in sheep's clothing but inside they are wild wolves. You will recognize them by their fruits. Do you ever pick grapes from thornbushes, or figs from this-tles?

"A good tree always produces good fruit, a rotten tree produces bad fruit. A good tree cannot produce bad fruit and a rotten tree cannot bear good fruit. Any tree that does not bear good fruit is cut down and thrown in the fire. So you will know them by their fruit."

2 4 **Thursday**

JUNE

Is 49:1-6   Acts 13:22-26   Lk 1:57-66, 80

When the time came for Elizabeth, she gave birth to a son. Her neighbors and relatives heard that the merciful Lord had done a wonderful thing for her and they rejoiced with her.

When on the eighth day they came to attend the circumcision of the child, they wanted to name him Zechariah after his father. But his mother said, "Not so; he shall be called John." They said to her, "No one in your family has that name"; and they asked the father by means of signs for the name he wanted to give. Zechariah asked for a writing tablet and wrote on it, "His name is John," and they were very surprised. Immediately Zechariah could speak again and his first words were in praise of God.

A holy fear came on all in the neighborhood, and throughout the Hills of Judea the people talked about these events. All who heard of it pondered in their minds and wondered, "What will this child be?" For they understood that the hand of the Lord was with him.

As the child grew up, he was seen to be strong in the Spirit; he lived in the desert till the day when he appeared openly in Israel.

John the Baptist is like a first draft for Jesus. They were alike in some ways; yet they were different. Despite all his fire, John's message in the end was rather conventional. He was, you might say, a moralist. The impact of Jesus on history has been infinitely greater. Jesus is more than a moralist. If he were only a moralist, he would be a very poor one, for his claims exceeded those of any moralist. He claimed that he and the Father were one. Any moralist making such a claim would not be credible for a moment. He was able to say, "The Kingdom of God is among you." This is much more powerful than all the moralism in the world. An ounce of "is" is better than a ton of "ought."

What are the contrasting phrases in this short reading? "Large crowds followed him," and "Do not tell anyone." Talk creates a crowd. Talk is itself a kind of crowd—a crowd of words. Like the sand, it drifts and blows here and there. Living today is like walking in a sandstorm of words (and here am I adding more!). But Jesus told the healed leper to tell no one about his healing. This tells us that sometimes it is necessary to stand in from the storm. Sometimes it is necessary to be alone and think one's own thoughts. Why not meditate on this today: the silence of Jesus?

When Jesus came down from the mountain, large crowds followed him.

Then a leper came forward. He knelt before him and said, "Sir, if you want to, you can make me clean." Jesus stretched out his hand, touched him, and said, "I want to, be clean again." At that very moment the man was cleansed from his leprosy. Then Jesus said to him, "See that you do not tell anyone, but go to the priest, have yourself declared clean, and offer the gift that Moses ordered as proof of it."

Lm 2:2,10-14,18-19   Mt 8:5-17

Today, meet a different approach to words: meet an army officer, used to giving and receiving commands. For this officer, language was as clear as everything else in army life. This clarity holds great attraction for some people, and they would love to impose it on the whole society. We have to beware of people who worship uniformity and "efficiency"—in Church and state alike. It is only about appearances. There is infinitely more vitality and creativity in the drift of ordinary life. There is hope for every one of us!

When Jesus entered Capernaum, an army captain approached him to ask his help, "Sir, my servant lies sick at home. He is paralyzed and suffers terribly." Jesus said to him, "I will come and heal him."

The captain answered, "I am not worthy to have you under my roof. Just give an order and my boy will be healed. For I myself, a junior officer, give orders to my soldiers. And if I say to one: 'Go,' he goes, and if I say to another: 'Come,' he comes, and to my servant: 'Do this,' he does it."

When Jesus heard this he was astonished and said to those who were following him, "I tell you, I have not found such faith in Israel. I say to you, many will come from east and west and sit down with Abraham, Isaac and Jacob at the feast in the kingdom of heaven; but the heirs of the kingdom will be thrown out into the darkness; there they will wail and grind their teeth."

Then Jesus said to the captain, "Go home now. As you believed, so let it be." And at that moment his servant was healed.

Jesus went to Peter's house and found Peter's mother-in-law in bed with fever. He took her by the hand and the fever left her; she got up and began to wait on him.

Towards evening they brought to Jesus many possessed by evil spirits, and with a word he drove out the spirits. He also healed all who were sick. In doing this he fulfilled what was said by the prophet Isaiah: He bore our infirmities and took on himself our diseases.

Sunday

The pattern is the same throughout. Jesus took people as they were, and through his influence they were transformed. He led them into the unknown. The later John—the John of the Letters, say—would have been the Unknown to the younger John. Jesus always leads into the Unknown. "The Son of Man has nowhere to lay his head," he said to the man who wanted to follow him. Leave the past behind. "Leave the dead to bury their dead." If I crave for security, if I have a horror of the unknown, if I use my religion only as an anchor in the past, then I am denying the Gospel more effectively than any atheist could. And I am laying the foundation for a very boring old age.

1K 19:16,19-21

Yahweh said to Elijah, "You shall also anoint Jehu, son of Nimshi, as king over Israel; and Elisha, son of Shaphat, from Abel Meholah, you shall anoint as prophet in your place. So Elijah left. He found Elisha, son of Shaphat, who was plowing a field of twelve acres and was at the end of the twelfth acre. Elijah passed by him and cast his cloak over him. Elisha left the oxen, ran after Elijah and said, "Let me say goodbye to my father and mother; then I will follow you." Elijah said to him, "Return if you want, don't worry about what I did." However, Elisha turned back, took the yoke of oxen and slew them. He roasted their meat on the pieces of the yoke and gave it to his people who ate of it. After this, he followed Elijah and began ministering to him.

Gal 5:1,13-18

Christ freed us to make us really free. So remain firm and do not submit again to the yoke of slavery. You, brothers and sisters, were called to enjoy freedom; I am not speaking of that freedom which gives free rein to the desires of the flesh, but of that which makes you slaves of one another through love. For the whole Law is summed up in this sentence: You shall love your neighbor as yourself. (...)

Lk 9:51-62

As the time drew near when Jesus would be taken up to heaven, he made up his mind to go to Jerusalem. He had sent ahead of him some messengers who entered a Samaritan village to prepare a lodging for him. But the people would not receive him because he was on his way to Jerusalem. Seeing this, James and John, his disciples said, "Lord, do you want us to call down fire from heaven to reduce them to ashes?" Jesus turned and rebuked them, and they went on to another village.

As they went on their way, a man said to him, "I will follow you wherever you go." Jesus said to him, "Foxes have holes and birds of the air have nests; but the Son of Man has nowhere to lay his head." To another he said, "Follow me." But he answered, "Let me go back now, for first I want to bury my father." And Jesus said to him, "Let the dead bury their dead; as for you, leave them and proclaim the kingdom of God." Another said to him, "I will follow you, Lord, but first let me say goodbye to my family." And Jesus said to him, "Whoever has put his hand to the plow and looks back is not fit for the kingdom of God."

J U N E

Monday

28

ORDINARY TIME
13th Week

St. Irenaeus

Am 2:6-10,13-16   Mt 8:18-22

Matthew gives us today what Luke gave us yesterday: those two sayings of Jesus. "The Son of Man has nowhere to lay his head," and "Leave the dead to bury their dead." It's not surprising; they are hard to forget. There is a great fascination about wanderers. We would love to have both—freedom and security—but they are incompatible. "Leave the dead to bury their dead." Jesus said come now! Postponement becomes a habit: after his father's death he would find another reason for delay, and another…. Putting the two sayings together, what do we get? He is saying to us: if you want to be free, be free now!

When Jesus saw the crowd press around him, Jesus gave orders to cross to the other shore. A teacher of the Law approached him and said, "Master, I will follow you wherever you go." Jesus said to him, "Foxes have holes and birds have nests, but the Son of Man has nowhere to lay his head."

Another disciple said to him, "Lord, let me go and bury my father first." But Jesus answered him, "Follow me, and let the dead bury their own dead."

Acts 12:1-11   2Tim 4:6-8,17-18   Mt 16:13-19

Jesus came to Caesarea Philippi. He asked his disciples, "Who do people say the Son of Man is?" They said, "For some of them you are John the Baptist, for others Elijah or Jeremiah or one of the prophets."

Jesus asked them, "But you, who do you say I am?" Peter answered, "You are the Messiah, the Son of the living God." Jesus replied, "It is well for you, Simon Bar-jona, for it is not flesh or blood that has revealed this to you but my Father in heaven.

"And now I say to you: You are Peter (or Rock) and on this rock I will build my Church; and never will the powers of death overcome it.

"I will give you the keys of the kingdom of heaven: whatever you bind on earth shall be bound in heaven, and what you unbind on earth shall be unbound in heaven."

"For some of them you are John the Baptist, for others Elijah or Jeremiah or one of the prophets,"... Could we say that there are two kinds of recognition: 1. when you check and are satisfied that something is just as you have always thought it to be; and 2. when something confronts you in that painfully familiar way of dragging you out of your rut and setting you naked in some new situation. Both are "recognition": knowing again. In the first case it's a repeat of the past, it's a refusal of life; in the second, it's the repeated call to be a living being. Peter had that moment of grace to see Jesus as God's new deed. It is on that faith that the community of the faithful is built.

JUNE

Wednesday

30

ORDINARY TIME
13th Week

First Martyrs of the Church of Rome

Am 5:14-15,21-24   Mt 8:28-34

For Jews, a dead body was "unclean", so tombs were "unclean" places. Only a demoniac would think of living there. Everything in this story, then, is unclean. At least it was appropriate that all unclean things and people should be in the one place. There's a kind of right order in that. By the end of the story Jesus has rearranged everything: the demons have gone into the pigs, which in turn have gone into the water. Thus, in this story, Jesus restores everything to its proper place. He establishes right order. That makes me think: what are the arrangements in my life that seem "right" to me (at least in the sense of being familiar), but which are not right at all...?

When Jesus reached Gadara on the other side, he was met by two demoniacs who came out from the tombs. They were so fierce that no one dared to pass that way. Suddenly they shouted, "What do you want with us, you, Son of God? Have you come to torture us before the time?"

At some distance away there was a large herd of pigs feeding. So the demons begged him, "If you drive us out, send us into that herd of pigs." Jesus ordered them, "Go." So they left and went into the pigs. The whole herd rushed down the cliff into the lake and drowned.

The men in charge of them ran off to the town, where they told the whole story, also what had happened to the men possessed with the demons. Then the whole town went out to meet Jesus; and when they saw him, they begged him to leave their area.

1 Thursday

JULY

Am 7:10-17   Mt 9:1-8

"This man is insulting God," they said. I think we can take it to mean, "This man is insulting us!" If God is "our" God, then to insult God is to insult us. In this way we make God our property. It's good to beware of the words "my" and "our." In the Our Father, of course, we call God "ours," but the very next thing we say is, "Holy be your name." In Hebrew the word for 'holy' is "kadosh." Its basic meaning is "separate, wholly other." We cannot put God in our pocket. God can be "ours" only in the sense that God is the One to whom we give ourselves. God is not subject to our will, but we to God's. Yes, let God do God's business, and beware of our clarity.

Jesus got back into the boat, crossed the lake again, and came to his hometown. Here they brought a paralyzed man to him, lying on a bed. Jesus saw their faith and said to the paralytic, "Courage, my son! Your sins are forgiven."

Then some teachers of the Law said to themselves, "This man insults God." Jesus was aware of what they were thinking, and said, "Why have you such evil thoughts? Which is easier to say: 'Your sins are forgiven' or 'Stand up and walk'? You must know that the Son of Man has authority on earth to forgive sins." He then said to the paralyzed man, "Stand up! Take your stretcher and go home." The man got up, and went home.

When the crowds saw this, they were filled with awe and praised God for giving such power to human beings.

Am 8:4-6,9-12   Mt 9:9-13

The ancient world generally did not see compassion as a high value. The Romans despised it as weakness. Clemency they valued, because it showed you in a good light: you were so powerful and confident that you didn't even need to take revenge. Compassion is seen as a high value now, even when it is being disregarded in practice. Most people would like to be regarded as compassionate—even politicians and bureaucrats. It's a tribute, even if sometimes half-hearted, to the man of Nazareth who sat down to eat with the despised of the land, and who laid down his life to prove that compassion was more than soft talk.

As Jesus moved on from there, he saw a man named Matthew at his seat in the custom-house, and he said to him, "Follow me." And Matthew got up and followed him. Now it happened, while Jesus was at table in Matthew's house, many tax collectors and other sinners joined Jesus and his disciples. When the Pharisees saw this they said to his disciples, "Why is it that your master eats with those sinners and tax collectors?"

When Jesus heard this he said, "Healthy people do not need a doctor, but sick people do. Go and find out what this means: What I want is mercy, not sacrifice. I did not come to call the righteous but sinners."

**ORDINARY TIME
13th Week**

St. Thomas, Apostle

Eph 2:19-22   Jn 20:24-29

3 Saturday

JULY

The others said to Thomas, "We have seen...." Thomas said, "Until I have seen...." What's the difference? None. The others believed because they had seen; why shouldn't Thomas insist on the same? Thomas has been unfairly nicknamed "Doubting Thomas." Of course the gospel writer has us in mind. Like Thomas, we're late on the scene—much later. We have to be reassured; we are the real Doubting Thomases. Like Thomas we are invited too to "put your finger here and see my hands; stretch out your hand and put it into my side." Most of us know the wounds of Christ firsthand.

Thomas, the Twin, one of the Twelve, was not with them when Jesus came. The other disciples told him, "We have seen the Lord." But he replied, "Until I have seen in his hands the print of the nails, and put my finger in the mark of the nails and my hand in his side, I will not believe."

Eight days later, the disciples were inside again and Thomas was with them. Despite the locked doors Jesus came and stood in their midst and said, "Peace be with you." Then he said to Thomas, "Put your finger here and see my hands; stretch out your hand and put it into my side. Resist no longer and be a believer."

Thomas then said, "You are my Lord and my God." Jesus replied, "You believe because you see me, don't you? Happy are those who have not seen and believe."

Every follower of Christ is called to proclaim the Kingdom of God. Even reluctant followers! To the man who was making excuses for not following, Jesus said, "Go and proclaim the Kingdom of God" (Lk 9:60). Do you need a diploma in catechetics? No! Not one of the 70 had a diploma of any kind—nor any of the Twelve. Jesus himself had no diplomas or degrees. But what you have to have is love. If you love genuinely, you are a missionary: you are going out of yourself. If you go out to even one stranger you are, in a way, going out "to the whole world." And if you go out to an enemy, you are standing on the highest peak of the Christian life.

Is 66:10-14

Rejoice for Jerusalem and be glad for her, all you who love her. Be glad with her, rejoice with her, all you who were in grief over her, that you may suck of the milk from her comforting breasts, that you may drink deeply from the abundance of her glory." For this is what Yahweh says: I will send her peace, overflowing like a river; and the nations' wealth, rushing like a torrent towards her. (...)

Gal 6:14-18

For me, I do not wish to take pride in anything except in the cross of Christ Jesus our Lord. Through him the world has been crucified to me and I to the world. Let us no longer speak of the circumcised and of non-Jews, but of a new creation. Let those who live according to this rule receive peace and mercy: they are the Israel of God! (...)

Lk 10:1-12,17-20

The Lord appointed seventy-two other disciples and sent them two by two ahead of him to every town and place, where he himself was to go. And he said to them, "The harvest is rich, but the workers are few. So you must ask the Lord of the harvest to send workers to his harvest. Courage! I am sending you like lambs among wolves. Set off without purse or bag or sandals; and do not stop at the homes of those you know. Whatever house you enter, first bless them saying: 'Peace to this house.' If a friend of peace lives there, the peace shall rest upon that person. But if not, the blessing will return to you. Stay in that house eating and drinking at their table, for the worker deserves to be paid. Do not move from house to house. When they welcome you in any town, eat what they offer you. Heal the sick who are there and say to them: 'The kingdom of God has drawn near to you.' But in any town where you are not welcome, go to the marketplace and proclaim: 'Even the dust of your town that clings to our feet, we wipe off and leave with you. But know and be sure that the kingdom of God had come to you.' I tell you that on the Judgment Day it will be better for Sodom than for this town. The seventy-two disciples returned full of joy. They said, "Lord, even the demons obeyed us when we called on your name." Then Jesus replied, "I saw Satan fall like lightning from heaven. You see, I have given you authority to trample on snakes and scorpions and to overcome all the power of the Enemy, so that nothing will harm you. Nevertheless, don't rejoice because the evil spirits submit to you; rejoice rather that your names are written in heaven."

JULY

Monday

5

**ORDINARY TIME
14th Week**

St. Anthony Zaccaria

Hos 2:16,17-18,21-22   Mt 9:18-26

"Courage, my daughter, your faith has saved you." It is interesting to see what happens when you emphasize a different word. You see that these words ("Your faith has saved you") are quite frequent in the gospels. Many people imagine that the life of faith is some kind of alienation, but here Jesus puts people's lives back in their own hands. Meister Eckhart wrote, "It is just as true to say that man became God as that God became man….And so whatever you have you have not got on loan from God, for God is your own." The "self" in question, is not the ego, but "your true life that is hidden with Christ in God" (Col 3:3). Faith then is not a kind of mental slavery, but a coming into your power.

While Jesus was speaking to them, an official of the synagogue came up to him, bowed before him and said, "My daughter has just died, but come and place your hands on her, and she will live." Jesus stood up and followed him with his disciples.

Then a woman who had suffered from a severe bleeding for twelve years came up from behind and touched the edge of his cloak. For she thought, "If I only touch his cloak, I will be healed." Jesus turned, saw her and said, "Courage, my daughter, your faith has saved you." And from that moment the woman was cured.

When Jesus arrived at the official's house and saw the flute players and the excited crowd, he said, "Get out of here! The girl is not dead. She is only sleeping!" And they laughed at him. But once the crowd had been turned out, Jesus went in and took the girl by the hand, and she stood up. The news of this spread through the whole area.

Hos 8:4-7,11-13   Mt 9:32-38

"He drives away demons with the help of the prince of demons." This is what you might call "the explanation from below." A great deal of modern psychology also offers explanations "from below." There is also the "explanation from above." That too has its dangers of course. It all makes you think: What are we doing when we look for explanations? What do we do with explanations when we get them? In truth: nothing! We pass on to something else. In Matthew's version of today's passage, Jesus ignored the jibe about Beelzebul. That's undoubtedly the best thing to do with explanations, especially explanations "from below." Trying to counter them only robs us of our power.

Some people brought to Jesus a man who was dumb because he was possessed by a demon. When the demon was driven out, the dumb man began to speak. The crowds were astonished and said, "Nothing like this has ever been seen in Israel." (But the Pharisees said, "He drives away demons with the help of the prince of demons.")

Jesus went around all the towns and villages, teaching in their synagogues and proclaiming the good news of the Kingdom, and he cured every sickness and disease. When he saw the crowds he was moved with pity, for they were harassed and helpless like sheep without a shepherd. Then he said to his disciples, "The harvest is abundant but the workers are only few. Ask the master of the harvest to send workers to gather his harvest."

Look at that list of twelve and try to imagine how they looked. They were simple men; to us today they would probably appear ragged and scruffy. Yet these are the men whose memory has been venerated by the saints and mystics of all ages. Recently I thumbed through an expensive large-format book on the treasures of the Vatican. We are used to witnessing such treasures, but the legend took me aback. Faith feeds upon symbols and images. The gold cardinal's cross is the symbol of the "Princes of the Church." I felt immensely sad. The Cross is a symbol of poverty and humility, not of worldly royalty. Poverty can go anywhere, but solid gold is a stranger to most places.

Jesus called his twelve disciples to him and gave them authority over the unclean spirits to drive them out and to heal every disease and sickness.

These are the names of the twelve apostles: first Simon, called Peter, and his brother Andrew; James, the son of Zebedee, and his brother John; Philip and Bartholomew, Thomas and Matthew, the tax collector; James, the son of Alphaeus, and Thaddaeus; Simon, the Canaanite, and Judas Iscariot, the man who would betray him.

Jesus sent these twelve on mission with the instruction: "Do not visit pagan territory and do not enter a Samaritan town. Go instead to the lost sheep of the people of Israel. Go and proclaim this message: The kingdom of heaven is near."

Hos 11:1,3-4,8-9   Mt 10:7-15

Jesus said to his disciples, "Go and proclaim this message: The kingdom of heaven is near. Heal the sick, bring the dead back to life, cleanse the lepers, and drive out demons. You received this as a gift, so give it as a gift. Do not carry any gold, silver or copper in your purses. Do not carry a traveler's bag, or an extra shirt, or sandals, or walking-stick: workers deserve their living.

"When you come to a town or a village, look for a worthy person and stay there until you leave.

"As you enter the house, wish it peace. If the people in the house deserve it, your peace will be on them; if they do not deserve it, your blessing will come back to you.

"And if you are not welcomed and your words are not listened to, leave that house or that town and shake the dust off your feet. I assure you, it will go easier for the people of Sodom and Gomorrah on the day of judgment than it will for the people of that town."

"You received this as a gift, so give it as a gift." Giving and receiving are the opposite of buying and selling. In the Anglican Book of Common Prayer there is a prayer for ourselves in time of wealth. "In all time of our tribulation; in all time of our wealth; in the hour of death, and in the day of judgment, Good Lord, deliver us."

This shows a wise understanding that we are in greater danger from wealth than from poverty. When we can buy our way we depend on no one, but when we are poor we depend on everyone, we are at everyone's mercy. And so we are well placed for learning something about the mercy of God.

JULY

Friday

9

**ORDINARY TIME
14th Week**

St. Augustine Zhao Rong

Hos 14:2-10   Mt 10:16-23

We associate intelligence with the ability to plan. We are impressed by planning, even when the objective is silly. Many things in life require planning, but it can become a compulsive habit. Compulsive planning ensures that I will always live in the past, that I will never fully meet a new situation. Intelligence isn't old hat; it's always new. We have to trust the intelligence that is in us. "When the hour comes, you will be given what you are to say." All the things that are very alive—faith, intelligence—don't keep till tomorrow; they are for now. That word "alertness" is probably much closer to the essence of intelligence and faith than "planning." Jesus kept saying, "Stay awake!"

Jesus said to his disciples, "Look, I send you out like sheep among wolves. You must be clever as snakes and innocent as doves. Be on your guard with respect to people, for they will hand you over to their courts and they will flog you in your synagogues. You will be brought to trial before rulers and kings because of me, and so you may witness to them and the pagans.

"But when you are arrested, do not worry about what you are to say and how you are to say it; when the hour comes, you will be given what you are to say. For it is not you who will speak; but it will be the Spirit of your Father in you.

"Brother will hand over brother to death, and a father his child; children will turn against parents and have them put to death. Everyone will hate you because of me, but whoever stands firm to the end will be saved.

"When they persecute you in one town, flee to the next. For sure, you will not have gone through all the towns of Israel before the Son of Man comes."

Is 6:1-8   Mt 10:24-33

Jesus said to his apostles, "A student is not above his teacher, or a slave above his master. A student should be glad to become like his teacher, and the slave like his master. If the head of the family has been called Beelzebul, how much more the members of the family! So, do not be afraid of them.

"There is nothing covered that will not be uncovered, and nothing hidden that will not be made known. What I am telling you in the dark, you must speak in the light. What you hear in private, proclaim from the housetops.

"Do not be afraid of those who kill the body, but have no power to kill the soul. Rather be afraid of him who can destroy both body and soul in hell. For only a few cents you can buy two sparrows, yet not one sparrow falls to the ground without your Father's consent. As for you, every hair of your head has been counted. So do not be afraid: you are worth much more than many sparrows.

"Whoever acknowledges me before others I will acknowledge before my Father in heaven. Whoever rejects me before others I will reject before my Father in heaven."

Here I will give you sentences and phrases of Meister Eckhart's sermon on it. It is probably his most obscure sermon. "When God works in the soul, He loves His work. Where the soul is in which God performs His work, that work is so great that it is nothing but love, and the love is nothing but God. God loves Himself and His nature, His being and His Godhead…. In the love in which God loves Himself, He loves all things… God is in the soul with His nature, with His being and with His Godhead, and yet He is not the soul. The reflection of the soul in God is God, and yet she is what she is....."

Sunday

"Do this and you will live," said Jesus to the teacher, referring to the answer the teacher had just given him. At the end of the reading he says again, "Go and do the same." Those scribes or teachers of the Law loved to quote texts, as this one does in today's reading. Life isn't a theory, or a quotation or piece of Scripture, Jesus seems to say to him. Holiness of life can never be pushed to the side in theology. "Whoever does not love does not know God, for God is love," wrote St. John (1Jn 4:8). Before the Faith was called 'Christianity' it was called "the Way" (Acts 19:9). It is a way of life before it is a way of thinking. The real test is in the field of action.

15TH SUNDAY IN ORDINARY TIME

11

Dt 30:10-14
Col 1:15-20

He is the image of the unseen God, and for all creation he is the firstborn, for in him all things were created, in heaven and on earth, visible and invisible: thrones, rulers, authorities, powers… All was made through him and for him. He is before all and all things hold together in him. And he is the head of the body, that is the Church, for he is the first, the first raised from the dead that he may be the first in everything, for God was pleased to let fullness dwell in him. Through him God willed to reconcile all things to himself, and through him, through his blood shed on the cross, God establishes peace, on earth as in heaven.

Lk 10:25-37

A teacher of the Law came and began putting Jesus to the test. And he said, "Master, what shall I do to receive eternal life?" Jesus replied, "What is written in the Scripture? How do you understand it?" The man answered, "It is written: You shall love the Lord your God with all your heart, with all your soul, with all your strength and with all your mind. And you shall love your neighbor as yourself." Jesus replied, "What a good answer! Do this and you shall live." The man wanted to keep up appearances, so he replied, "Who is my neighbor?"

Jesus then said, "There was a man going down from Jerusalem to Jericho, and he fell into the hands of robbers. They stripped him, beat him and went off leaving him half-dead. It happened that a priest was going along that road and saw the man, but passed by on the other side. Likewise a Levite saw the man and passed by on the other side. But a Samaritan, too, was going that way, and when he came upon the man, he was moved with compassion. He went over to him and treated his wounds with oil and wine and wrapped them with bandages. Then he put him on his own mount and brought him to an inn where he took care of him. The next day he had to set off, but he gave two silver coins to the innkeeper and told him: 'Take care of him and whatever you spend on him, I will repay when I come back.'"

Jesus then asked, "Which of these three, do you think, made himself neighbor to the man who fell into the hands of robbers?" The teacher of the Law answered, "the one who had mercy on him." And Jesus said, "Go then and do the same."

Is 1:10-17   Mt 10:34—11:1

Kierkegaard distinguished three stages in our spiritual development: the aesthetic, the moral, and the spiritual. In the first stage a person is governed by the senses, impulse, and emotion. In the second, you begin to take moral standards and responsibilities seriously and in the third, you take a leap of faith in God. It's true. We can detain ourselves for years at the aesthetic level, reading beautiful books and yet taking few or no steps to lead a spiritual life. Many people become locked in stage two, and their religion remains grim and judgmental. But God will take us beyond it: one day we will get the grace to "take up our cross, follow him, and to lose our life for his sake...."

Jesus said to his disciples, "Do not think that I have come to establish peace on earth. I have not come to bring peace, but a sword. For I have come to set a man against his father and daughter against her mother; a daughter-in-law against her mother-in-law. Each one will have as enemies those of one's own family.

"Whoever loves father or mother more than me is not worthy of me. And whoever loves son or daughter more than me is not worthy of me. And whoever does not take up his cross and come after me is not worthy of me. One who wants to benefit from his life will lose it; one who loses his life for my sake will find it.

"Whoever welcomes you welcomes me, and whoever welcomes me welcomes him who sent me. The one who welcomes a prophet as a prophet will receive the reward of a prophet; the one who welcomes a just man because he is a just man will receive the reward of a just man. And if anyone gives even a cup of cold water to one of these little ones, because he is a disciple of mine, I assure you, he will not go unrewarded."

When Jesus had finished giving his twelve disciples these instructions, he went on from there to teach and to proclaim his message in their towns.

ORDINARY TIME
15th Week

St. Henry

Is 7:1-9   Mt 11:20-24

13 Tuesday

JULY

Jesus worked great miracles in Chorazin and Bethsaida, he said. Yet there is no account of them. The Son of God walked their streets, healed their sick tormented people, spoke to them about a new hope and a new world. Gospels could have been written, filled with his words and his deeds.... Instead, there is total silence. It doesn't read like a success story. It is the mystery of divine grace and the human will. This is the greatest drama in the world, and there are no clichés or platitudes in it. It is a heart-rending story, and who could even begin to guess the ending?

Jesus began to denounce the cities in which he had performed most of his miracles, because the people there did not change their ways, "Alas for you Chorazin and Bethsaida! If the miracles worked in you had taken place in Tyre and Sidon, the people there would have repented long ago in sackcloth and ashes. But I assure you, for Tyre and Sidon it will be more bearable on the day of judgment than for you. And you, Capernaum, will you be lifted up to heaven? You will be thrown down to the place of the dead! For if the miracles which were performed in you had taken place in Sodom, it would still be there today! But I tell you, it will be more bearable for Sodom on the day of judgment than for you."

J U L Y

Wednesday

14

**ORDINARY TIME
15th Week**

Bl. Kateri Tekakwitha

Is 10:5-7,13-16   Mt 11:25-27

It is when Jesus had spoken of the dismal failures of Chorazin, Bethsaida and Capernaum that he suddenly burst out, "Father, Lord of heaven and earth, I praise you, because you have hidden these things from the wise and learned and revealed them to simple people." We must not be against human wisdom: this would do no service to God. Intelligence is one of God's most shining gifts. But it has to be a kind of wisdom that remains open to extension beyond itself: to a deeper wisdom that must look at first like foolishness. A child can cut through all our evasions and ask a question that goes straight to the heart. To such as these, said Jesus, the Kingdom of God has been revealed.

On one occasion Jesus said, "Father, Lord of heaven and earth, I praise you, because you have hidden these things from the wise and learned and revealed them to simple people. Yes, Father, this is what pleased you.

"Everything has been entrusted to me by my Father. No one knows the Son except the Father, and no one knows the Father except the Son and those to whom the Son chooses to reveal him."

Is 26:7-9,12,16-19   Mt 11:28-30

Johann Tauler preached this: "If people could discover and realize and contemplate how God has founded the innermost depth of the soul, how God dwells there hidden and concealed, they would indeed be blessed. And even though people have turned their eyes away from all this and wandered far away, still they are constantly drawn and attracted back to it. As long as they wander away from it they can never find rest, for there is nothing else that can satisfy them. Though they may not know it, this pulls and draws them all the time, for this is what they were made for. All things find rest in their own proper state; the stone lies on the ground, fire rises into the air, and the human soul is drawn to God."

Jesus spoke thus, "Come to me, all you who work hard and who carry heavy burdens and I will refresh you. Take my yoke upon you and learn from me for I am gentle and humble of heart; and you will find rest. For my yoke is good and my burden is light."

JULY

Friday

16

ORDINARY TIME
15th Week

Our Lady of Mt. Carmel

Is 38:1-6,21-22,7-8   Mt 12:1-8

There was a time in the Church, not long ago, when rubics and regulations about minutiae were given an inordinate importance. Rules are brought into ridicule when there is no room left for common sense. In reaction people swing to the opposite extreme. The law tried to be spirit; it tried to go into every nook and cranny of our lives and guide us from within. We need spirit, or rather the Spirit, to guide us wisely. I often come back to these words from the Sequence to the Holy Spirit at Pentecost: Bend the rigid, Warm the frigid, Straighten out the quirks! (Flecte quod est rigidum, Fove quod est frigidum, Rege quod est devium.)

It happened that Jesus walked through the wheat fields on a Sabbath. His disciples were hungry, and began to pick some heads of wheat and crush them to eat the grain. When the Pharisees noticed this, they said to Jesus, "Look at your disciples; they are doing what is prohibited on the Sabbath!"

Jesus answered, "Have you not read what David did when he and his men were hungry? He went into the house of God, and they ate the bread offered to God, although neither he nor his men had the right to eat it, but only the priests. And have you not read in the Law that on the Sabbath the priests in the Temple break the Sabbath rest, yet they are not guilty?

"I tell you, there is greater than the Temple here. If you really knew the meaning of the words: It is mercy I want, not sacrifice, you would not have condemned the innocent. Besides the Son of Man is Lord of the Sabbath."

Mic 2:1-5   Mt 12:14-21

We need not think that legalism gives up easily. It continually tries to make a comeback. What's the difference between the Pharisees measuring out tithes of "mint, dill, and cumin" (Mt 23:23), and Catholics up the 1960s weighing food by the ounce on fast days? The difference is that we had no excuse. We had been hearing the Gospel all our lives. When he has spoken the truth there is nothing else he can do. Even he cannot force them to live with open hearts. Someone can shout at you, but understanding is a silent subtle movement, like a bud opening in the mind. At a certain point there is nothing to do but wait. He gives us time to ripen.

The Pharisees went out and made plans to get rid of him. As Jesus was aware of the plot, he went away from that place. Many people followed him and he cured all who were sick. Then he gave them strict orders not to make him known.

In this way Isaiah's prophecy was fulfilled: Here is my servant whom I have chosen, the one I love, and with whom I am pleased. I will put my Spirit upon him†and he will announce my judgment to the nations.

He will not argue or shout, nor will his voice be heard in the streets. The bruised reed he will not crush, nor snuff out the smoldering wick. He will persist until justice is made victorious and in him all the nations will put their hope.

Sunday

Martha and Mary: work and contemplation. If you had only a slight acquaintance with Meister Eckhart you might expect him to favor Mary over Martha. But surprisingly he regards Martha as having it more together than Mary. We suspect that Mary sat at the Lord's feet a little more for her own happiness than for spiritual profit. Martha stood maturely and well grounded in virtue…. Martha says, "Lord, tell her to help me." This was said not in anger, but it was rather affection that constrained her…Temporal work is as noble as any communing with God, for it joins us to Him as closely as the highest that can happen to us except the vision of God in His naked nature.

Gen 18:1-10

Yahweh appeared to Abraham near the oak of Mamre. Abraham was sitting at the entrance to his tent, in the heat of the day, when he looked up and saw three men standing nearby. When he saw them he ran from the entrance of the tent to meet them. He bowed to the ground and said, "My Lord, if I have found favor in your sight, do not pass your servant by. Let a little water be brought. Wash your feet and then rest under the trees. I shall fetch some bread so that you can be refreshed and continue on your way, since you have come to your servant." They then said, "Do as you say." Abraham hurried into the tent to Sarah and said to her, "Quick, take three measures of flour, knead it and make cakes." Abraham then ran to the herd, took a fine, tender calf, gave it to the servant who hurried to prepare it. He took butter and milk and together with the calf he had prepared laid it all before them. And while he remained standing, they ate. They then asked, "Where is Sarah, your wife?" Abraham answered, "She is in the tent." And the visitor said, "At this same time next year I will return and Sarah by then will have a son."

Col 1:24-28

At present I rejoice when I suffer for you; I complete in my own flesh what is lacking in the sufferings of Christ for the sake of his body, which is the Church. For I am serving the Church since God entrusted to me the ministry to make the word of God fully known. I mean that mysterious plan that for centuries and generations remained secret, and which God has now revealed to his holy ones. God willed to make known to them the riches and even the Glory that his mysterious plan reserved for the pagan nations: Christ is in you and you may hope God's Glory. This Christ we preach. We warn and teach everyone true wisdom, aiming to make everyone perfect in Christ.

Lk 10:38-42

As Jesus and his disciples were on their way, he entered a village and a woman called Martha welcomed him to her house. She had a sister named Mary who sat down at the Lord's feet to listen to†this words. Martha, meanwhile, was busy with all the serving and finally she said, "Lord, don't you care that my sister has left me to do all the serving?" But the Lord answered, "Martha, Martha, you worry and are troubled about many things, whereas only one thing is needed. Mary has chosen the better part, and it will not be taken away from her."

The time in which Jesus lived was a time of fervid enthusiasms and political meltdown. The people were looking for "signs and wonders." Naturally, people expected something similar from Jesus. "No sign will be given to this wicked generation," he told them, "but the sign of Jonah!" Matthew seems to have interpreted this very fancifully, comparing the "three days and three nights" that Jesus was to spend in the tomb (factually inaccurate) with the three days and nights that Jonah spent in the whale's belly. (Lk 11:29-32 does not make this comparison.) Jonah himself was the sign to the Ninevites. Jesus is saying, "You are seeking a sign—I am God's sign!"

Some teachers of the Law and some Pharisees spoke up, "Teacher, we want to see a sign from you." Jesus answered them, "An evil and unfaithful people want a sign, but no sign will be given them except the sign of the prophet Jonah. In the same way that Jonah spent three days and three nights in the belly of the monster fish, so will the Son of Man spend three days and three nights in the depths of the earth.

"At the judgment, the people of Niniveh will rise with this generation and condemn it, because they reformed their lives at the preaching of Jonah, and here there is greater than Jonah. At the judgment, the Queen of the South will stand up and condemn you. She came from the ends of the earth to listen to the wisdom of Solomon, and here there is greater than Solomon."

Mic 7:14-15,18-20   Mt 12:46-50

While Jesus was still talking to the people, his mother and his brothers wanted to speak to him and they waited outside. So someone said to him, "Your mother and your brothers are just outside; they want to speak with you."

Jesus answered, "Who is my mother? Who are my brothers?" Then he pointed to his disciples and said, "Look! Here are my mother and my brothers. Whoever does the will of my Father in heaven is for me brother, sister, or mother."

"This fair lovely word 'mother' is so sweet and so kind in itself that it cannot truly; be said of anyone nor to anyone except of him [Jesus] and to him who is true Mother of life and of all." Thus wrote Julian of Norwich, the 14th-century English anchoress. What are we to make of Julian's calling Jesus our Mother? No feminist today has gone this far! But Julian always has good reasons for what she says. She is not saying that Jesus is like your mother, but the reverse: your mother is like Jesus. "A mother's is the most intimate of all services, because it is the truest of all. None has been able to fulfill it properly but Christ.... He bears us to joy and eternal life! Blessings on him!"

J U L Y

Wednesday **21**

ORDINARY TIME
16th Week

St. Lawrence of Brindisi

Jer 1:1,4-10   Mt 13:1-9

The word of God is fruitful in itself, but we have the ability to make it fruitless. Here is the timeless question of the interplay of grace and freewill. Theologians had many a bitter battle over it in past centuries. Once it becomes an abstract question it has no context any more, and the debate can go on forever. It was never settled in fact. But of course when you bring it back to the personal sphere it is a very pointed question, and it is settled every moment of one's life. It becomes the question, "How is my heart today?" Our job now is to find good soil in the heart, where the seeds of the Gospel can sprout.

Jesus left the house and sat down by the lakeside. As many people gathered around him, he got in a boat. There he sat while the whole crowd stood on the shore, and he spoke to them in parables about many things.

Jesus said, "The sower went out to sow and, as he sowed, some seeds fell along the path and the birds came and ate them up. Other seeds fell on rocky ground where there was little soil, and the seeds sprouted quickly because the soil was not deep. But as soon as the sun rose the plants were scorched and withered because they had no roots. Again other seeds fell among thistles; and the thistles grew and choked the plants. Still other seeds fell on good soil and produced a crop; some produced a hundredfold, others sixty and others thirty. If you have ears, then hear!"

Now, on the first day after the Sabbath, Mary of Magdala came to the tomb early in the morning, while it was still dark and she saw that the stone blocking the tomb had been moved away. She ran to Peter and the other disciple whom Jesus loved. And she said to them, "They have taken the Lord out of the tomb and we don't know where they have laid him."

Mary stood weeping outside the tomb, and as she wept she bent down to look inside; she saw two angels in white sitting where the body of Jesus had been, one at the head, and the other at the feet. They said, "Woman, why are you weeping?" She answered, "Because they have taken my Lord and I don't know where they have put him."

As she said this, she turned around and saw Jesus standing there, but she did not recognize him. Jesus said to her, "Woman, why are you weeping? Who are you looking for?" She thought it was the gardener and answered him, "Lord, if you have taken him away, tell me where you have put him, and I will go and remove him."

Jesus said to her, "Mary." She turned and said to him, "Rabboni"—which means, Master. Jesus said to her, "Do not cling to me; you see I have not yet ascended to the Father. But go to my brothers and say to them: I am ascending to my Father, who is your Father, to my God, who is your God."

So Mary of Magdala went and announced to the disciples, "I have seen the Lord, and this is what he said to me."

A woman's evidence carried no weight in first-century cultures; only men could be proper witnesses. Yet all four gospels testify in different ways that Mary Magdalene was the first to see the risen Christ. She was the first bearer of the distinctive Christian message: that Jesus is risen from the dead. For this reason tradition has called her "the apostle to the apostles." She was the first Christian preacher! She had been searching for him ("They have taken the Lord out of the tomb, and we don't know where they have laid him."), and now that she found him she wasn't going to let him go! But he said, "Go to my brothers and tell them...." She learned to move from contemplation to action.

J U L Y

Friday

23

ORDINARY TIME
16th Week
St. Bridget

Jer 3:14-17   Mt 13:18-23

This passage is generally regarded by scholars not as words of Jesus but as an interpretation by the earliest Christian community. It was not Jesus' way to explain parables. In fact explaining a story is like explaining a joke: it only flattens it. The parables don't need explanation— unless it be to fill in some historical facts that have become obscured by the passage of time. But we can meditate on them, as those early Christians did, and all Christians through the ages. In our individual selves perhaps we can distinguish all four kinds of hearers. Or days when we are one of them in particular....

Jesus said to his disciples, "Now listen to the parable of the sower.

"When a person hears the message of the Kingdom but without taking it to himself, the devil comes and snatches away what was sown in his heart. This is the seed that fell along the footpath.

"The seed that fell on rocky ground stands for the one who hears the word and accepts it at once with joy. But this fickle and has no roots. No sooner is he harassed or persecuted because of the word, than he gives up.

"The seed that fell among the thistles is the one who hears the word, but then the worries of this life and the love of money choke the word, and it does not bear fruit.

"As for the seed that fell on good soil it is the one who hears the word and understands it; this bears fruit and produces a hundred, or sixty, or thirty times more."

**ORDINARY TIME
16th Week**

St. Sharbel Makhluf

24 Saturday

JULY

Jer 7:1-11   Mt 13:24-30

The infant Church soon experienced "weeds among the wheat." Paul mentions as one of his greatest difficulties "danger from false brothers" (2 Cor 11:26). The weed in the parable was darnel, a plant that has a resemblance to wheat. Evil takes care to look like good. If everything evil looked evil, our life would have wonderful clarity, but alas! it isn't so. Our world today pays incredibly detailed attention to image: it's the age of the image, almost to the point of discarding substance. The parable summons us to careful discernment.

Jesus told his disciples another parable, "The kingdom of heaven can be compared to a man who sowed good seed in his field. While everyone was asleep, his enemy came and sowed weeds among the wheat and left. When the plants sprouted and produced grain, the weeds also appeared. Then the servants of the owner came to him and said: 'Sir, was it not good seed that you sowed in your field? Where did the weeds come from?'

"He answered them: 'This is the work of an enemy.' They asked him: 'Do you want us to go and pull up the weeds?' He told them: 'No, when you pull up the weeds, you might uproot the wheat with them. Let them just grow together until harvest; and at harvest time I will say to the workers: Pull up the weeds first, tie them in bundles and burn them; then gather the wheat into my barn.'"

Sunday

Christianity appeared first as a "mystery religion." Christians did not speak about the inner mysteries to outsiders. The Our Father was one of those mysteries. Tertullian (born about 160 AD) prepared them for the moment they would address God for the first time as Father. "You blessed ones, when you come up from that sacred washing of the new birth, and when for the first time you spread out your hands with your brothers and sisters in your mother's house [the Church], ask of your Father…for special graces…. 'Ask,' Jesus says, 'and you shall receive.' So now, you have sought, and have found. You have knocked, and it has been opened to you."

Gen 18:20-32
Col 2:12-14

I refer to baptism. On receiving it you were buried with Christ; and you also rose with him for having believed in the power of God who raised him from the dead. You were dead. You were in sin and uncircumcised at the same time. But God gave you life with Christ. He forgave all our sins. He canceled the record of our debts, those regulations which accused us. He did away with all that and nailed it to the cross.

Lk 11:1-13

One day Jesus was praying in a certain place and when he had finished, one of his disciples said to him, "Lord, teach us to pray, just as John taught his disciples." And Jesus said to them, "When you pray, say this:

Father, hallowed be your name, may your kingdom come, give us each day the kind of bread we need, and forgive us our sins, for we also forgive all who do us wrong, and do not bring us to the test."

Jesus said to them, "Suppose one of you has a friend and goes to his house in the middle of the night and says: 'Friend, lend me three loaves, for a friend of mine who is traveling has just arrived and I have nothing to offer him.' Maybe your friend will answer from inside: 'Don't bother me now; the door is locked and my children and I are in bed, so I can't get up and give you anything.' But I tell you, even though he will not get up and attend to you because you are a friend, yet he will get up because you are a bother to him, and he will give you all you need.

And so I say to you, 'Ask and it will be given to you; seek and you will find; knock and it will be opened to you. For the one who asks receives, and the one who searches finds, and to him who knocks the door will be opened.

If your child asks for a fish, will you give a snake instead? And if your child asks for an egg, will you give a scorpion? Even you evil people know how to give good gifts to your children, how much more then will the Father in heaven give holy spirit to those who ask him!"

JULY

Monday

26

ORDINARY TIME
17th Week

Sts. Joachim & Ann

Sir 44:1,10-15   Mt 13:16-17

Christianity is a mystery religion; it can only be understood from the inside. To the outsider, for example, the Eucharist is just a crowd of people eating little morsels of bread; but to the insider it is "the mystery of faith: Christ has died, Christ has risen, Christ will come again." Western culture equips us poorly for understanding anything from the inside. We have specialized in analysis, the view from the outside. "But blessed are your eyes, for they see, and your ears, for they hear." In other words, don't let anyone do your hearing or your seeing for you. They can do their own, and offer to share it with you, but don't let them presume that they can do yours.

Jesus said to his disciples, "But blessed are your eyes because they see, and your ears, because they hear.

"For I tell you that many prophets and upright people would have longed to see the things you see, but they did not, and to hear the things you hear, but they did not hear it."

Jer 14:17-22   Mt 13:36-43

Aha! They are looking for explanations! They want to get their minds around this parable, so that they can put it "out there" from them: that's what explanations do. Still, it must be all right to look for explanations—so long as we don't put too much store by them, or imagine that the one we find is the only possible one. It is about seeds. Seeds are the beginning of things, not the end. Good and evil will be separated out only at the end of time. That means, in practical terms, never! In the ultimate, yes, in eternity; but not in time—at no time! Let's not be too surprised at evil deeds: we are part of the picture ourselves.

Jesus sent the crowds away and went into the house. And his disciples came to him saying, "Explain to us the parable of the weeds in the field." He answered them, "The one who sows the good seed is the Son of Man. The field is the world; the good seed are the people of the Kingdom; the weeds are those who follow the evil one. The enemy who sows them is the devil; the harvest is the end of time and the workers are the angels.

"Just as the weeds are pulled up and burned in the fire, so will it be at the end of time. The Son of Man will send his angels, and they will weed out of his kingdom all that is scandalous and all who do evil. And these will be thrown in the blazing furnace, where there will be weeping and gnashing of teeth. Then the just will shine like the sun in the kingdom of their Father. If you have ears, then hear."

We see ourselves reflected in the eyes of others as in a mirror. A mirror reflects only the surface, so we see only the surface of ourselves and not the reality. We have to become frustrated with surfaces sooner or later. We have to fail in some significant way. Richard Rohr said (speaking particularly about men): we spend the first half of life building our tower (our career, our savings, etc.), and this is right. But in the second half of our life we have to fall off our tower! Unless you fall off your tower—unless you have a broken heart—he said, you will be of no use to anyone. It is failure that will open up the heart; and in that deep inner place we will find the hidden treasure, the pearl of great price.

Jesus said to the crowds, "The kingdom of heaven is like a treasure hidden in a field. The one who finds it buries it again; and so happy is he, that he goes and sells everything he has, in order to buy that field.

"Again the kingdom of heaven is like a trader who is looking for fine pearls. Once he has found a pearl of exceptional quality, he goes away, sells everything he has and buys it."

1Jn 4:7-16   Jn 11:19-27

A little beyond the end of today's reading there is the shortest verse in the Bible. It is Jn 11:35, and it says simply, "Jesus wept." It shows sensitivity in the people who first divided the Scriptures into chapters and verses. They could easily have put these words with the following verse; it would even have been logical: the following verse is, "So the Jews said, 'See how he loved him!'" When someone weeps you just have to give them time to weep. Weeping may be saying a lot, but it is not language, and it doesn't require an answer or an explanation.

Many Jews had come to Martha and Mary to offer consolation at their brother's death.

When Martha heard that Jesus was coming, she went to meet him while Mary remained sitting in the house. And she said to Jesus, "If you had been here, my brother would not have died. But I know that whatever you ask from God, God will give you." Jesus said, "Your brother will rise again."

Martha replied, "I know that he will rise in the resurrection, at the last day." But Jesus said to her, "I am the resurrection; whoever believes in me, though he die, shall live. Whoever is alive by believing in me will never die. Do you believe this?"

Martha then answered, "Yes, Lord, I have come to believe that you are the Christ, the Son of God, he who is coming into the world."

J U L Y

Friday

30

ORDINARY TIME
17th Week
St. Peter Chrysologus

Jer 26:1-9   Mt 13:54-58

In the church of the Monastery of Jeronimos in Lisbon, built in 1498 and dedicated to "Our Lady of the Kings," there is a statue of King Manuel, surrounded by symbolic figures of all the virtues. One of those virtues, to our surprise, is wealth! It must have taken a lot of misreading of the New Testament to put that statue there! Jesus had nowhere to lay his head. You cannot serve God and wealth, he said. Because we worship wealth we are impressed by the renunciation of wealth. That is still a kind of worship of wealth. Jesus was neither wealthy, nor had he renounced great wealth. He's a nobody; we know all about him; why should anyone bother with a carpenter? Wealth is a key to the mind.

Jesus went to his hometown and taught the people in their synagogue. They were amazed and said, "Where did he get this wisdom and these special powers? Isn't he the carpenter's son? Isn't Mary his mother and aren't James, Joseph, Simon and Judas his brothers? Aren't all his sisters living here? How did he get all this?" And so they took offense at him.

Jesus said to them, "The only place where prophets are not welcome is their hometown and in their own family." And he did not perform many miracles there because of their lack of faith.

Jer 26:11-16,24   Mt 14:1-12

On one occasion the news about Jesus reached King Herod. And he said to his servants, "This man is John the Baptist. John has risen from the dead, and that is why miraculous powers are at work in him."

Herod had, in fact, ordered that John be arrested, bound in chains and put in prison because of Herodias, the wife of his brother Philip. For John had said to him, "It is not right for you to have her as wife." Herod wanted to kill him but he did not dare, because he feared the people who regarded John as a prophet.

On Herod's birthday the daughter of Herodias danced in the midst of the guests; she so delighted Herod that he promised under oath to give her anything she asked. The girl, following the advice of her mother, said, "Give me the head of John the Baptist here on a dish."

The king was very displeased, but because he had made this promise under oath in the presence of the guests, he ordered it to be given her. So he had John beheaded in prison and his head brought on a dish and given to the girl. The girl then took it to her mother.

Then John's disciples came to take his body and bury it. And they went to bring the news to Jesus.

When Herod the Great died, he divided his kingdom among his four sons; known as "tetrarch," meaning "ruler of a quarter." When one died, the Emperor gave the dead man's quarter to Agrippa, with the title "king." This maddened Herodias with jealousy, because her husband was known only as a tetrarch. She persuaded her husband to beg the Emperor for the title of king. Agrippa sent word ahead that Herod was organizing a rebellion. The Emperor took Herod's tetrarchy from him, and sent him and Herodias into exile. It was a lot of trouble for the title "king," which is only a word. They were probably still haunted by the ghost of John the Baptist. Words and spirits: all just wind, just nothing.

Sunday

Jesus takes up this theme in the gospel reading, expressing it typically as a story. But there is a difference. Qoheleth says the rich man is foolish because he "must leave all to someone who has not worked for it." In other words, he is foolish to have worked, because he cannot enjoy all the fruits of it himself. Jesus said the rich man is foolish because he does not "amass for God." That expression meant almsgiving. Though these two readings are alike in subject and even in the direction of what they say, they are worlds apart. Two lines of T.S. Eliot's come to mind, "The last temptation is the greatest treason: / To do the right thing for the wrong reason."

18TH SUNDAY IN ORDINARY TIME 1

Ecl 1:2;2:21-23

All is meaningless—says the Teacher—meaningless, meaningless! For here was a man who toiled in all wisdom, knowledge and skill and he must leave all to someone who has not worked for it. This is meaningless and a great misfortune. For what profit is there for a man in all his work and heart-searching under the sun? All his days bring sorrow, his work grief; he hasn't, moreover, peaceful rest at night: that too is meaningless.

Col 3:1-5,9-11

So then, if you are risen with Christ, seek the things that are above, where Christ is seated at the right hand of God. Set your mind on the things that are above, not on earthly things. For you have died and your life is now hidden with Christ in God. When Christ, who is your life, reveals himself, you also will be revealed with him in Glory. Therefore, put to death what is earthly in your life, that is immorality, impurity, inordinate passions, wicked desires and greed which is a way of worshiping idols. Do not lie to one another. You have been stripped of the old self and its way of thinking to put on the new, which is being renewed and is to reach perfect knowledge and the likeness of its creator. There is no room for destination between Greek or Jew, circumcised or uncircumcised, barbarian, foreigner, slave or free, but Christ is all and in all.

Lk 12:13-21

Someone in the crowd spoke to Jesus, "Master, tell my brother to share with me the family inheritance." He replied, "My friend, who has appointed me as your judge or your attorney?" Then Jesus said to the people, "Be on your guard and avoid every kind of greed, for even though you have many possessions, it is not that which gives you life."

And Jesus continued with this story, "There was a rich man and his land had produced a good harvest. He thought: 'What shall I do? For I am short of room to store my harvest.' So this is what he planned: 'I will pull down my barns and build bigger ones to store all this grain, which is my wealth. Then I may say to myself: My friend, you have a lot of good things put by for many years. Rest, eat, drink and enjoy yourself.' But God said to him: 'You fool! This very night your life will be taken from you; tell me who shall get all you have put aside?' This is the lot of the one who stores up riches instead of amassing for God."

Monday

2

This account of the feeding of the multitudes has strong echoes of the Exodus event which took place more than twelve centuries before. There are many points of convergence. Even the wording is the same in places, "they all ate and were filled." In turn, both stories carry echoes of the "messianic banquet." This was the imagined absolute future in which God would be all in all. God would prepare on Mount Zion a banquet for all the redeemed (see Isaiah 25:6). Jesus uses this image to describe the beatitude of heaven (Mt 8:11). Our Eucharist retains this theme. Thus, everything in the Faith echoes everything else. It is a living body, not a loose collection of thoughts.

On hearing the death of John the Baptist, Jesus set out secretly by boat for a secluded place. But the people heard of it, and they followed him on foot from their towns. When Jesus went ashore, he saw the crowd gathered there and he had compassion on them. And he healed their sick.

Late in the afternoon, his disciples came to him and said, "We are in a lonely place and it is now late. You should send these people away, so they can go to the villages and buy something for themselves to eat."

But Jesus replied, "They do not need to go away; you give them something to eat." They answered, "We have nothing here but five loaves and two fishes." Jesus said to them, "Bring them here to me."

Then he made everyone sit down on the grass. He took the five loaves and the two fishes, raised his eyes to heaven, pronounced the blessing, broke the loaves and handed them to the disciples to distribute to the people. And they all ate, and everyone had enough; then the disciples gathered up the leftovers, filling twelve baskets. About five thousand men had eaten there besides women and children.

3 Tuesday

A U G U S T

Jer 30:1-2,12-15,18-22   Mt 14:22-36

After the crowds has eaten their fill, Jesus obliged his disciples to get into the boat and go ahead of him to the other side, while he sent the crowd away.

And having sent the people away, he went up the mountain by himself to pray. At nightfall, he was there alone. Meanwhile, the boat was very far from land, dangerously rocked by the waves for the wind was against it.

At daybreak, Jesus came to them walking on the lake. When they saw him walking on the sea, they were terrified, thinking that it was a ghost. And they cried out in fear. But at once Jesus said to them, "Courage! Don't be afraid. It's me!" Peter answered, "Lord, if it is you, command me to come to you walking on the water."

Jesus said to him, "Come." And Peter got out of the boat, walking on the water to go to Jesus. But, in face of the strong wind, he was afraid and began to sink. So he cried out, "Lord, save me!" Jesus immediately stretched out his hand and took hold of him, saying, "Man of little faith, why did you doubt?"

As they got into the boat, the wind dropped. Then those in the boat bowed down before Jesus saying, "Truly, you are the Son of God!"

They came ashore at Gennesareth. The local people recognized Jesus and spread the news throughout the region. So they brought all the sick to him, begging him to let them touch just the fringe of his cloak. All who touched it became perfectly well.

Here too, of course, everything echoes everything else. As God calms the sea (Psalm 76:16), Jesus calms the storm and walks on the water. As God rescued his people by making "a path through the mighty waters" (Isaiah 43:16), Jesus comes over the water to rescue a hesitant Peter and his terrified companions. Today we have to chase down these references and echoes, but to the earliest Christians these were instantly self-evident. They had a whole symbolic world through which to interpret the actions of Jesus, and so they recognized him as "the one who was to come." Against this, we have the assurance that the word of God cannot return empty.

AUGUST

Wednesday 4

ORDINARY TIME
18th Week

St. John Vianney

Jer 31:1-7   Mt 15:21-28

Here is a little of what Johann Tauler (1300-1361) said about this passage, "Oh, children, if only we could all have this real insight into the depths of truth; not through learned explanations, not through words; not through our senses at all, but in the very depths of our soul! We would know then that neither God nor all His creatures can so oppress and abase us that we cannot sink still more deeply into the truth…. My children, if we could understand that everything depends on this, we should have grasped a vital truth. This is the only way that leads us straight to God without any intermediary…."

Jesus withdrew to the region of Tyre and Sidon. Now a Canaanite woman came from those borders and began to cry out, "Lord, Son of David, have pity on me! My daughter is tormented by a demon." But Jesus did not answer her, not even a word. So his disciples approached him and said, "Send her away: see how she is shouting after us." Then Jesus said to her, "I was sent only to the lost sheep of the nation of Israel."

But the woman was already kneeling before Jesus and said, "Sir, help me!" Jesus answered, "It is not right to take the bread from the children and throw it to the little dogs." The woman replied, "It is true, sir, but even the little dogs eat the crumbs which fall from their master's table." Then Jesus said, "Woman, how great is your faith! Let it be as you wish." And her daughter was healed at that moment.

Jer 31:31-34   Mt 16:13-23

Jesus came to Caesarea Philippi. He asked his disciples, "Who do people say the Son of Man is?" They said, "For some of them you are John the Baptist, for others Elijah or Jeremiah or one of the prophets."

Jesus asked them, "But you, who do you say I am?" Peter answered, "You are the Messiah, the Son of the living God." Jesus replied, "It is well for you, Simon Barjona, for it is not flesh or blood that has revealed this to you but my Father in heaven.

"And now I say to you: You are Peter (or Rock) and on this rock I will build my Church; and never will the powers of death overcome it.

"I will give you the keys of the kingdom of heaven: whatever you bind on earth shall be bound in heaven, and what you unbind on earth shall be unbound in heaven."

Then he ordered his disciples not to tell anyone that he was the Christ.

From that day Jesus began to make it clear to his disciples that he must go to Jerusalem; he would suffer many things from the Jewish authorities, the chief priests and the teachers of the Law. He would be killed and be raised on the third day.

Then Peter took him aside and began to reproach him, "Never, Lord! No, this must never happen to you." But Jesus turned to him and said, "Get behind me, Satan! You would have me stumble. You are their king not as God does, but as people do."

This was Peter's moment. His profession of faith echoes all the more loudly against the pagan background, "You are the Christ, the Son of the living God." Peter spoke with the voice of God. But very soon he was to speak with the voice of Satan! That was Peter's fickle nature. At one moment he would draw his sword in defense of Jesus (Jn 18:10), but very soon he would deny that he ever even knew him (18:25). That is why Christian art represents him now as a proud figure holding the keys of the kingdom, and now with the cock crowing beside him. He is like everyone: strong and weak, faithful and faithless, good and bad....

Dn 7:9-10,13-14   2P 1:16-19   Lk 9:28-36

When Jesus said so often to people, "Stay awake!" he didn't mean half-awake and half-asleep. I take it that those three were as good as asleep. So don't feel so bad if you feel drowsy or fall asleep at prayer! Peter, James and John did! It says, "They awoke and saw his glory." Had they been in a zen monastery the monitor would have kept them awake with the kyosaku, the 'awakening stick'! Someone asked a zen master once, "Could I become enlightened during sleep?" And he replied, "If it doesn't happen to you during sleep it will never happen, because what you call your waking life is only another form of sleep!"

About eight days after Jesus had said all this, he took Peter, John and James and went up the mountain to pray. And while he was praying, the aspect of his face was changed and his clothing became dazzling white. Two men were talking with Jesus: Moses and Elijah. They had just appeared in heavenly glory and were telling him about his departure that had to take place in Jerusalem.

Peter and his companions had fallen asleep, but they awoke suddenly and saw Jesus' Glory and the two men standing with him. As Moses and Elijah were about to leave, Peter said to him, "Master, how good it is for us to be here for we can make three tents, one for you, one for Moses and one for Elijah." For Peter didn't know what to say. And no sooner had he spoken than a cloud appeared and covered them; and the disciples were afraid as they entered the cloud. Then these words came from the cloud, "This is my Son, my Chosen one, listen to him." And after the voice had spoken, Jesus was there alone.

The disciples kept this to themselves at the time, telling no one of anything they had seen.

Hb 1:12–2:4   Mt 17:14-20

A man approached Jesus, knelt before him and said, "Sir, have pity on my son who is an epileptic and is in a wretched state. He has often fallen into the fire and at other times into the water. I brought him to your disciples but they could not heal him."

Jesus replied, "You, faithless and evil people! How long must I be with you? How long must I put up with you? Bring him here to me." And Jesus commanded the evil spirit to leave the boy, and the boy was immediately healed.

The disciples then gathered around Jesus and asked him privately, "Why couldn't we drive out the spirit?" Jesus said to them, "Because you have little faith. I say to you: if only you had faith the size of a mustard seed, you could tell that mountain to move from here to there, and the mountain would obey. Nothing would be impossible to you."

The disciples were in the valley. Mountains are for the big vision. Now in the valley they wonder why they can't do anything. Their faith, said Jesus, was less than the size of a mustard seed. This was the small vision! But if their faith were the size of a mustard seed, he told them, they could move mountains. Even if they were not up to the big vision, they could still do great work. How he stretched them! How humble they must have felt, and how uneasy with themselves! There's not one of us who hasn't slept through mysteries; we are those sleepy disciples. When we want to feel 'comfortable with our faith' he wakes us up. How? Through disappointments, through unflattering insights into ourselves, through suffering....

Sunday

This is a "stay awake!" reading. Jesus keeps saying: "The Son of Man will come at an hour you do not expect." He comes every moment, does he not? But if he had put it that way we would surely go back to sleep. Anything that happens all the time loses its mystery for us. Our attention is intermittent…. I remember a carpenter's workshop in Germany: on the wall was a piece of wood with the word "Achtung!" carved on it. It has the double meaning of "attention" and "respect." What a fine word! How good it is to keep them together in one word! Attention because of respect; respect because of attention. Attention as a form of respect; respect as a form of attention.

19TH SUNDAY IN ORDINARY TIME 8

Wis 18:6-9

That night had been foretold to our fathers, and knowing in what promise they trusted, they could rejoice in all surety. Your people waited for both the salvation of the just and the downfall of their enemies, for the very punishment of our enemies brought glory to the people you have called—that is, to us. The holy race secretly offered the Passover sacrifice and really agreed on this worthy pact: that they would share alike both blessings and dangers. And forthwith they began to sing the hymns of their fathers.

Heb 11:1-2,8-19

Faith is the assurance of what we hope for, being certain of what we cannot see. Because of their faith our ancestors were approved. It was by faith that Abraham, called by God, set out for a country that would be given to him as an inheritance; for he parted without knowing where he was going. By faith he lived as a stranger in that promised land. There he lived in tents, as did Isaac and Jacob, beneficiaries of the same promise. Indeed, he looked forward to that city of solid foundation of which God is the architect and builder. (...) Death found all these people strong in their faith. They had not received what was promised, but they had looked ahead and had rejoiced in it from afar, saying that they were foreigners and travelers on earth. Those who speak in this way prove that they are looking for their own country. For if they had longed for the land they had left, it would have been easy for them to return, but no, they aspired to a better city, that is, a supernatural one; so God, who prepared the city for them is not ashamed of being called their God. (...)

Lk 12:35-40

Jesus said to his disciples, "Be ready, dressed for service, and keep your lamps lit, like people waiting for their master to return from the wedding. As soon as he comes and knocks, they will open to him. Happy are those servants whom the master finds wide-awake when he comes. Truly, I tell you, he will put on an apron and have them sit at table and he will wait on them. Happy are those servants if he finds them awake when he comes at midnight or daybreak! Pay attention to this: If the master of the house had known at what time the thief would come, he would not have let his house be broken into. You also must be ready, for the Son of Man will come at an hour you do not expect."

Monday

9

AUGUST

ORDINARY TIME
19th Week

St. Teresiae Benedicta of the Cross

Ezk 1:2-5,24-28   Mt 17:22-27

Everyone paid this Temple tax; it became almost a badge of Jewish identity. But in secular kingdoms taxes were not paid by a ruler's family. So if the Temple was indeed "his Father's house," then Jesus should be exempt from the Temple tax. The implications went far beyond the single case of Jesus, of course. Matthew was a Jewish Christian, writing for Jewish Christians, and no doubt this Temple tax was a burning question for them. In his gospel he has Jesus say: you are exempt, really, but so as not to give offence, pay it anyway. In other words, you don't have to fight every battle, you don't have to take on everyone; let side-issues be side-issues.

While Jesus was in Galilee with the Twelve, he said to them, "The Son of Man will be delivered into human hands, and they will kill him. But he will rise on the third day." The Twelve were deeply grieved.

On returning to Capernaum, the Temple tax collectors came to Peter and asked him, "Does your master pay the temple tax?" He answered, "Certainly."

Peter then entered the house, but immediately Jesus asked him, "What do you think, Simon? Who pay taxes or tributes to the kings of the earth: their sons or the other people?" Peter replied, "The others." And Jesus told him, "The sons, then, are tax-free. But so as not to offend these people, go to the sea, throw in a hook and open the mouth of the first fish you catch. You will find a coin in it, take it and let it pay for you and for me."

10

Tuesday

AUGUST

2Cor 9:6-10   Jn 12:24-26

St. Lawrence was martyred in Rome in 258 during the persecution under the Romans. When he was challenged to hand over the Church's treasure to the authorities, he asked for a few days' grace; then "he went all over the city, seeking out in every street the poor who were supported by the Church, and with whom no other was so well acquainted. On the third day, he gathered a great number of them before the church and placed them in rows: the decrepit, the blind, the lame, the maimed, the lepers, orphans and widows; then he went to the prefect, invited him to come and see the treasure of the Church." The Basilica of San Lorenzo, Rome, was built over his burial place.

Jesus said, "Truly, I say to you, unless the grain of wheat falls to the earth and dies, it remains alone; but if it dies, it produces much fruit.

"Those who love their life destroy it, and those who despise their life in this world keep it for everlasting life.

"Whoever wants to serve me, let him follow me and wherever I am, there shall my servant be also. If anyone serves me, the Father will honor him."

AUGUST

Wednesday
11

ORDINARY TIME
19th Week

St. Clare

Ezk 9:1-7;10:18-22   Mt 18:15-20

Jesus told his followers to expect hatred, "If the world hates you, be aware that it hated me before you" (Jn 15:18). This does not come from a feeling of superiority; it comes from a realistic knowledge of the world. The Christian does not depend on anyone's hatred, but tries to disarm hatred with love. "Owe no one anything, except to love one another" wrote St. Paul (Rom 13:8). Today's reading tells how we should deal with the criminality of another Christian, in the light of the Father's concern that "not one should perish." It is not about punishment, nor about feeling superior to them, nor about "restoring the balance of justice," but about sincerely trying to win back an erring brother or sister.

Jesus said to his disciples, "If your brother or sister has sinned against you, go and point out the fault when the two of you are in private, and if he listens to you, you have won your brother. If you are not listened to, take with you one or two others so that the case may be decided by the evidence of two or three witnesses. If he still refuses to listen to them, tell it to the assembled Church. But if he does not listen to the Church, then regard such a one as a pagan or a publican.

"I say to you: whatever you bind on earth, heaven will keep bound; and whatever you unbind on earth, heaven will keep unbound.

"In like manner, I say to you: if on earth two of you are united in asking for anything, it will be granted to you by my heavenly Father. For where two or three are gathered in my Name, I am there among them."

12 Thursday

AUGUST

Ezk 12:1-12   Mt 18:21—19:1

Peter asked Jesus, "Lord, how many times must I forgive the offenses of my brother or sister? Seven times?" Jesus answered, "No, not seven times, but seventy-seven times. This story throws light on the kingdom of heaven. A king decided to settle the accounts of his servants. Among the first was one who owed him ten thousand gold ingots. As the man could not repay the debt, the king commanded that he be sold as a slave with his wife, children and all his goods in payment. The official threw himself at the feet of the king and said, 'Give me time, and I will pay you back everything.' The king took pity on him and not only set him free but even canceled his debt. This official then left the king's presence and he met one of his companions who owed him a hundred pieces of silver. He grabbed him by the neck and almost strangled him, shouting, 'Pay me what you owe!' His companion threw himself at his feet and asked him, 'Give me time, and I will pay everything.' The other did not agree, but sent him to prison until he had paid all his debt. His companions saw what happened. They were indignant and so they went and reported everything to their lord. Then the lord summoned his official and said, 'Wicked servant, I forgave you all that you owed when you begged me to do so. Weren't you bound to have pity on your companion as I had pity on you?' The lord was now angry, so he handed his servant over to be punished, until he had paid his whole debt." Jesus added, "So will my heavenly Father do with you unless each of you sincerely forgive your brother or sister." (...)

We are bound to forgive others, and to believe that God forgives us; but it is not so often said that we must forgive ourselves. It is easier to forgive others than to forgive oneself. Karl Jung wrote, "What I do to the least of my brothers and sisters I do to Christ. But what if I should discover that the least among them all, the poorest of all the beggars, the most impudent of all offenders, the very enemy himself—that these are within me, and that I myself stand in need of the alms of my own kindness—that I am myself the enemy who must be loved—what then?"

AUGUST

Friday

13

ORDINARY TIME
19th Week

Sts. Pontian & Hippolytus

Ezk 16:59-63   Mt 19:3-12

In Genesis 1:27 there is a lyrical description of the creation of man and woman, "God made human beings in his own image; male and female he created them." All this, of course, is before the Fall! After the Fall, all is changed. Human beings damaged their original innocence, and they suffer differently for it. The woman suffers by becoming subject to man and dependent on him, but this was not God's intention. This Genesis story reflects the actual social position of woman in the ancient Near East, which was one of subjection first to her father and then to her husband. It is the story of the corruption of God's image. What Jesus had to say about divorce was an affirmation of the original state over the corrupted one.

Some Pharisees approached Jesus. They wanted to test him and asked, "Is a man allowed to divorce his wife for any reason he wants?"

Jesus replied, "Have you not read that in the beginning the Creator made them male and female, and he said: Man has now to leave father and mother, and be joined to his wife, and the two shall become one body? So they are no longer two but one body; let no one separate what God has joined."

They asked him, "Then, why did Moses command us to write a bill of dismissal in order to divorce?" Jesus replied, "Moses knew your stubborn heart, so he allowed you to divorce your wives, but it was not so in the beginning. Therefore I say to you: whoever divorces his wife, unless it be for concubinage, and marries another, commits adultery."

The disciples said, "If that is the condition of a married man, it is better not to marry." Jesus said to them, "Not everybody can accept what you have just said, but only those who have received this gift. Some are born incapable of marriage. Some have been made that way by others. But there are some who have given up the possibility of marriage for the sake of the kingdom of heaven. Let the one who can accept it, accept it."

**ORDINARY TIME
19th Week**

St. Maximilian Mary Kolbe

14 Saturday

AUGUST

Ezk 18:1-10,13,30-32   Mt 19:13-15

A good day to recall the words of Kalhil Gibran: "Your children are not your children. / They are the sons and daughters of Life's longing for itself. / They came through you but not from you; / And though they are with you yet they belong not to you. / You may give them your love but not your thoughts, / For they have their own thoughts / You may house their bodies but not their souls, / For their souls dwell in the house of tomorrow, which you cannot visit, not even in your dreams… The Prophet (1923) "On Children"

Little children were brought to Jesus that he might lay his hands on them with a prayer. But the disciples scolded those who brought them. Jesus then said, "Let them be! Do not stop the children from coming to me, for the king-dom of heaven belongs to people such as these." So Jesus laid his hands on them and went his way.

Sunday

Scholars are able to see the antecedents of the Magnificat in the Old Testament: in Isaiah 29:14, etc., and in the Canticle of Hannah, the mother of Samuel (1Sam 2:1-10, "My heart exults in Yahweh, I feel strong in my God.... The bow of the mighty is broken, but the weak are girded with strength…). Mary is repeating, you might say, what others had said long before she was born. But when Mary (or indeed anyone) says "My soul glorifies the Lord," it's a leap of joy and praise in the present moment; it may have been said many times before, but it's new now. A prayer could be as old as the hills, but it is perfectly new if it comes from the heart.

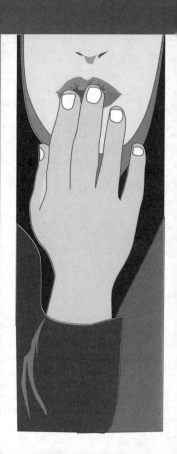

ASSUMPTION OF MARY 15

Rev 11:19;12:1-6,10
1Cor 15:20-27

Christ has been raised from the dead and he comes before all those who have fallen asleep. A human being brought death; a human being also brings resurrection of the dead. All die for being Adam's, and in Christ all will receive life. However, each one in his own time: first Christ, then Christ's people, when comes. Then the end will come, when Christ delivers the kingdom to God the Father, after having destroyed every rule, authority and power. For he must reign and put all enemies under his feet. The last enemy to be destroyed will be death. As Scripture says: God has subjected everything under his feet. When we say that everything is put under his feet, we exclude, of course, the Father who subjects everything to him.

Lk 1:39-56

Mary then set out for a town in the Hills of Judah. She entered the house of Zechariah and greeted Elizabeth. When Elizabeth heard Mary's greeting, the baby leapt in her womb. Elizabeth was filled with holy spirit, and giving a loud cry, said, "You are most blessed among women and blessed is the fruit of your womb! How is it that the mother of my Lord comes to me? The moment your greeting sounded in my ears, the baby within me suddenly leapt for joy. Blessed are you who believed that the Lord's word would come true!"

And Mary said: "My soul proclaims the greatness of the Lord, my spirit exults in God my savior! He has looked upon his servant in her lowliness, and people forever will call me blessed. The Mighty One has done great things for me, Holy is his Name! From age to age his mercy extends to those who live in his presence. He has acted with power and done wonders, and scattered the proud with their plans. He has put down the mighty from their thrones and lifted up those who are downtrodden. He has filled the hungry with good things but has sent the rich away empty. He held out his hand to Israel, his servant, for he remembered his mercy, even as he promised our fathers, Abraham and his descendants forever."

Mary remained with Elizabeth about three months and then returned home.

AUGUST

Monday

16

ORDINARY TIME
20th Week
St. Stephen of Hungary

Ezk 24:15-24   Mt 19:16-22

Today's reading touches the DIY person in all of us, the "self-made man." We all want to succeed at what we do—who would set out to fail?—but we know when it goes into exaggeration. Nothing fails like success, someone said. I suppose that means, in part, that while we nearly always learn from failure we seldom learn from success. The young man in today's reading was a success. He had a certain openness to something beyond that. But it didn't prove to be a real openness; he refused to take the step. We have to be at the end of our tether before we really change. We have to fail. This is the pattern of Christ's own life and death.

A young man approached him and asked, "Master, what good work must I do to receive eternal life?" Jesus answered, "Why do you ask me about what is good?" Only one is Good. If you want to enter eternal life, keep the commandments." The young man said, "Which commandments?" Jesus replied, "Do not kill, do not commit adultery, do not steal, do not bear false witness, honor your father and mother, and love your neighbor as yourself."

The young man said to him, "I have kept all these commandments, what is still lacking?" Jesus answered, "If you wish to be perfect, go and sell all that you possess and give the money to the poor and you will become the owner of a treasure in heaven. Then come back and follow me."

On hearing this answer, the young man went away sad for he was a man of great wealth.

Ezk 28:1-10   Mt 19:23-30

Jesus said to his disciples, "Truly I say to you: it will be hard for one who is rich to enter the kingdom of heaven. Yes, believe me: it is easier for a camel to go through the eye of a needle than for the one who is rich to enter the kingdom of heaven."

On hearing this the disciples were astonished and said, "Who, then, can be saved?" Jesus looked steadily at them and answered, "For humans it is impossible, but for God all things are possible."

Then Peter spoke up and said, "You see we have given up everything to follow you: what will be our lot?"

Jesus answered, "You who have followed me, listen to my words: on the Day of Renewal, when the Son of Man sits on his throne in glory, you, too, will sit on twelve thrones to rule the twelve tribes of Israel. As for those who have left houses, brothers, sisters, father, mother, children or property for my Name's sake, they will receive a hundredfold and given eternal life. Many who are now first will be last, and many who are now last will be first."

"Easier for a camel..." This colorful language is typical of Aramaic. There have been attempts to "explain" it: someone suggested that "camel" may have been some kind of thick cord; and someone else suggested that the "eye of the needle" may have been a narrow pass in the mountains. Jesus spoke more than a poet, a prophet. Peter and the others had not made sensible calculations; they had taken a risk. It may not have been much that they gave up, but it was everything they had. And they gave themselves. The two things go together: giving things and giving oneself. It is not wealth in itself that keeps the rich from entering the kingdom, but the habit of not giving it away.

A U G U S T

Wednesday **18**

ORDINARY TIME
20th Week

St. Jane Frances de Chantal

Ezk 34:1-11   Mt 20:1-16

"A landowner went out early…" Johann Tauler (14th century) focused on the word "early." God takes the first step, God always works "early," he said. It's a great word: "early." It expresses readiness, eagerness, determination. The way you get up in the morning shows how your day will be. If you roll out of bed at the last minute you are telling yourself, body and soul, that life is just dragging you along. When we do get the idea of "early" we tend to overdo it! Everyone wants to be the first note! We race one another for the first place. But "early" doesn't have to mean "first." If I'm in the middle of a piece, or at the end, surely that's the right time, and I can give myself as fully as if I were the first note!

Jesus said to his disciples, "This story throws light on the kingdom of heaven. A landowner went out early in the morning to hire workers for his vineyard. He agreed to pay the workers a salary of a silver coin for the day, and sent them to his vineyard. He went out again at about nine in the morning, and seeing others idle in the square, he said to them: 'You, too, go to my vineyard and I will pay you what is just.' So they went. The owner went out at midday and again at three in the afternoon, and he did the same. Finally he went out at the last working hour—it was the eleventh—and he saw others standing there. So he said to them: 'Why do you stay idle the whole day?' They answered: 'Because no one has hired us.' The master said: 'Go and work in my vineyard.'

"When evening came, the owner of the vineyard said to his manager: 'Call the workers and pay them their wage, beginning with the last and ending with the first.' Those who had come to work at the eleventh hour turned up and were given a denarius each (a silver coin). When it was the turn of the first, they thought they would receive more. But they, too, received a denarius each. So, on receiving it, they began to grumble against the landowner. They said: 'These last hardly worked an hour, yet you have treated them the same as us who have endured the day's burden and heat.' The owner said to one of them: 'Friend, I have not been unjust to you. Did we not agree on a denarius a day? So take what is yours and go. I want to give to the last the same as I give to you. Don't I have the right to do as I please with my money? Why are you envious when I am kind?' So will it be: the last will be first, the first will be last."

ORDINARY TIME
20th Week

St. John Eudes

19 Thursday

AUGUST

Ezk 36:23-28   Mt 22:1-14

Jesus began to address the chief priests and elders of the people, once more using parables:

"This story throws light on the kingdom of heaven. A king celebrated the wedding of his son. He sent his servants to call the invited guests to the wedding feast, but the guests refused to come.

"Again he sent other servants ordering them to say to the invited guests: 'I have prepared a banquet, slaughtered my fattened calves and other animals, and now everything is ready; come then, to the wedding feast.' But they paid no attention and went away, some to their fields, and others to their work. While the rest seized the servants of the king, insulted them and killed them.

"The king became angry. He sent his troops to destroy those murderers and burn their city. Then he said to his servants: 'The wedding banquet is prepared, but the invited guests were not worthy. Go, then, to the crossroads and invite everyone you find to the wedding feast.'

"The servants went out at once into the streets and gathered everyone they found, good and bad alike, so that the hall was filled with guests.

"The king came in to see those who were at table, and he noticed a man not wearing the festal garment. So he said to him: 'Friend, how did you get in without the wedding garment?' But the man remained silent. So the king said to his servants: 'Bind his hands and feet and throw him into the dark where there is weeping and gnashing of teeth.' Know that many are called, but few are chosen."

Tauler wants to be with us again today! "The Lord Jesus Christ is the bridegroom, and we are the bride, your soul and mine. We are called and invited, everything is all prepared for the union between God and His bride, the soul who loves Him. This is something indescribable. This love is so close, so interior, so secret, so tender and so ardent as to be beyond all comprehension. All the great theologians of Paris, with all their wisdom, could never express what it is. However much they wanted to speak about it they could only keep silence. The more we want to say what it is, the less we can say and the less we understand it...."

AUGUST

Friday

20

**ORDINARY TIME
20th Week**

St. Bernard

Ezk 37:1-14   Mt 22:34-40

I mentioned my rediscovery of the penny catechism after many years: the one that tried to equip us for life with knowledge of God, but forgot to mention that God was love. Older people grew up with that, and we pray that it didn't sink in too deeply! But it did go deep with many sensitive people. I don't know the motives of the publishers who recalled this nightmare stuff to us; perhaps they believe that people are longing for old certitudes in a world of rapid change. That is undoubtedly true, and it's a good thing to get down to basics at such a time. But the basics are the gospels, and not a dated catechism. The word that renews and strengthens us and sets us free is the word of God.

When the Pharisees heard how Jesus had silenced the Sadducees, they came together. One of them, a teacher of the Law, tried to test him with this question, "Teacher, which is the most important commandment in the Law?"

Jesus answered, "You shall love the Lord, your God, with all your heart, with all your soul and with all your mind. This is the first and the most important of the commandments. But after this there is another one very similar to it: You shall love your neighbor as yourself. The whole Law and the Prophets are founded on these two commandments."

Ezk 43:1-7   Mt 23:1-12

Every word of the Gospel is addressed to every Christian without distinction: to the one who proclaims it, as much as to the ones who hear it proclaimed. It is "alive and active, sharper than any two-edged sword" (Hebrews 4:12). It can never be used, though it has often been used, by one person against another. It is not a dead instrument to be brandished at will; it is alive with a life of its own. The preacher cannot say, "You sinners…" but "We sinners…."—because one edge of that sword is always turned towards the speaker. That word of God does two apparently opposite things: it pulls down and it builds up.

Jesus said to the crowds and to his disciples, "The teachers of the Law and the Pharisees sat on the seat of Moses. So you shall do and observe all they say, but do not do as they do, for they do not do what they say. They tie up heavy burdens and load them on the shoulders of the people, but they do not even raise a finger to move them. They do everything in order to be seen by people; so they wear very wide bands of the Law around their foreheads, and robes with large tassels. They enjoy the first place at feasts and reserved seats in the synagogues, and being greeted in the marketplace and being called 'Master' by the people.

"But you, do not let yourselves be called Master because you have only one Master, and all of you are brothers and sisters. Neither should you call anyone on earth Father, because you have only one Father, he who is in heaven. Nor should you be called leader, because Christ is the only leader for you. Let the greatest among you be the servant of all. For whoever makes himself great shall be humbled, and whoever humbles himself shall be made great."

Sunday

AUGUST

In today's reading, Jesus did not answer the question, "Is it true that few people will be saved?" It may have been this text that set the early custom of not trying to answer it. Among the mediaeval, Julian of Norwich was exceptional in her insistence on leaving such questions unanswered. There are two aspects to revealed truth, she said. The first is what we know of "our Savior and our salvation." This is "open and clear, lovely and light, and plentiful." The other is "our Lord's secret counsel (privy councell)," and we should not "pry into those secrets (not to wel wetyn his conselye)." God gives us everything needed for our salvation, it seems, and statistics are no part of that.

21ST SUNDAY IN ORDINARY TIME 22

Is 66:18-21

The Lord says this, "Now I am going to gather the nations of every tongue, and they will witness my glory, for I will perform a wonderful thing among them. Then I will send some of their survivors to the nations (...) to the distant islands where no one has ever heard of me or seen my glory. They will proclaim my glory among the nations. They will bring your brothers from all the nations as an offering to Yahweh on horses, in chariots, in litters, on mules, on camels to my holy mountain in Jerusalem, says Yahweh, just as the Israelites bring oblations in clean vessels to the house of Yahweh. Then I will choose priests and Levites even from them, says Yahweh.

Heb 12:5-7, 11-13

Do not forget the comforting words that Wisdom addresses to you as children: My son, pay attention when the Lord corrects you and do not be discouraged when he punishes you. For the Lord corrects those he loves and chastises everyone he accepts as a son. What you endure is in order to correct you. God treats you like sons and what son is not corrected by his father? All correction is painful at the moment, rather than pleasant; later it brings the fruit of peace, that is, holiness to those who have been trained by it. Lift up, then, your drooping hands, and strengthen your trembling knees; make level the ways for your feet, so that the lame may not be disabled, but healed.

Lk 13:22-30

Jesus went through towns and villages teaching and making his way to Jerusalem. Someone asked him, "Lord, is it true that few people will be saved?" And Jesus answered, "Do your best to enter by the narrow door, for many, I tell you, will try to enter and will not be able. When once the master of the house has got up and locked the door, you will stand outside; then you will knock at the door calling: 'Lord, open to us.' But he will say to you: 'I do not know where you come from.' Then you will say: We ate and drank with you and you taught in our streets! But he will reply: 'I don't know where you come from. Away from me all you workers of evil.' You will weep and grind your teeth when you see Abraham and Jacob and all the prophets in the kingdom of God, and you yourselves left outside. Others will sit at table in the kingdom of God, people coming from east and west, from north and south. Some who are among the last will be the first, and others who were first will be last!"

Monday

23

**ORDINARY TIME
21st Week**

St. Rose of Lima

AUGUST

2Thes 1:1-5,11-12   Mt 23:13-22

This passage has been used by Christians in the past to fuel anti-Jewish polemic. But clearly it is not Judaism itself that Matthew's gospel had in focus, but those Pharisees who opposed and ultimately destroyed Jesus. The problem with the Pharisees was the absence of an interior spirit to give life to their religious practices. They are a warning headline for all time, because any group in any religion is capable of going their way. The Pharisees get harsh treatment especially in Matthew's gospel. The word 'Pharisee' has come to mean hypocrite. Does that remind you of the difference between Protestant and Catholic? If so, then the gospels are even a better mirror to us all.

Jesus said, "Woe to you, teachers of the Law and Pharisees, you hypocrites! You shut the door to the kingdom of heaven in people's faces. You yourselves do not enter, nor do you allow others to do so.

"Woe to you, teachers of the Law and Pharisees, you hypocrites! You travel by sea and land to win a single convert, yet once he is converted, you turn him twice as fit for hell as yourselves.

"Woe to you, blind guides! You say: To swear by the Temple is not binding, but to swear by the treasure of the Temple is. Blind fools! Which is of more worth? The gold in the Temple or the Temple which makes the gold a sacred treasure? You say: To swear by the altar is not binding, but to swear by the offering on the altar is. How blind you are! Which is of more value: the offering on the altar or the altar which makes the offering sacred? Whoever swears by the altar is swearing by the altar and by everything on it. Whoever swears by the Temple is swearing by it and by God who dwells in the Temple. Whoever swears by heaven is swearing by the throne of God and by him who is seated on it."

Rev 21:9-14   Jn 1:45-51

Philip found Nathanael and said to him, "We have found the one that Moses wrote about in the Law, and the prophets as well: he is Jesus, son of Joseph, from Nazareth."

Nathanael replied, "Can anything good come from Nazareth?" Philip said to him, "Come and see." When Jesus saw Nathanael coming, he said of him, "Here comes an Israelite, a true one; there is nothing false in him." Nathanael asked him, "How do you know me?" And Jesus said to him, "Before Philip called you, you were under the fig tree and I saw you."

Nathanael answered, "Master, you are the Son of God! You are the King of Israel!" But Jesus replied, "You believe because I said: 'I saw you under the fig tree.' But you will see greater things than that.

"Truly, I say to you, you will see the heavens opened and the angels of God ascending and descending upon the Son of Man."

Bartholomew is a surname: "Bar" means "son of," just like Mc and O' in some surnames. The first three gospels never mention Nathanael, and the fourth gospel never mentions Bartholomew. It's probable, scholars say, that they were one and the same person under different names. In the first three gospels Bartholomew is always mentioned with Philip, and in the fourth gospel Nathanael is always mentioned with Philip—a further reason to suspect that Bartholomew and Nathanael are one man.

Under the name of Bartholomew nothing is said of him in the first three gospels; he is only a name on the list. But there is an apocryphal Gospel of Bartholomew, which is known for the splendor of its prayers.

2Thes 3:6-10,16-18   Mt 23:27-32

One of the things that Jesus condemned in the Pharisees was their exclusiveness and their tendency to judge people. When we read an ancient writing we assume that it is only about ancient people. But the fact that we are reading it today raises it beyond its past and extends it into the present. I'm very struck by the fact that the Liturgy puts these texts before us at Mass. The Liturgy of the Word is not a history lesson; it is the application of the word of God to ourselves. The Liturgy is saying: we are the Pharisees, the Sadducees,, the Herod and Pilate, and Peter, James and John, and the Marys; we are standing in the shoes of every figure in the New Testament: from Judas to Jesus himself.

Jesus said, "Woe to you, teachers of the Law and Pharisees, you hypocrites! You are like whitewashed tombs beautiful in appearance, but inside there are only dead bones and uncleanness. In the same way you appear as religious to others, but you are full of hypocrisy and wickedness within.

"Woe to you, teachers of the Law and Pharisees, you hypocrites! You build tombs for the prophets and decorate the monuments of the righteous. You say: Had we lived in the time of our ancestors, we would not have joined them in the blood of prophets. So, you yourselves confess to be kins of those who murdered the prophets. And now, finish off what your ancestors began!"

1Cor 1:1-9   Mt 24:42-51

Jesus said to his disciples, "Stay awake, then, for you do not know on what day your Lord will come. Just think about this: if the owner of the house knew that the thief would come by night around a certain hour, he would stay awake to prevent his house to be broken into. So be alert, for the Son of Man will come at the hour you least expect.

"Imagine a capable servant whom his master has put in charge of his household to give them food at the proper time. Fortunate indeed is that servant whom his master will find at work when he comes. Truly, I say to you, his lord will entrust that one with everything he has.

"Not so with the bad servant who thinks: My master is delayed. And he begins ill-treating his fellow servants while eating and drinking with drunkards. But his master will come on the day he does not know and at the hour he least expects. He will dismiss that servant and deal with him as with the hypocrites, where there will be weeping and gnashing of teeth."

All real religious teachers, whatever their differences, have one thing in common: they all say, "Wake up!" Sometimes a psychotherapist will try to help someone make these unconscious games conscious. The whole world, you might say, is trying to wake up. Perhaps it's still early morning in human civilization! When Zuigan said to himself, "Never be deceived by others," I presume he didn't mean only people. He also meant circumstances. Don't be deceived by anything. But ultimately it's not circumstances that deceive us; it's only we who can deceive ourselves.

1Cor 1:17-25   Mt 25:1-13

Today's reading is giving us the same lesson as yesterday's: wakefulness. No one could like those wise bridesmaids in today's parable, I think. They remain awake all right, but they are not the kind of people you would go to if you had a problem. Some "good" people are like that. But this is to misread this parable, which is not an allegory. An allegory has points of application all along the line, but a parable has only one point. The point of this one is the need to stay awake. The meaning of the parable is in the last line, "Stay awake!"

Jesus said to his disciples, "This story throws light on what will happen in the kingdom of heaven. Ten bridesmaids went out with their lamps to meet the bridegroom. Five of them were careless while the others were sensible.

"The careless bridesmaids took their lamps as they were and did not bring extra oil. But those who were sensible, brought with their lamps flasks of oil. As the bridegroom delayed, they all grew drowsy and fell asleep.

"But at midnight, a cry rang out: 'The bridegroom is here, come out and meet him!' All the maidens woke up at once and trimmed their lamps. Then the careless ones said to the sensible ones: 'Give us some oil, for our lamps are going out.' The sensible ones answered: 'There may not be enough for both you and us. You had better go to those who sell and buy for yourselves.'

"They were out buying oil when the bridegroom came, and those who were ready went with him to the wedding feast, and the doors were shut.

"Later the rest of the bridesmaids arrived and called out: 'Lord, Lord, open to us.' But he answered: 'Truly, I do not know you.' So, stay awake, for you do not know the day nor the hour."

**ORDINARY TIME
21st Week**

St. Augustine

28 Saturday

AUGUST

1Cor 1:26-31   Mt 25:14-30

Jesus told this parable to his disciples, "Imagine someone who, before going abroad, summoned his servants to entrust his property to them. He gave five talents of silver to one, then two to another, and one to a third, each one according to his ability; and he went away. He who received five talents went at once to do business with the money and gained another five. The one who received two did the same and gained another two. But the one with one talent dug a hole and hid his master's money. After a long time, the master of those servants returned and asked for a reckoning. The one who received five talents came with another five talents, saying: 'Lord, you entrusted me with five talents, but see I have gained five more with them.' The master answered: 'Very well, good and faithful servant, since you have been faithful in a few things, I will entrust you with much more. Come and share the joy of your master.' Then the one who had two talents came and said: 'Lord, you entrusted me with two talents; I have two more which I gained with them.' The master said: 'Well, good and faithful servant, since you have been faithful in little things, I will entrust you with much more. (...).' Finally, the one who had received one talent came and said: 'Master, I know that you are an exacting man. You reap what you have not sown and gather what you have not invested. I was afraid, so I hid your money in the ground. Here, take what is yours.' But his master replied: 'Wicked and worthless servant, you know that I reap where I have not sown and gather where I have not invested. Then you should have deposited my money in the bank, and you would have given it back to me with interest on my return (...).'"

To say that the spiritual world is all "gift" is to say the truth. But to say no more would be to make it a purely passive thing. In reality we know that nothing deep or "inner" can ever be given to us without our effort. Even God's gifts, poured out without measure, cannot really become mine unless I interiorize them myself. Struggle is part of the spiritual life, even though it remains true that everything is gift. And it's a fact of experience that the more I have the more I will receive. The more I know the more I am capable of knowing; the more I love the more I am capable of loving; the more I pray the more I am able to pray.... And likewise the less.

Sunday

AUGUST

Thomas Merton gave us this story by Chuang Tzu. "The Prince of Chu sent two vice-chancellors with a formal document: 'We hereby appoint you Prime Minister.' He answered, 'I am told there is a sacred tortoise, canonized three thousand years ago, in a precious shrine on an altar in the Temple. What do you think: is it better to give up one's life and leave a sacred shell as an object of cult in a cloud of incense three thousand years, or better to live as a plain turtle dragging its tail in the mud?' 'For the turtle,' said the Vice-Chancellor, 'better to live and drag its tail in the mud!' 'Go home!' said Chuang Tzu. 'Leave me here to drag my tail in the mud!'"

Sir 3:17-18,20,28-29

My son, conduct your affairs with discretion and you will be loved by those who are acceptable to God. The greater you are, the more you should humble yourself and thus you will find favor with God. For great is the power of the Lord and it is the humble who give him glory. For the sufferings of the proud man there is no remedy, the roots of evil are implanted in him. The wise man reflects on proverbs. What the wise man desires is an attentive ear.

Heb 12:18-24

What you have come to is nothing known to the senses nor heat of a blazing fire, darkness and gloom and storms, blasts of trumpets or such a voice that the people pleaded that no further word be spoken. But you came near to Mount Zion, to the city of the living God, to the heavenly Jerusalem with its innumerable angels. You have come to the solemn feast, the assembly of the firstborn of God, whose names are written in heaven. There is God (...).

Lk 14:1, 7-14

One Sabbath Jesus had gone to eat a meal in the house of a leading Pharisee, and he was carefully watched. Jesus then told a parable to the guests, for he had noticed how they tried to take the places of honor. And he said, "When you are invited to a wedding party, do not choose the best seat. It may happen that someone more important than you has been invited, and your host, who invited both of you, will come and say to you: 'Please give this person your place.' What shame is yours when you take the lowest seat!

"Whenever you are invited, go rather to the lowest seat, so that your host may come and say to you: 'Friend, you must come up higher.' And this will be a great honor for you in the presence of all the other guests. For whoever makes himself out to be great will be humbled, and whoever humbles himself will be raised."

Jesus also addressed the man who had invited him and said, "When you give a lunch or a dinner, don't invite your friends, or your brothers and relatives and wealthy neighbors. For surely they will also invite you in return and you will be repaid. When you give a feast, invite instead the poor, the crippled, the lame and the blind. Fortunate are you then, because they can't repay you; you will be repaid at the Resurrection of the upright."

"Today these words come true, even as you listen." Today is the most difficult day. Yesterday and tomorrow are no trouble; perhaps that's why I spend so much time there! Imagine: if they were places. I would seldom be at home! I would zip by now and then to see that my place hadn't been robbed, but I would leave again immediately. Really, I'm robbing myself! What use is my place to me? If all the prophecies of all time are not fulfilled today, when will they be fulfilled? Nothing ever happens unless it happens today. Yesterday and tomorrow are only escapes from home; they are absences. I can be present only in the present.

When Jesus came to Nazareth where he had been brought up, he entered the synagogue on the Sabbath as he usually did. He stood up to read and they handed him the book of the prophet Isaiah. Jesus then unrolled the scroll and found the place where it is written: "The Spirit of the Lord is upon me. He has anointed me to bring good news to the poor, to proclaim liberty to captives and new sight to the blind; to free the oppressed and announce the Lord's year of mercy." Jesus then rolled up the scroll, gave it to the attendant and sat down, while the eyes of all in the synagogue were fixed on him. Then he said to them, "Today these prophetic words come true even as you listen."

All agreed with him and were lost in wonder, while he kept on speaking of the grace of God. Nevertheless they asked, "Who is this but Joseph's son?" So he said, "Doubtless you will quote me saying: Doctor, heal yourself! Do here in your town what they say you did in Capernaum." Jesus added, "No prophet is honored in his own country. Truly, I say to you, there were many widows in Israel in the days of Elijah, when the heavens withheld rain for three years and six months and a great famine came over the whole land. Yet Elijah was not sent to any of them, but to a widow of Zarephath, in the country of Sidon. There were also many lepers in Israel in the time of Elisha, the prophet, and no one was healed except Naaman, the Syrian." On hearing these words, the whole assembly became indignant. They rose up and brought him out of the town, to the edge of the hill on which Nazareth is built, intending to throw him down the cliff. But he passed through their midst and went his way.

1Cor 2:10-16   **Lk 4:31-37**

Jesus went down to Capernaum, a town of Galilee, and began teaching the people at the sabbath meetings. They were astonished at the way he taught them, for his word was spoken with authority.

In the synagogue there was a man possessed by an evil spirit who shouted in a loud voice, "What do you want with us, Jesus of Nazareth? Have you come to destroy us? I recognize you: you are the Holy One of God." Then Jesus said to him sharply, "Be silent and leave this man!" The evil spirit then threw the man down in front of them and came out of him without doing him harm.

Amazement seized all these people and they said to one another, "What does this mean? He commands the evil spirits with authority and power. He orders, and you see how they come out!" And news about Jesus spread throughout the surrounding area.

We have to be careful with our explanations. What are they for? What are we doing with them? Sometimes (I know from experience) we "explain" something in order to avoid facing it. "Children are dumb to say how hot the day is, / How hot the scent is of the summer rose, / How dreadful the black wastes of evening sky, / How dreadful the tall soldiers drumming by. / But we have speech, to chill the angry day, / And speech, to dull the rose's cruel scent. / We spell away the overhanging night, / We spell away the soldiers and the fright...." (Robert Graves)

1Cor 3:1-9   Lk 4:38-44

Dreadful thought: like the people of Nazareth, we have the power to prevent miracles. The chances are that we all have prevented many miracles, just by filling the air with criticism or cynicism. Some people have a presence that is quite negative. In their atmosphere we die a little: we keep our stories and anecdotes to ourselves, we talk "safe." This is how human community is corroded. It is also how faith is corroded. We talk about "denying the faith," as if words were the worst we could do. We can do much worse than that! Words at least are explicit. But by a look, by our very presence, our atmosphere, we can corrode the faith subtly and silently and deeply. And we may not even be aware that we have done it.

Leaving the synagogue, Jesus went to the house of Simon. His mother-in-law was suffering from high fever and they asked him to do something for her. Bending over her, he rebuked the fever, and it left her. Immediately she got up and waited on them.

At sunset, people suffering from many kinds of sickness were brought to Jesus. Laying his hands on each one, he healed them. Demons were driven out, howling as they departed from their victims, "You are the Son of God!" He rebuked them and would not allow them to speak, for they knew he was the Messiah.

Jesus left at daybreak and looked for a solitary place. People went out in search of him and, finding him, they tried to dissuade him from leaving. But he said, "I have to go to other towns to announce the good news of the kingdom of God. That is what I was sent to do." So Jesus continued to preach in the synagogues of the Jewish country.

2. Thursday

S E P T E M B E R

1Cor 3:18-23   Lk 5:1-11

One day, as Jesus stood by the Lake of Gennesaret, with a crowd gathered around him listening to the word of God, he caught sight of two boats left at the water's edge by the fishermen now washing their nets. He got into one of the boats, the one belonging to Simon, and asked him to pull out a little from the shore. There he sat and continued to teach the crowd.

When he had finished speaking he said to Simon, "Put out into deep water and lower your nets for a catch." Simon replied, "Master, we worked hard all night and caught nothing. But if you say so, I will lower the nets." This they did and caught such a large number of fish that their nets began to break. They signaled their partners in the other boat to come and help them. They came and filled both boats almost to the point of sinking.

Upon seeing this, Simon Peter fell at Jesus' knees, saying, "Leave me, Lord, for I am a sinful man!" For he and his companions were amazed at the catch they had made and so were Simon's partners, James and John, Zebedee's sons.

Jesus said to Simon, "Do not be afraid. You will catch people from now on." So they brought their boats to land and followed him, leaving everything.

In today's reading, if Peter had made a large catch by his own skill, the further large catch on Jesus' instructions would not have been at all surprising. But because he came empty-handed, the Lord was able to catch him! The fish in that miraculous catch was Peter himself! The most pathetic words in the New Testament: "That night they caught nothing." But look! There on the shore stood Jesus! Had they caught a lot of fish that night, they might not have seen him at all. He was their catch that night! So when have I failed? When have I succeeded? The wonder of it is that I can never say for sure. (How unbearable life would be if I could!)

1Cor 4:1-5   Lk 5:33-39

This says to us: don't let your mind become like an old wine-skin. Our faith makes unconditional demands on us throughout our lives. It requires us to make immense leaps of sympathy and forgiveness; it asks us to live for God, not for earthly power and wealth; it asks us to put aside self-will and to live for others; it asks us to put to death our worldly pride and vanity, and to imitate the self-emptying (kenosis), the poverty of Christ; it asks us to lay down our very lives for our brothers and sisters; most challenging of all, it asks us to love our enemies. This was a new way to live, it was the new wine, requiring a new mind, new structures.

Some people asked Jesus, "The disciples of John fast often and say long prayers, and so do the disciples of the Pharisees. Why is it that your disciples eat and drink?" Then Jesus said to them, "You can't make wedding guests fast while the bridegroom is with them. But later the bridegroom will be taken from them and they will fast in those days."

Jesus also told them this parable, "No one tears a piece from a new coat to put it on an old one; otherwise the new will be torn and the piece taken from the new will not match the old. No one puts new wine into old wineskins; otherwise the new wine will burst the skins and be spilled, and the skins will be destroyed as well. But new wine must be put into fresh skins. Yet no one who has tasted old wine is eager to get new wine, but says: The old is good."

1Cor 4:9-15   Lk 6:1-5

How do you take it when some people are observing you and waiting for you to make a mistake? That kind of scrutiny causes you to make mistakes; so the critical attitude finds only what it is looking for. If you often suffer from this kind of attack, it is interesting to see how Jesus handled it. He gave them no ground; he didn't apologize even though his own argument was not very strong! It is impossible to engage in argument with fanatical legalists without becoming a legalist yourself. It is better not to enter into details, but simply to take the ground from under their whole system—which is what the Lord did. "The Son of Man," he said, "is Lord of the Sabbath."

One Sabbath Jesus was going through the corn fields and his disciples began to pick heads of grain crushing them in their hands for food. Some of the Pharisees asked them, "Why do you do what is forbidden on the Sabbath?" Then Jesus spoke, "Have you never read what David did when he and his men were hungry?" He entered the house of God, took and ate the bread of the offering and even gave some to his men, though only priests are allowed to eat that bread." And Jesus added, "The Son of Man is Lord and rules over the Sabbath."

Sunday

Aramaic idiom dispensed with qualifiers: if you don't love, you hate; if you're not first, you're last… In modern languages we are able to say something and then qualify it out of existence. The shock of a literal translation from Aramaic is probably good for us! What that particular verse is saying is that discipleship is to come before all other relationships. It even comes before one's relationship to oneself, "Those who lose their life for my sake will find it" (Mt 10:39). Discipleship doesn't mean fawning on a teacher, but being moved with the help of that teacher to a position where everything isn't corrupted by the ego.

23RD SUNDAY IN ORDINARY TIME

5

Wis 9:13-18

Indeed, what man can know the intentions of God? Who can discern the plan of the Lord? For human reasoning is timid, our notions misleading; a perishable body is a burden for the soul and our tent of clay weighs down the active mind. We are barely able to know about the things of earth and it is a struggle to understand what is close to us; who then may hope to understand heavenly things? (...)

Phlm 9-10,12-17

Yet I prefer to request you in love. The one talking is Paul, the old man, now prisoner for Christ. And my request is on behalf of Onesimus, whose father I have become while I was in prison. In returning him to you, I am sending you my own heart. I would have liked to keep him at my side, to serve me on your behalf while I am in prison for the Gospel, but I did not want to do anything without your agreement, nor impose a good deed upon you without your free consent. Perhaps Onesimus has been parted from you for a while so that you may have him back forever, no longer as a slave, but better than a slave. For he is a very dear brother to me, and he will be even dearer to you. And so, because of our friendship, receive him as if he were I myself.

Lk 14:25-33

One day, when large crowds were walking along with Jesus, he turned and said to them, "If you come to me, without being ready to give up your love for your father and mother, your spouse and children, your brothers and sisters, and indeed yourself, you cannot be my disciple. Whoever does not follow me carrying his own cross cannot be my disciple. Do you build a house without first sitting down to count the cost to see whether you have enough to complete it? Otherwise, if you have laid the foundation and are not able to finish it, everyone will make fun of you: This fellow began to build and was not able to finish.' And when a king wages war against another king, does he go to fight without first sitting down to consider whether his ten thousand can stand against the twenty thousand of his opponent? And if not, while the other is still a long way off he sends messengers for peace talks. In the same way, none of you may become my disciple if he doesn't give up everything he has."

Monday 6

ORDINARY TIME
23rd Week

Labor Day

1Cor 5:1-8   Lk 6:6-11

If religion penetrates the head only, it will serve to divide people from one another, because left to itself that's what the head does best: it makes distinctions and oppositions. Religion brings out the best and the worst. This is very clear to us nowadays. Many religious people are not worshipping God but themselves: there is no ego quite so poisonous as the religious one. It bends the language of religion to its own ends, and is quite indifferent to God. In the 17th century, Pascal could write, "Men never do evil so completely and cheerfully as when they do it from religious conviction." The test, as always, is not what we say but what we do.

On another Sabbath Jesus entered the synagogue and began teaching. There was a man with a paralyzed right hand and the teachers of the Law and the Pharisees watched him: Would Jesus heal the man on the Sabbath? If he did, they could accuse him.

But Jesus knew their thoughts and said to the man, "Get up and stand in the middle." Then he spoke to them, "I want to ask you: what is allowed by the Law on the Sabbath, to do good or to do harm, to save life or destroy it?" And Jesus looked around at them all.

Then he said to the man, "Stretch out your hand." He stretched it out and his hand was restored, becoming as whole as the other. But they were furious and began to discuss with one another how they could deal with Jesus.

1Cor 6:1-11   Lk 6:12-19

Here is a taste of C.H. Spurgeon, the great English 19th-century Baptist preacher. "We cannot watch with Him one hour, but He watched for us whole nights. The occasion for this prayer is notable; it was after His enemies had been enraged—prayer was His refuge and solace; it was before He sent forth the twelve apostles—prayer was the gate of His enterprise, the herald of His new work. Should we not learn from Jesus to resort to special prayer when we are under peculiar trial, or contemplate fresh endeavors for the Master's glory? Lord Jesus, teach us to pray."

Jesus went out into the hills to pray, spending the whole night in prayer with God. When day came, he called his disciples to him and chose twelve of them whom he called apostles: Simon, whom he named Peter, and his brother Andrew, James and John; Philip and Bartholomew; Matthew and Thomas; James son of Alpheus and Simon called the Zealot; Judas son of James, and Judas Iscariot, who would be the traitor.

Coming down the hill with them, Jesus stood on a level place. Many of his disciples were there and a large crowd of people who had come from all parts of Judea and Jerusalem and from the coastal cities of Tyre and Sidon. They gathered to hear him and be healed of their diseases; likewise people troubled by evil spirits were healed. The entire crowd tried to touch him because of the power that went out from him and healed them all.

Mic 5:1-4 or Rom 8:28-30   Mt 1:18-23

Of course there is nothing in the gospels about the birth of Mary. But it's interesting that the text used for this feast is an account of the birth of Jesus. In a sense, when a child is born a mother is born. When a child is born, its mother begins to be a mother. Even if she was already mother to other children this new child makes her a new mother; a new chapter in her mothering begins. In the birth of the Son of God, Mary begins to be the Mother of God. When a Child is born, a Mother is born.

This is how Jesus Christ was born. Mary his mother had been given to Joseph in marriage but before they lived together, she was found to be pregnant through the Holy Spirit.

Then Joseph, her husband, made plans to divorce her in all secrecy. He was an upright man, and in no way did he want to discredit her.

While he was pondering over this, an angel of the Lord appeared to him in a dream and said, "Joseph, descendant of David, do not be afraid to take Mary as your wife. She has conceived by the Holy Spirit, and now she will bear a son. You shall call him 'Jesus' for he will save his people from their sins."

All this happened in order to fulfill what the Lord had said through the prophet: The virgin will conceive and bear a son, and he will be called Emmanuel which means: God-with-us.

9 Thursday

SEPTEMBER

1Cor 8:1-7,11-13   Lk 6:27-38

Jesus said to his disciples, "But I say to you who hear me: Love your enemies, do good to those who hate you. Bless those who curse you and pray for those who treat you badly. To the one who strikes you on the cheek, turn the other cheek; from the one who takes your coat, do not keep back your shirt. Give to the one who asks and if anyone has taken something from you, do not demand it back.

"Do to others as you would have others do to you. If you love only those who love you, what kind of graciousness is yours? Even sinners love those who love them. If you do favors to those who are good to you, what kind of graciousness is yours? Even sinners do the same. If you lend only when you expect to receive, what kind of graciousness is yours? For sinners also lend to sinners, expecting to receive something in return.

"But love your enemies and do good to them, and lend when there is nothing to expect in return. Then will your reward be great and you will be sons and daughters of the Most High. For he is kind towards the ungrateful and the wicked. Be merciful, just as your Father is merciful.

"Don't be a judge of others and you will not be judged; do not condemn and you will not be condemned; forgive and you will be forgiven; give and it will be given to you, and you will receive in your sack good measure, pressed down, full and running over. For the measure you give will be the measure you receive back."

Loving your enemy is the clearest evidence that you are no longer making yourself the measure of love. By some miracle the axis of your life has moved elsewhere. The self-centered self, which seemed fixed forever and which controlled everything you did and saw, is no longer the main center of reference. Suddenly the world is immense! And the very idea of competition dies. I can force myself to do good for others. This is very good and heroic, but the problem is that resistance may be growing within me at some deep level. If I have outbursts of anger and impatience, this is a sign that my virtue is forced. I still don't have the skill. There has been no "release."

1Cor 9:16-19,22-27   Lk 6:39-42

We are still looking at that extraordinary teaching by Jesus. "Judge not!" is the same as "Love your enemies." In both cases it is the self-centered basis that is being removed. I read where a scholar translated this "Judge not" as "Try to be more lenient in your judgments!" This misses the point exactly. If you judge, even leniently, you are still on your throne of judgment—probably admiring yourself for your leniency! St. Paul wrote, "Why do you pass judgment on your brother or sister…? For we will all stand before the judgment seat of God" (Rom 14:10). That was calculated to dampen our enthusiasm for judging one another.

Jesus offered this example, "Can a blind person lead another blind person? Surely both will fall into a ditch. A disciple is not above the master; but when fully trained, he will be like the master. So why do you pay attention to the speck in your brother's eye while you have a log in your eye and are not conscious of it? How can you say to your neighbor: 'Friend, let me take this speck out of your eye,' when you can't remove the log in your own? You hypocrite! First remove the log from your own eye and then you will see clearly enough to remove the speck from your neighbor's eye."

11 Saturday

SEPTEMBER

1Cor 10:14-22   Lk 6:43-49

Trees don't tell lies; only human beings tell lies. Jesus faced this fundamental lie in his adversaries, "You are from your father the devil.... He does not stand in the truth, because there is no truth in him. When he lies, he speaks according to his own nature, for he is a liar and the father of lies. But because I tell the truth, you do not believe me" (Jn 8:44-45). But the truth emerges eventually. One day we will be completely truthful. Perhaps that is the attraction that trees have —and nature generally: those are being that are already true to the core. Sit under a tree for an hour, and it will become harder to tell a lie afterwards!

Jesus said to the crowd, "No healthy tree bears bad fruit, no poor tree bears good fruit. And each tree is known by the fruit it bears: you don't gather figs from thorns, or grapes from brambles. Similarly the good person draws good things from the good stored in the heart, and an evil person draws evil things from the evil stored in the heart. For the mouth speaks from the fullness of the heart.

"Why do you call me: 'Lord! Lord!' and not do what I say? I will show you what the one who comes to me and listens to my words and acts accordingly, is like. That one is like the builder who dug deep and laid the foundations of his house on rock. The river overflowed and the stream dashed against the house, but could not carry it off because the house had been well built.

"But the one who listens and does not act, is like a man who built his house on the ground without a foundation. The flood burst against it, and the house fell at once: and what a terrible disaster that was!"

Sunday

"This man welcomes sinners and eats with them." This is the theme of chapter 15 of Luke's gospel. The chapter has three parables of God's mercy: the lost sheep, coin and the prodigal son. In fact Luke's could be called the gospel of the lost. But these parables would be better named "the found sheep," "the found coin" and "the found son"; the point of the parables is that God's mercy comes after us and finds us. Each of them mentions joy, "rejoice with me!" says the shepherd who found the lost sheep; says the woman who found the coin; "it was right we should celebrate and rejoice," said the father of the lost son. That is a theme to stay with: God's joy in us.

24TH SUNDAY IN ORDINARY TIME

Ex 32:7-11,13-14
1Tim 1:1,2-17

I give thanks to Christ Jesus, our Lord, who is my strength, who has considered me trustworthy and appointed me to his service, although I had been a blasphemer, a persecutor and a rabid enemy. However he took mercy on me because I did not know what I was doing when I opposed the faith; and the grace of our Lord was more than abundant, together with faith and love that are in Christ Jesus.

This saying is true and worthy of belief: Christ Jesus came into the world to save sinners, of whom I am the first. Because of that I was forgiven; Christ Jesus wanted to display his utmost patience in me so that I might be an example for all who are to believe and obtain eternal life. To the King of ages, the only God who lives beyond every perishable and visible creation—to him be honor and glory forever. Amen!

Lk 15:1-32

(...) Jesus continued, "There was a man with two sons. The younger said to his father: 'Give me my share of the estate.' So the father divided his property between them. Some days later, the younger son gathered all his belongings and started off for a distant land where he squandered his wealth in loose living. Having spent everything, he was hard pressed when a severe famine broke out in that land. So he hired himself out to a well-to-do citizen of that place and was sent to work on a pig farm. So famished was he that he longed to fill his stomach even with the food given to the pigs, but no one offered him anything. Finally coming to his senses, he said: 'How many of my father's hired workers have food to spare, and here I am starving to death! I will get up and go back to my father and say to him: Father, I have sinned against God and before you. I no longer deserve to be called your son. Treat me then as one of your hired servants.' With that thought in mind he set off for his father's house. He was still a long way off when his father caught sight of him. His father was so deeply moved with compassion that he ran out to meet him, threw his arms around his neck and kissed him. The son said: 'Father, I have sinned against Heaven and before you. I no longer deserve to be called your son…'

But the father turned to his servants: 'Quick! Bring out the finest robe and put it on him. Put a ring on his finger and sandals on his feet. Take the fattened calf and kill it. We shall celebrate and have a feast, for this son of mine was dead and has come back to life. He was lost and is found.' And the celebration began. (...)

Monday 13

1Cor 11:17-26,33   Lk 7:1-10

The "captains" of this translation are the "centurions" of other translations. The centurion in today's reading left more than a good impression; "he loves our people, and it is he who built our synagogue for us." He was also particularly sensitive to Jewish custom. He knew that Jews would not allow Gentiles to enter their houses, and vice versa, so he sent messengers to Jesus. When Jesus came near the house, the centurion said, "Sir, I am not worthy to receive you in my house...." Which goes to show that an army man doesn't have to give his soul to the army; he can be a human being at the same time.

When Jesus had finished teaching to the people, he went to Capernaum.

There was a captain whose servant was very sick and near to death, a man very dear to him. So when he heard about Jesus, he sent some elders of the Jews to persuade him to come and save his servant's life. The elders came to Jesus and begged him earnestly, saying, "He deserves this of you, for he loves our people and even built a synagogue for us."

Jesus went with them. He was not far from the house when the captain sent friends to give this message, "Sir, do not trouble yourself for I am not worthy to welcome you under my roof. You see I didn't approach you myself. Just give the order and my servant will be healed. For I myself, a junior officer, give orders to my soldiers and I say to this one: 'Go,' and he goes; and to the other: 'Come,' and he comes; and to my servant: 'Do this,' and he does it."

On hearing these words, Jesus was filled with admiration. He turned and said to the people with him, "I say to you, not even in Israel have I found such great faith." The people sent by the captain went back to his house; there they found that the servant was well.

Num 21:4-9   Phil 2:6-11   Jn 3:13-17

Nicodemus cannot have been a very great teacher—and Jesus hinted it—because Jews at that time spoke of converts to Judaism as people who were "born again." He didn't seem quite to understand this expression. These are still battling it out, under new names: "creation-centered spirituality" versus "sin/redemption spirituality." Original blessing or original sin? Nature or the Cross? But we mustn't forget that it was the same Jesus who said, "Behold the lilies of the field…" and who died on the Cross. The challenge, as always, is to refuse to become partisan, but rather to enter into the drama and refuse to be limited by labels.

Jesus said to Nicodemus, "No one has ever gone up to heaven except the one who came from heaven, the Son of Man.

"As Moses lifted up the serpent in the desert, so must the Son of Man be lifted up, so that whoever believes in him may have eternal life.

"Yes, God so loved the world that he gave his only Son that whoever believes in him may not be lost, but may have eternal life. God did not send the Son into the world to condemn the world; instead, through him the world is to be saved."

SEPTEMBER

Wednesday 15

ORDINARY TIME
24th Week

Our Lady of Sorrows

Heb 5:7-9   Jn 19:25-27

I came across this remarkable prayer from the Methodist Service Book, "I am no longer my own, but yours. Put me to what you will, rank me with whom you will; put me to doing, put me to suffering; let me be employed for you or laid aside for you, exalted for you or brought low for you; let me be full, let me be empty; let me have all things, let me have nothing." That prayer may appear to some as an expression of purely passive spirituality; or some may describe it as "feminine." But just think: how could you defeat a person who could truly pray that prayer? It would be impossible.

Near the cross of Jesus stood his mother, his mother's sister Mary, who was the wife of Cleophas, and Mary of Magdala. When Jesus saw the Mother, and the disciple whom he loved, he said to the Mother, "Woman, this is your son." Then he said to the disciple, "There is your mother." And from that moment the disciple took her to his own home.

1Cor 15:1-11   Lk 7:36-50

One of the Pharisees asked Jesus to share his meal, so he went to the Pharisee's home and as usual reclined on the sofa to eat. And it happened that a woman of this town, who was known as a sinner, heard that he was in the Pharisee's house. She brought a precious jar of perfume and stood behind him at his feet, weeping. She wet his feet with tears, she dried them with her hair and kissed his feet and poured the perfume on them. The Pharisee who had invited Jesus was watching and thought, "If this man were a prophet, he would know what sort of person is touching him; isn't this woman a sinner?"

Then Jesus spoke to the Pharisee and said, "Simon, I have something to ask you." He answered, "Speak, master." And Jesus said, "Two people were in debt to the same creditor. One owed him five hundred silver coins, and the other fifty. As they were unable to pay him back, he graciously canceled the debts of both. Now, which of them will love him more?" Simon answered, "The one, I suppose, who was forgiven more." And Jesus said, "You are right." And turning toward the woman, he said to Simon, "Do you see this woman? You gave me no water for my feet when I entered your house, but she has washed my feet with her tears and dried them with her hair. You didn't welcome me with a kiss, but she has not stopped kissing my feet since she came in. You provided no oil for my head, but she has poured perfume on my feet. This is why, I tell you, her sins, her many sins, are forgiven, because of her great love. But the one who is forgiven little, has little love." (...)

It was probably to get a better look at him that Simon the Pharisee invited Jesus to a meal. He omitted all the normal courtesies for receiving a guest. There is great irony in the fact that, without knowing it, a woman of the streets paid him the very courtesies that his host had so rudely omitted. Meanwhile Simon thought to himself, "If this man were a prophet...." For Simon, a prophet would be someone who pried into people's hearts in order to judge and condemn them. A prophet would be someone who kept the line of division clear. He wasn't ready and he couldn't imagine a Messiah who would "welcome sinners and eat with them."

Friday

17

1Cor 15:12-20   Lk 8:1-3

Every morning of life Jewish men gave thanks to God for not having been born Gentiles, nor slaves, nor women. A rabbi would not be seen speaking to a woman in public. But Jesus was followed around the country by a mixed band of men and women. Luke's gospel particularly teems with women: Elizabeth, Anna, the widow of Naim, and the woman who anointed Jesus' feet in the house of Simon the Pharisee; it is Luke who gives us the scene of Jesus in the house of Mary and Martha. And see the litany of names in today's reading. Scholars say that Luke was probably from Macedonia, where women were more emancipated than elsewhere.

Jesus walked through towns and countryside, preaching and giving the good news of the kingdom of God. The Twelve followed him, and also some women who had been healed of evil spirits and diseases: Mary called Magdalene, who had been freed of seven demons; Joanna, wife of Chuza, Herod's steward; Suzanna and others who provided for them out of their own funds.

Sunday

This parable has been a problem from the beginning. A scholar says that the second part is "early Christian moralizing." Every character in the story, even the owner, was dishonest. Someone said that the meaning of a text is the history of its meaning. In other words, it means all the things that people have ever thought it to mean. This seems a very unruly principle, but it's not as bad as it sounds: 1. our Christian instinct will be a fairly reliable guide in excluding any unchristian interpretations; and 2. it means that we really respect and listen to every interpretation it has ever received. (And that means respecting the people who went before us.)

1Cor 15:35-37,42-49   Lk 8:4-15

As a great crowd gathered and people came to him from every town, Jesus began teaching them through stories, or parables, "The sower went out to sow the seed. And as he sowed, some of the grain fell along the way, was trodden on and the birds of the sky ate it up. Some fell on rocky ground, and no sooner had it come up than it withered, because it had no water. Some fell among thorns; the thorns grew up with the seed and choked it. But some fell on good soil and grew, producing fruit—a hundred times as much." And Jesus cried out, "Listen then, if you have ears to hear!"

The disciples asked him, "What does this story mean?" And Jesus answered, "You have been granted to know the mystery of the kingdom of God. But to others it is given in the form of stories, or parables, so that seeing they may not perceive and hearing they may not understand."

"Now, this is the point of the parable:

"The seed is the word of God. Those along the wayside are people who hear it, but immediately the devil comes and takes the word from their minds, for he doesn't want them to believe and be saved. Those on the rocky ground are people who receive the word with joy, but they have no root; they believe for a while and give way in time of trial. Among the thorns are people who hear the word but as they go their way, are choked by worries, riches, and the pleasures of life; they bring no fruit to maturity. The good soil, instead, are people who receive the word and keep it in a gentle and generous mind, and persevering patiently, they bear fruit."

The soil is the heart, the place where the seed of God's word is to be received and hidden, and from where it will appear in its own time in a revolution of freshness. But "some seed fell along the path." The path is where everyone walks: If I'm always somewhere else I'm nowhere, and the word of God cannot find a place in me. "Some on rocky ground." The heart can be like a rock: solid, separate, unloving and unloved. "Some among thorns." Everything else is growing there too. My power is divided into a thousand parts, and only one is available for the word of God. "Some on good soil." It's good soil when none of the above applies. Then the heart is deep and soft and silent. Then I may hear the word of God.

Hear this, you who trample on the needy to do away with the weak of the land. You who say, "When will the new moon or the sabbath feast be over that we may open the store and sell our grain? Let us lower the measure and raise the price; let us cheat and tamper with the scales, and even sell the refuse with the whole grain. We will buy up the poor for money and the needy for a pair of sandals." Yahweh, the pride of Jacob, has sworn by himself, "I shall never forget their deeds."

Am 8:4-7

Jesus told his disciples, "There was a rich man whose steward was reported to him for fraudulent service. He summoned the steward and asked him: 'What is this I hear about you? I want you to render an account of your service for it is about to be terminated.' The steward thought to himself: 'What am I to do now? My master will surely dismiss me. I am not strong enough to do hard work, and I am ashamed to beg. I know what I will do: I must make sure that when I am dismissed, there will be some people to welcome me into their house.'

1Tim 2:1-8
Lk 16:1-13

"So he called his master's debtors one by one. He asked the first who came: 'How much do you owe my master?' The reply was: 'A hundred jars of oil.' The steward said: 'Here is your bill. Sit down quickly and write there fifty.' To the second he put the same question: 'How much do you owe?' The answer was: 'A thousand measures of wheat.' Then he said: 'Take your bill and write eight hundred.'

"The master commended the dishonest steward for his astuteness. For the people of this world are more astute in dealing with their own kind than are the people of light. And so I tell you: use filthy money to make friends for yourselves, so that when it fails, these people may welcome you into the eternal homes.

"Whoever can be trusted in little things can also be trusted in great ones; whoever is dishonest in slight matters will also be dishonest in greater ones. So if you have not been trustworthy in handling filthy money, who could entrust you with true wealth? And if you have not been trustworthy with things which are not really yours, who will give you the wealth which is your own? No servant can serve two masters. Either he does not like the one and is fond of the other, or he regards one highly and the other with contempt. You cannot give yourself both to God and to Money."

SEPTEMBER

Monday

20

St. Andrew Kim Taegon & Companions

ORDINARY TIME
25th Week

Pro 3:27-34   Lk 8:16-18

Matthew's gospel too has this image of a light on a lamp stand; but there's a subtle difference. "It gives light to all who are in the house" (Mt 5:15); while here in Luke's gospel, it gives light to those who enter the house. Matthew was Jewish and writing for Christians of Jewish origin, but Luke was a Gentile writing for Gentile Christians. Gentiles are coming to the house of faith from the outside. Read in connection with this, Ephesians 5:8-9. "Once you were darkness, but now in the Lord you are light. Live as children of light—for the fruit of the light is found in all that is good and right and true."

Jesus said to his disciples, "No one, after lighting a lamp covers it with a bowl or puts it under the bed; rather he puts it on a lampstand so that people coming in may see the light. In the same way, there is nothing hidden that shall not be uncovered; nothing kept secret that shall not be known clearly. Now, take care how well you listen, for whoever produces will be given more, but from those who do not produce, even what they seem to have will be taken away from them."

Eph 4:1-7,11-13   Mt 9:9-13

As Jesus moved on, he saw a man named Matthew at his seat in the custom-house, and he said to him, "Follow me." And Matthew got up and followed him. Now it happened, while Jesus was at table in Matthew's house, many tax collectors and other sinners joined Jesus and his disciples. When the Pharisees saw this they said to his disciples, "Why is it that your master eats with those sinners and tax collectors?"

When Jesus heard this he said, "Healthy people do not need a doctor, but sick people do. Go and find out what this means: What I want is mercy, not sacrifice. I did not come to call the righteous but sinners."

St. Augustine thinks Matthew wasn't called at the same time as the others because he had some financial matters to finish off. Business people tend to be hard-headed, and perhaps his conversion took a little longer. But a 6th-century writer took it that Matthew left his affairs in disorder, a thing that greatly impressed him. It must be particularly difficult for someone who deals with figures to leave them unbalanced. His must have been a powerful conversion, because he had been in the service of Mammon, God's greatest rival. Do we have to balance our books before we set out on the Gospel path?

Wednesday 22

SEPTEMBER

Why would I spend every day worrying about the next day and trying to provide for it? Because I don't believe in Providence, which means literally to see to something. God is a Father who sees to things, not a cold pagan God. The Father of Jesus is a warm God. But can you trust this warm God? People who believe in God and in God's Providence don't have it any easier than others; in fact they often have it harder. The language of business corrupts religion. It makes self-interest a first principle. Jesus tells us to "take nothing for the journey." He tells us to love God with the whole heart: that means we are to take our eyes off the returns, stop calculating chances and giving up our lives to anxiety.

Jesus called his twelve disciples and gave them power and authority to drive out all evil spirits and to heal diseases. And he sent them to proclaim the kingdom of God and to heal the sick. He instructed them, "Don't take anything for the journey, neither walking stick, nor bag, nor bread, nor silver coins; and don't even take a spare tunic. Whatever house you enter, remain there until you leave that place. And wherever they don't welcome you, leave the town and shake the dust from your feet: it will be as a testimony against them."

So they set out and went through the villages, proclaiming the good news and healing people everywhere.

ORDINARY TIME
25th Week

St. Pio of Piatrelcina

23 **Thursday**

SEPTEMBER

Ecl 1:2-11   Lk 9:7-9

Herod, Luke says, was
"anxious to see Jesus."
Later in the gospel he
hadn't lost this interest.
"Herod was delighted to
see Jesus; he had heard
about him and had been
wanting for a long time to
set eyes on him" (23:8).
The tone of Luke's
gospel is a great
openness to the future.
We can be so absorbed
in our past that the
present seems less real,
and the future only a
threat. When we look at
one another we should
see living people, not
ghosts. Ghosts are
creatures who have
nothing but a past.

King Herod heard of all that Jesus was and
did not know what to think, for people said, "This is John,
raised from the dead." Others believed that Elijah or one
of the ancient prophets had come back to life. As for Herod,
he said, "I had John beheaded; who is this man about
whom I hear such wonders?" And he was anxious to see
him.

Ecl 3:1-11   Lk 9:18-22

"What do people say about me?" Jesus asked. People say everything! It was scarcely necessary to ask. They gave the usual list of false identities. He seemed to have a presentiment of this. "The Son of Man must suffer many things." Jesus would never be popular. He lost to Barabbas. I always feel uncomfortable when I hear people reciting Church statistics—percentages and numbers. What's a statistic? Does it exist in the singular? When you figure in statistics are you one of a community, or of a crowd, or a mob? Any calculation that fails to distinguish between these can't be very useful for anything.

One day when Jesus was praying alone, not far from his disciples, he asked them, "What do people say about me?" And they answered, "Some say that you are John the Baptist; others say that you are Elijah, and still others that you are one of the former prophets risen from the dead." Again Jesus asked them, "Who then do you say I am?" Peter answered, "The Messiah of God." Then Jesus spoke to them, giving them strict orders not to tell this to anyone.

And he added, "The Son of Man must suffer many things. He will be rejected by the elders and chief priests and teachers of the Law, and put to death. Then after three days he will be raised to life."

"Something prevented them from grasping what he meant...." It's always "something" when we don't understand it, or want to understand it, or even want to look at it. "There's no need to be afraid of the truth," we were often told as children. There's every reason! In fact there's no reason to be afraid of anything else. To lie is to look away from the truth, because I'm afraid of it. Lies are evasions for the sake of comfort. Lies are afraid of nothing so much as the truth, because it has power to destroy them. "The light has come into the world, and people loved darkness rather than light..." (Jn 3:19). "Are you afraid of the dark?" "No, I'm afraid of the light!"

While all were amazed at everything Jesus did, he said to his disciples, "Listen and remember what I tell you now: The Son of Man will be delivered into human hands." But the disciples didn't understand this saying; something prevented them from grasping what he meant, and they were afraid to ask him about it.

Sunday

Rich and poor: we'd like to be both. It would be nice to be rich: we would be very secure, everything provided for (and against), we would be very comfortable. But on the other hand we would have a lot of worries.. Sometimes we would think: how nice if we were poor! we only have to worry about small immediate things. If we were rich we would be secure; if we were poor we would be free. How nice if we could be both: secure, and free at the same time. Today's parable makes it clear that we can't have it both ways, and that the consequences of our choice reach into eternity. The parable is a warning to the rich to wake up from their beautiful dream.

26TH SUNDAY IN ORDINARY TIME 26

Am 6:1,4-7

Woe to those proud people who live, over-confident on the hill of Samaria! Woe to you, men of renown, from the first among the nations, to whom the people of Israel come! You lie on beds inlaid with ivory and sprawl on your couches (...). Therefore you will be the first to go into exile; and the feast of sprawlers will be over.

1Tim 6:11-16

You, man of God, shun all this. Strive to be holy and godly. Live in faith and love, with endurance and gentleness. Fight the good fight of faith and win everlasting life to which you were called when you made the good profession of faith in the presence of so many witnesses. Now, in the presence of God who gives life to all things, and of Christ Jesus who gave the good testimony before Pontius Pilate, I command you to keep the commandment. (...)

Lk 16:19-31

Jesus said to the Pharisees, "Once there was a rich man who dressed in purple and fine linen and feasted every day. At his gate lay Lazarus, a poor man covered with sores, who longed to eat just the scraps falling from the rich man's table. Even dogs used to come and lick his sores. It happened that the poor man died and angels carried him to take his place with Abraham. The rich man also died and was buried. From hell where he was in torment, he looked up and saw Abraham afar off, and with him Lazarus at rest. He called out: 'Father Abraham, have pity on me and send Lazarus with the tip of his finger dipped in water to cool my tongue, for I suffer so much in this fire.' Abraham replied: 'My son, remember that in your lifetime you were well-off while the lot of Lazarus was misfortune. Now he is in comfort and you are in agony. But that is not all. Between your place and ours a great chasm has been fixed, so that no one can cross over from here to you or from your side to us.' The rich man implored once more: 'Then I beg you, Father Abraham, to send Lazarus to my father's house where my five brothers live. Let him warn them so that they may not end up in this place of torment.' Abraham replied: 'They have Moses and the prophets. Let them listen to them.' But the rich man said: 'No, Father Abraham. But if someone from the dead goes to them, they will repent.' Abraham said: 'If they will not listen to Moses and the prophets, they will not be convinced even if someone rises from the grave.'"

SEPTEMBER

Monday

27

ORDINARY TIME
26th Week
St. Vincent de Paul

Job 1:6-22   Lk 9:46-50

Someone said that neurosis is a secret you don't know you're keeping. There must exist somewhere deep in us the mother of all neuroses. It has been given a name: it is the ego. It's not me, it's the idea I have of me. That makes two of me. The disciples of Jesus, like all of us, had a problem. Each had to be reassured that each one was doing well. They were "arguing about which of them was the most important." Jesus took a child and said, You must become like children. Children were not romanticized in those days: a child was a nobody. You must become nobody, then there will be room in you for you—and for all the others.

One day the disciples were arguing about which of them was the most important. But Jesus knew their thoughts, so he took a little child and stood him by his side. Then he said to them, "Whoever welcomes this little child in my name welcomes me; and whoever welcomes me, welcomes the one who sent me. And listen: the one who is found to be the least among you all, is the one who is the greatest."

Then John spoke up, "Master, we saw someone who drove out demons by calling upon your name, and we tried to forbid him because he doesn't follow you with us." But Jesus said, "Don't forbid him. He who is not against you is for you."

Job 3:1-3,11-17,20-23   Lk 9:51-56

There was once a great saint who wandered around the country, always giving thanks to God, "Thank you, Lord, you always give us everything we need!" Some people were attracted to his lifestyle and took to wandering with him. One day they were given nothing to eat. But the saint continued, "Thank you, Lord, you always give us everything we need!" For the next two days they fared no better. Still the old man continued thanking Gad. This was too much for one of the disciples, and he said, "Haven't you noticed that for the past three days the Lord has given us nothing?" "Well then," said the old man, "it must be that we needed three days of hunger. Thank you, Lord, you give us everything we need."

As the time drew near when Jesus would be taken up to heaven, he made up his mind to go to Jerusalem. He had sent ahead of him some messengers who entered a Samaritan village to prepare a lodging for him. But the people would not receive him because he was on his way to Jerusalem. Seeing this, James and John, his disciples said, "Lord, do you want us to call down fire from heaven to reduce them to ashes?" Jesus turned and rebuked them, and they went on to another village.

SEPTEMBER

Wednesday **29**

**ORDINARY TIME
26th Week**

Michael, Gabriel & Raphael, Archangels

Rev 12:7-12   Jn 1:47-51

The word "angel" means "messenger" (Greek, angelos). In the Old Testament the Hebrew word mal'ak was applied to both human and divine messengers. The more remote God seemed, the greater became the need for intermediaries. Certain mighty figures, later known as archangels, appear in the Book of Daniel, and the process of naming angels began. A confusing variety of functions and names are found, probably because angels were important in popular devotion. All these names have meanings. Early Christianity inherited Jewish beliefs about angels, but the interest is much diminished.

When Jesus saw Nathanael coming, he said of him, "Here comes an Israelite, a true one; there is nothing false in him." Nathanael asked him, "How do you know me?" And Jesus said to him, "Before Philip called you, you were under the fig tree and I saw you."

Nathanael answered, "Master, you are the Son of God! You are the King of Israel!" But Jesus replied, "You believe because I said: 'I saw you under the fig tree.' But you will see greater things than that.

"Truly, I say to you, you will see the heavens opened and the angels of God ascending and descending upon the Son of Man."

Job 19:21-27 | **Lk 10:1-12**

"I am sending you out like lambs among wolves." Jesus had a right to say this because he himself was like a lamb among wolves. The Christian Gospel proclaims that the deepest wisdom is hidden in suffering. This is not to love suffering for itself, but to understand that "power is made perfect in weakness" (2Cor 12:9). It is very paradoxical. Any deep teaching is full of paradox. Hard outer shells go with inner mushiness. One of the things we learn as we grow older is the difference between neurotic self-inflicted suffering and genuine suffering. "By their fruits you shall know them." Even by the skin of their fruits you shall know them.

The Lord appointed seventy-two other disciples and sent them two by two ahead of him to every town and place, where he himself was to go. And he said to them, "The harvest is rich, but the workers are few. So you must ask the Lord of the harvest to send workers to his harvest. Courage! I am sending you like lambs among wolves. Set off without purse or bag or sandals; and do not stop at the homes of those you know.

"Whatever house you enter, first bless them saying: 'Peace to this house.' If a friend of peace lives there, the peace shall rest upon that person. But if not, the blessing will return to you. Stay in that house eating and drinking at their table, for the worker deserves to be paid. Do not move from house to house.

"When they welcome you in any town, eat what they offer you. Heal the sick who are there and say to them: 'The kingdom of God has drawn near to you.'

"But in any town where you are not welcome, go to the marketplace and proclaim: Even the dust of your town that clings to our feet, we wipe off and leave with you. But know and be sure that the kingdom of God had come to you.' I tell you that on the Judgment Day it will be better for Sodom than for this town."

OCTOBER

Friday

1

ORDINARY TIME
26th Week
St. Thérèse of the Child Jesus

Job 38:1,12-21,40:3-5   Lk 10:13-16

There is good silence, but this was not good silence. It's the silence of the barren ground where the seed of God's Word could not find soil. It's the barrenness of the heart. How amazing to think how much in the world has never come to fruit! Even the words and actions of Jesus seem to leave no trace in so many places. How can one live with such a thought? But we are not the measure. We can't even say when we ourselves have failed. What looks like total failure and emptiness is often the doorway to a new life. How could we say that Jesus failed, except in a material sense? If he is to teach us to stop trying to measure success, there has to be a Chorazin, there has to be a Bethsaida.

Jesus said, "Alas for you Chorazin! Alas for you Bethsaida! So many miracles have been worked in you! If the same miracles had been performed in Tyre and Sidon, they would already be sitting in ashes and wearing the sackcloth of repentance. Surely for Tyre and Sidon it will be better than for you on the Judgment Day. And what of you, city of Capernaum? Will you be lifted up to heaven? You will be thrown down to the place of the dead.

"Whoever listens to you listens to me, and whoever rejects you rejects me; and he who rejects me, rejects the one who sent me."

Ex 23:20-23   Mt 18:1-5,10

Jockeying for first place in the kingdom of heaven is not better—in fact it's worse—than jockeying for first place here. Having read the verse "Their angels in heaven continually see the face of my heavenly Father," Chrysostom wrote, "Here Jesus is speaking not of any angels, but of the higher sort; for when he says, 'They see the face of my Father,' he shows that their honor is great."

But not everyone agreed. Someone said recently, with wonderful simplicity, that angels are "God's thoughts." It's wise to put them as close to God as possible. It's only when creatures are far from God that they start jockeying for position.

At that time the disciples came to Jesus and asked him, "Who is the greatest in the kingdom of heaven?"

Then Jesus called a little child, set the child in the midst of the disciples, and said, "I assure you that unless you change and become like little children, you cannot enter the kingdom of heaven. Whoever becomes lowly like this child is the greatest in the kingdom of heaven, and whoever receives such a child in my name receives me.

"See that you do not despise any of these little ones, for I tell you: their angels in heaven continually see the face of my heavenly Father."

Sunday

The theme of today's Liturgy is
faith. The faith is a light only for
people who are searching. The
moment we stop searching we
no longer need the light. The
end of the gospel passage is a
warning. We are capable of
turning our faith into a crusade,
an ego-plan. But if after all our
efforts we can still call
ourselves unprofitable
servants, the ego has nothing
to cling to.

27TH SUNDAY IN ORDINARY TIME

3

Hb 1:2-3;2:2-4

Yahweh, how long will I cry for help while you pay no attention to me? I denounce the oppression and you do not save. Why do you make me see injustice? Are you pleased to look on tyranny? All I see is outrage, violence and quarrels. Then Yahweh answered me and said, "Write down the vision, inscribe it on tables so it can be easily read, since this is a vision for an appointed time; it will not fail but will be fulfilled in due time. If it delays, wait for it, for it will come and will not be deferred. Look: I don't look with favor on the one who gives way; the upright, on the other hand, will live by his faithfulness."

2Tim 1:6-8,13-14

I invite you to fan into a flame the gift of God you received through the laying on of my hands. For God did not confer on us a spirit of bashfulness, but of strength, love and good judgment. Do not be ashamed of testifying to our Lord, nor of seeing me in chains. On the contrary, do your share in laboring for the Gospel with the strength of God.

Follow the pattern of the sound doctrine which you have heard from me, concerning faith and love in Christ Jesus. Keep this precious deposit with the help of the Holy Spirit who lives within us.

Lk 17:5-10

The apostles said to the Lord, "Increase our faith." And the Lord said, "If you have faith even the size of a mustard seed, you may say to this tree: 'Be uprooted and plant yourself in the sea,' and it will obey you.

"Who among you would say to your servant coming in from the fields after plowing or tending sheep: 'Come at once and sit down at table'? No, you tell him: 'Prepare my dinner. Put on your apron and wait on me while I eat and drink; you can eat and drink afterwards.' Do you thank this servant for doing what you commanded? So for you. When you have done all that you have been told to do, you must say: 'We are no more than servants; we have only done our duty.'"

OCTOBER

John Tauler (14th century) commented: "Genuine illumination makes us sink down and melt away in all our nothingness and littleness. The brighter and purer the light shed on us by the greatness of God, the more clearly do we see our own littleness and nothingness. In fact this is how we may discern the genuineness of this illumination; for it is the divine God shining into our very being, not through images, not through our faculties, but in the very depths of our souls." We cannot love or serve our neighbor from any other place. This alone undermines the ego and its hidden strategies.

A teacher of the Law came and began putting Jesus to the test. And he said, "Master, what shall I do to receive eternal life?" Jesus replied, "What is written in the Scripture? How do you understand it?" The man answered, "It is written: You shall love the Lord your God with all your heart, with all your soul, with all your strength and with all your mind. And you shall love your neighbor as yourself." Jesus replied, "What a good answer! Do this and you shall live." The man wanted to keep up appearances, so he replied, "Who is my neighbor?"

Jesus then said, "There was a man going down from Jerusalem to Jericho, and he fell into the hands of robbers. They stripped him, beat him and went off leaving him half-dead.

"It happened that a priest was going along that road and saw the man, but passed by on the other side. Likewise a Levite saw the man and passed by on the other side. But a Samaritan, too, was going that way, and when he came upon the man, he was moved with compassion. He went over to him and treated his wounds with oil and wine and wrapped them with bandages. Then he put him on his own mount and brought him to an inn where he took care of him.

"The next day he had to set off, but he gave two silver coins to the innkeeper and told him: 'Take care of him and whatever you spend on him, I will repay when I come back.'" Jesus then asked, "Which of these three, do you think, made himself neighbor to the man who fell into the hands of robbers?" The teacher of the Law answered, "The one who had mercy on him." And Jesus said, "Go then and do the same."

Spurgeon again, "Martha's fault was not that she served: the condition of a servant well becomes every Christian.... Nor was it her fault that she had "much serving." We cannot do too much.... Her fault was that she grew "encumbered with much serving," so that she forgot Him, and only remembered the service. She allowed service to override communion, and so presented one duty stained with the blood of another. We ought to be Martha and Mary in one: we should do much service, and have much communion at the same time. For this we need great grace. It is easier to serve than to commune."

As Jesus and his disciples were on their way, he entered a village and a woman called Martha welcomed him to her house. She had a sister named Mary who sat down at the Lord's feet to listen to his words. Martha, meanwhile, was busy with all the serving and finally she said, "Lord, don't you care that my sister has left me to do all the serving?"

But the Lord answered, "Martha, Martha, you worry and are troubled about many things, whereas only one thing is needed. Mary has chosen the better part, and it will not be taken away from her."

OCTOBER

Wednesday 6

ORDINARY TIME
27th Week

St. Bruno & Bl. Marie-Rose Durocher

Gal 2:1-2,7-14   Lk 11:1-4

In the Scriptures we see the intimacy of the relationship between Jesus and his Father. When he spoke about his Father in heaven he did so with tenderness and affection. He was therefore able to say that we must become as children if we are to enter the Kingdom (Mt 18:1). But what if you have had an unhappy relationship, or none much at all, with your father? May I suggest this thought? To call God "Father" is to go beyond human fatherhood! "Call no one on earth your father; you have only one father, who is in heaven" (Mt 23:9). Like Mary, but in our own way, we disciples are called to give birth to the Word; but that Word has no human father, the only father is God.

One day Jesus was praying in a certain place and when he had finished, one of his disciples said to him, "Lord, teach us to pray, just as John taught his disciples." And Jesus said to them, "When you pray, say this:
Father, hallowed be your name,
may your kingdom come,
give us each day the kind of bread we need,
and forgive us our sins, for we also forgive all who do us wrong,
and do not bring us to the test."

Gal 3:1-5   Lk 11:5-13

Prayer isn't just a way of getting what you want. Some people go to the opposite extreme of never asking God for anything (while having no problem with prayer of praise, thanks, and so on). If it makes sense to thank God for something, it must make sense to ask God for it. We needn't feel abased by that: we stand in need of everything! Prayer is a way of relating with frankness to the God who loves us. God's mind is fixed in love for us; it doesn't need to be changed. Prayer doesn't change God's mind; it changes us.

Jesus said to his disciples, "Suppose one of you has a friend and goes to his house in the middle of the night and says: 'Friend, lend me three loaves, for a friend of mine who is traveling has just arrived and I have nothing to offer him.' Maybe your friend will answer from inside: 'Don't bother me now; the door is locked and my children and I are in bed, so I can't get up and give you anything.' But I tell you, even though he will not get up and attend to you because you are a friend, yet he will get up because you are a bother to him, and he will give you all you need.

"And so I say to you, 'Ask and it will be given to you; seek and you will find; knock and it will be opened to you. For the one who asks receives, and the one who searches finds, and to him who knocks the door will be opened.

"If your child asks for a fish, will you give a snake instead? And if your child asks for an egg, will you give a scorpion? Even you evil people know how to give good gifts to your children, how much more then will the Father in heaven give holy spirit to those who ask him!"

Gal 3:7-14   Lk 11:15-26

It's often said that there is a diminishing sense of sin in modern times. How is it when there is so much evidence of its reality? We are aware of the sins of the world, but we have a diminished sense of personal sin because we feel powerless. This feeling is the hatching ground of extensive evil. This undermines the very source of action, for it robs my actions of their meaning. This emptiness of meaning cannot be endured for long. The human heart abhors a vacuum. It is quickly filled with anger. Jesus is the "Logos"—a Greek word usually translated as "Word," but equally well as "Meaning," or "Harmony." "In the beginning was the Meaning....In the beginning was the Harmony."

As Jesus was casting out a devil some of the people said, "He drives out demons by the power of Beelzebul, the chief of the demons." So others wanted to put him to the test by asking him for a heavenly sign.

But Jesus knew their thoughts and said to them, "Every nation divided by civil war is on the road to ruin, and will fall. If Satan also is divided, his empire is coming to an end. How can you say that I drive out demons by calling upon Beelzebul? If I drive them out by Beelzebul, by whom do your fellow members drive out demons? They will be your judge, then.

"But suppose I drive out demons by the finger of God; would not this mean that the kingdom of God has come upon you? As long as the strong and armed man guards his house, his goods are safe. But when a stronger one attacks and overcomes him, the challenger takes away all the weapons he relied on and disposes of his spoils.

"Whoever is not with me is against me, and whoever does not gather with me, scatters.

"When the evil spirit goes out of a person, it wanders through dry lands looking for a resting place. And finding none, it says, 'I will return to my house from which I came.' When it comes, it finds the house swept and everything in order. Then it goes to fetch seven other spirits even worse than itself. They move in and settle there, so that the last state of that person is worse than the first."

**ORDINARY TIME
27th Week**

Sts. Denis & John Leonardi

Gal 3:22-29   Lk 11:27-28

9 Saturday

OCTOBER

Time to return to Eckhart after long absence! "If I, Eckhart, had said this and if it were my word, that that person is more blessed who hears God's word and keeps it than Mary is by giving birth and being Christ's bodily mother - I repeat, if I had said this, people would be surprised. But Christ himself has said it, and therefore we must believe him that it is the truth, for Christ is the Truth....The whole of Christendom pays our Lady great honor and respect because she is the bodily mother of Christ, and that is right and proper!... And if Christendom pays her such honor, as indeed is fitting, nevertheless Christendom should pay even greater honor and glory to that person who hears God's word and keeps it...."

As Jesus was speaking, a woman spoke from the crowd and said to him, "Blessed is the one who bore you and nursed you!" Jesus replied, "Surely blessed are those who hear the word of God and keep it as well."

Sunday

Shared misery had brought Jewish and Samaritan lepers together! Had they not been lepers, they would never have been found in one another's company! And the only leper who came back to give thanks to God was a Samaritan, a heretic! There's hope for us all! The Indian poet and philosopher, Rabindranath Tagore, wrote, "We are beginning to discover that our problem is world wide, and no one people of the earth can work out its salvation by detaching itself from others. Either we shall be saved together or drawn together into destruction." If love doesn't bring us together, adversity will. We are perhaps already those Ten Lepers, waiting for the Lord to stretch out his hand and touch us.

28TH SUNDAY IN ORDINARY TIME

10

2K 5:14-17

Naaman went down to the Jordan where he washed himself seven times as Elisha had ordered. His skin became soft like that of a child and he was cleansed. Then Naaman returned to the man of God with all his men. He entered and said to him, "Now I know that there is no other God anywhere in the world but in Israel. I ask you to accept these gifts from your servant." But Elisha answered, "I swear by Yahweh whom I serve, I will accept nothing." And however much Naaman insisted, Elisha would not accept his gifts. So Naaman told him, "Since you refuse, let me get some sacks of soil from your land—the amount that two mules can carry. I shall use it to build an altar to Yahweh, for I shall not offer sacrifices to any other god but him."

2Tim 2:8-13

Remember Christ Jesus, risen from the dead, Jesus, son of David, as preached in my Gospel. For this Gospel I labor and even wear chains like an evildoer, but the word of God is not chained. And so I bear everything for the sake of the chosen people, that they, too, may obtain the salvation given to us in Christ Jesus and share eternal glory. This statement is true: If we have died with him, we shall also live with him; If we endure with him, we shall reign with him; If we deny him, he will also deny us; If we are unfaithful, he remains faithful for he cannot deny himself.

LK 17:11-19

On the way to Jerusalem, Jesus was passing along the border between Samaria and Galilee, and as he entered a village, ten lepers came to meet him. Keeping their distance, they called to him, "Jesus, Master, have pity on us!" Then Jesus said to them, "Go and show yourselves to the priests." Now, as they went their way, they found they were cured. One of them, as soon as he saw he was cleansed, turned back praising God in a loud voice, and throwing himself on his face before Jesus, he gave him thanks. This man was a Samaritan.

Then Jesus said, "Were not all ten healed? Where are the other nine? Was no one found to return and give praise to God but this alien?" And Jesus said to him, "Stand up and go your way; your faith has saved you."

Monday 11

Gal 4:22–5:1   Lk 11:29-32

The basic and more usual meaning of sign in the Scriptures is: something that indicates the existence or the presence of what it signifies; it points beyond itself to something present. Only rarely does "sign" mean an omen or portent: these would refer to future events, but a sign is about the present. The best sign would not draw attention to itself, but to what it signifies. The simpler and the less distracting it is, the better. The whale's belly hardly bears thinking about, and for that very reason it holds our attention (disgusting things do). But the preaching of Jesus is clear and it points our attention directly to God.

As the crowd increased, Jesus began to speak in this way, "People of the present time are evil people. They ask for a sign, but no sign will be given to them except the sign of Jonah. As Jonah became a sign for the people of Nineveh, so will the Son of Man be a sign for this generation. The Queen of the South will rise up on Judgment Day with the people of these times and accuse them, for she came from the ends of the earth to hear the wisdom of Solomon; and here there is greater than Solomon. The people of Nineveh will rise up on Judgment Day with the people of these times and accuse them, for Jonah's preaching made them turn from their sins, and here there is greater than Jonah."

12 Tuesday

Gal 5:1-6   **Lk 11:37-41**

Jesus was invited to a meal by the Pharisees, and he didn't think that it was going to be like dining at the high table at Oxford. It was more like an interrogation. They immediately found fault with him: he hadn't observed the ritual washing of hands. He called them hypocrites, but he never called them the embodiment of evil. His anger came from compassion, not from hatred. Explaining why a heretical teacher should meet with no mercy, John Henry Newman wrote: "He assumes the office of the Tempter; and so far forth as his error goes, must he be dealt with by a competent authority, as if he were embodied evil." It's very hard even for the greatest to pitch their anger right.

As Jesus was speaking, a Pharisee asked him to have a meal with him. So he went and sat at table. The Pharisee then wondered why Jesus did not first wash his hands before dinner. But the Lord said to him, "So then, you Pharisees, you clean the outside of the cup and the dish, but inside yourselves you are full of greed and evil. Fools! He who made the outside, also made the inside. But according to you, by the mere giving of alms everything is made clean."

Gal 5:18-25   Lk 11:42-46

In the absence of love, everything goes wrong. This has always been the message of the world's greatest teachers. But love can be extremely arduous, and—like anger—hard to pitch right. Too often when the word-package is opened there's nothing in it; or there are foul substitutes: lust, self-flattery, the will to power.... It must be the study and struggle of a lifetime to learn how to love. There has never been a shortage of people who legislate for others, but without love. The fame of the Scribes and Pharisees lies in that alone. But they have many successors, perhaps even oneself. Brrrr!

Jesus said, "A curse is on you, Pharisees; for the Temple you give a tenth of all, including mint and rue and the other herbs, but you neglect justice and the love of God. This ought to be practiced, without neglecting the other. A curse is on you, Pharisees, for you love the best seats in the synagogues and to be greeted in the marketplace. A curse is on you for you are like tombstones of the dead which can hardly be seen; people don't notice them and make themselves unclean by stepping on them."

Then a teacher of the Law spoke up and said, "Master, when you speak like this, you insult us, too." And Jesus answered, "A curse is on you also, teachers of the Law. For you prepare unbearable burdens and load them on the people, while you yourselves don't move a finger to help them."

ORDINARY TIME
28th Week

St. Callistus I

14 Thursday

OCTOBER

Eph 1:3-10   Lk 11:47-54

"You have taken away the key of knowledge!" This is the abiding challenge to every teacher: even when they are dedicated they could well be sowing discouragement and defeat in the minds of their students. But I've seen a few who adjust to your capacity, who have no urge to show off, who really want you to be able to do it yourself. These are the real teachers. Teachers! Teaching must be one of the hardest things in the world to do. As hard as loving—because it's akin to it.

Jesus said to the Pharisees, "A curse is on you, for you build memorials to the prophets your ancestors killed. So you approve and agree with what your ancestors did. Is it not so? They got rid of the prophets, and now you can build!"

(The Wisdom of God also said,) "I will send prophets and apostles and this people will kill and persecute some of them. But the present generation will have to answer for the blood of all the prophets that has been shed since the foundation of the world, from the blood of Abel to the blood of Zechariah, who was murdered between the altar and the sanctuary. Yes, I tell you, the people of this time will have to answer for them all.

"A curse is on you, teachers of the Law, for you have taken the key of knowledge. You yourselves have not entered, and you prevented others from entering."

As Jesus left that place, the teachers of the Law and the Pharisees began to harass him, asking him endless questions, setting traps to catch him in something he might say.

OCTOBER

Friday

15

ORDINARY TIME
28th Week

St. Teresa of Jesus

Eph 1:11-14   Lk 12:1-7

"Nothing is covered that will not be uncovered." Everything becomes visible eventually. People who thought they took secrets with them to the grave would be surprised if they could see how much we knew! And secrets have ways of creeping even out of graves. So why make an absolute division between the inside and the outside? They are partners! The heart is a fertile place; anything hidden there will grow for sure. If you can't keep grass from growing up through your paths, you should take that as fair warning about the heart! It would be wise to ensure that only the best things are planted in that secret place: love, goodness, truth....

Such a numerous crowd had gathered that they crushed one another. Then Jesus spoke to his disciples in this way,

"Beware of the yeast of the Pharisees which is hypocrisy. Nothing is covered that will not be uncovered, or hidden that will not be made known. Whatever you have said in the darkness will be heard in daylight, and what you have whispered in hidden places, will be proclaimed from the housetops.

"I tell you, my friends, do not fear those who put to death the body and after that can do no more. But I will tell you whom to fear: Fear the One who after killing you is able to throw you into hell. This one you must fear. Don't you get five sparrows for two pennies? Yet not one of them has been forgotten by God. Even the hairs of your head have been numbered. So do not fear: are you not worth more than a flock of sparrows?"

16 Saturday

OCTOBER

Eph 1:15-23   Lk 12:8-12

The Holy Spirit is "the Spirit of Truth." The sin against the Holy Spirit is the sin against the truth. It is to call white black and black white. Then nothing stands: nothing has any color any more. There is no forgiveness, Jesus said, for the sin against the Holy Spirit. This comes as a shock, because we rightly say that nothing is beyond the mercy of God. The blockage is not on God's side but on ours. We have turned the signpost right around; and that, is like turning the earth in the other direction; and that, in turn, is like turning back all the stars in the sky, like trying to live in a different universe. The trouble is that there isn't any!

Jesus said to his disciples, "I tell you, whoever acknowledges me before people, the Son of Man will also acknowledge before the angels of God. But the one who denies me before others will be denied before the angels of God.

"There will be pardon for the one who criticizes the Son of Man, but there will be no pardon for the one who slanders the Holy Spirit.

"When you are brought before the synagogues, governors and rulers, don't worry about how you will defend yourself or what to say. For the Holy Spirit will teach you at that time what you have to say."

Sunday

If anything is to become part of your life it must become part of your life today; and not even later today, but now. We learn this the hard way. Throughout one's life, thousands of wonderful things—millions!—have been part of our life tomorrow. Always tomorrow. Which means never. "Knock and the door will be opened to you," Jesus said (Mt 7:7). Yes, but only if you actually knock now instead of just thinking about it. Some door will open. Jesus told a parable about the need to pray continually and never lose heart" (Lk 18:1). That's what we mean by perseverance.

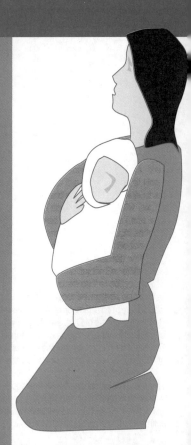

Ex 17:8-13

When the Israelites were at Rephidim, the Amalekites came and attacked them. So Moses said to Joshua, "Choose some of our men and go out to fight the Amalekites in the morning. As for me, I will stand with God's staff in my hand at the top of the hill." Joshua fought the Amalekites as Moses had directed, while Moses, Aaron and Hur went to the top of the hill. It happened that when Moses raised his hands, the Israelites would win but when he lowered them, the Amalekites would have the advantage. As Moses' arms grew weary they placed a stone for him to sit on while Aaron and Hur on either side held up his arms which remained steadily raised until sunset. (...)

2Tim 3:14-4:2

As for you, continue with what you have learned and what has been entrusted to you, knowing from whom you received it. Besides, you have known the Scriptures from childhood; they will give you the wisdom that leads to salvation through faith in Christ Jesus. All Scripture is inspired by God and is useful for teaching, refuting error, for correcting and training in Christian life. Through Scripture the man of God is made expert and thoroughly equipped for every good work. (...) I urge you to preach the Word, in season and out of season, reproving, rebuking or advising, always with patience and providing instruction.

Lk 18:1-8

Jesus told his disciples a parable to show them that they should pray continually and not lose heart. He said, "In a certain town there was a judge who neither feared God nor people. In the same town was a widow who kept coming to him, saying: 'Defend my rights against my opponent.' For a time he refused, but finally he thought: 'Even though I neither fear God nor care about people, this widow bothers me so much I will see that she gets justice; then she will stop coming and wearing me out.'"

And Jesus explained, "Listen to what the evil judge says. Will God not do justice for his chosen ones who cry to him day and night even if he delays in answering them? I tell you, he will speedily do them justice. Yet, when the Son of Man comes, will he find faith on earth?"

OCTOBER

Monday

18

**ORDINARY TIME
29th Week**

St. Luke, Evangelist

2Tim 4:9-17   **Lk 10:1-9**

Let's think about Luke, whose feast is today. He was in the first wave of foreign converts to the Faith, and his Gospel could be said to be for foreigners: for people who were not familiar with Jewish Law and custom. It is distinctive in many ways: 1) It was not written for Jews but for Gentiles, in other words, for the likes of you and me. 2) Women feature very distinctively. For example, the nativity story is told from Mary's point of view. 3) It is especially a Gospel of prayer and praise. He shows Jesus praying at all key moments of his life. What we would lack if we didn't have Luke's gospel: a) the infancy stories, b) seventeen parables, c) the three canticles mentioned above…

The Lord appointed seventy-two other disciples and sent them two by two ahead of him to every town and place, where he himself was to go. And he said to them, "The harvest is rich, but the workers are few. So you must ask the Lord of the harvest to send workers to his harvest. Courage! I am sending you like lambs among wolves. Set off without purse or bag or sandals; and do not stop at the homes of those you know.

"Whatever house you enter, first bless them saying: 'Peace to this house.' If a friend of peace lives there, the peace shall rest upon that person. But if not, the blessing will return to you. Stay in that house eating and drinking at their table, for the worker deserves to be paid. Do not move from house to house.

"When they welcome you in any town, eat what they offer you. Heal the sick who are there and say to them: 'The kingdom of God has drawn near to you.'

Eph 2:12-22   Lk 12:35-38

We say we keep some people "in our heart." Is it a place? What kind of place would it be? Very different, I imagine, from other places. It has some kind of reverse geometry: when there are many people in it there's room for more, but when there's no one in it there's no room for anyone. And in the matter of love (because that's what the heart stands for) one and one are still one. How hard it is to understand the heart! If we understood the heart fully we would lose all sense of wonder. But instead we have to be on the alert! "Be ready," today's reading tells us, "and keep your lamps lit!"

Jesus said to his disciples, "Be ready, dressed for service, and keep your lamps lit, like people waiting for their master to return from the wedding. As soon as he comes and knocks, they will open to him. Happy are those servants whom the master finds wide-awake when he comes. Truly, I tell you, he will put on an apron and have them sit at table and he will wait on them. Happy are those servants if he finds them awake when he comes at midnight or daybreak!"

Eph 3:2-12   Lk 12:39-48

The geometry of the heart becomes even more strange when we think of it in relation to God. St. Augustine, the great 5th century seeker after God, wrote, "God is within the inmost heart, yet the heart has wandered away from him." To keep gazing into one's own heart could be one of two things: it could be pure egoism, or it could be a search for God. It depends on how we approach it and do it. We find it natural to look inwards, but we are not always seeking God there. As soon as we open the door, a thousand things blow in there as well! In old-fashioned language we have to "keep vigil at the door of the heart."

Jesus said to his disciples, "Pay attention to this: If the master of the house had known at what time the thief would come, he would not have let his house be broken into. You also must be ready, for the Son of Man will come at an hour you do not expect."

Peter said, "Lord, did you tell this parable only for us, or for everyone?" And the Lord replied, "Imagine, then, the wise and faithful steward whom the master sets over his other servants to give them food rations at the proper time. Fortunate is this servant if his master on coming home finds him doing his work. Truly, I say to you, the master will put him in charge of all his property.

"But it may be that the steward thinks: 'My Lord delays in coming,' and he begins to abuse the menservants and the servant girls, eating and drinking and getting drunk. Then the master will come on a day he does not expect him and at an hour he doesn't know. He will discharge his servant and number him among the unreliable.

"The servant who knew his master's will, but did not prepare to do what his master wanted, will be punished with sound blows; but the one who did what deserved a punishment without knowing it shall receive fewer blows. Much will be required of the one who has been given much, and more will be asked of the one entrusted with more."

Eph 3:14-21   Lk 12:49-53

Jesus was a young man, full of fire. When we get older we lose our fire and settle for a little warmth. But it is fire that transforms and purifies. I never imagine Jesus now as he was portrayed in repository art: with sad dreamy eyes (blue!), hair in ringlets, tenuously masculine…. I think of him with fire in his eyes, with searing clarity in his speech and his actions, showing for the first time what a human being is, and what God is. It's unlikely that he came by it without a struggle. When he climbed a mountain late in the evening or stayed there all night in prayer, all labels, all old identities, were left far below. It may have been in times like those that he realized, "I and the Father are one" (Jn 10:30).

Jesus said to his disciples, "I have come to bring fire upon the earth and how I wish it were already kindled; but I have a baptism to undergo and what anguish I feel until it is over!

"Do you think that I have come to bring peace on earth? No, I tell you, but rather division. From now on, in one house five will be divided; three against two, and two against three. They will be divided, father against son and son against father; mother against daughter and daughter against mother; mother-in-law against her daughter-in-law, and daughter-in-law against her mother-in-law."

Eph 4:1-6   Lk 12:54-59

How are we going to read the signs of the times? What's happening in society? What's happening in the Church? One negative sign in most western countries is that very many young people are disillusioned with politics: both of society and of the Church, and they vote with their feet—they drop out. A positive sign is the widespread interest in meditation and the spiritual search. Anything not born of the Spirit is dying. But to say this is to speak again in generalities. We should look more often into one another's eyes!

Jesus said to the crowds, "When you see a cloud rising in the west, you say at once: 'A shower is coming.' And so it happens. And when the wind blows from the south, you say: 'It will be hot'; and so it is. You superficial people! You understand the signs of the earth and the sky, but you don't understand the present times. And why do you not judge for yourselves what is fit? When you go with your accuser before the court, try to settle the case on the way, lest he drag you before the judge and the judge deliver you to the jailer, and the jailer throw you in prison. I tell you, you will not get out until you have paid the very last penny."

Eph 4:7-16   Lk 13:1-9

One day some persons told Jesus what had occurred in the Temple: Pilate had Galileans killed and their blood mingled with the blood of their sacrifices. Jesus replied, "Do you think that these Galileans were worse sinners than all the other Galileans because they suffered this? I tell you: no. But unless you change your ways, you will all perish as they did.

And those eighteen persons in Siloah who were crushed when the tower fell, do you think they were more guilty than all the others in Jerusalem? I tell you: no. But unless you change your ways, you will all perish as they did."

And Jesus continued with this story, "A man had a fig tree growing in his vineyard and he came looking for fruit on it, but found none. Then he said to the gardener: 'Look here, for three years now I have been looking for figs on this tree and I have found none. Cut it down, why should it use up the ground?' The gardener replied: 'Leave it one more year, so that I may dig around it and add some fertilizer; and perhaps it will bear fruit from now on. But if it doesn't, you can cut it down.'"

I talk to myself about evil this way: there is no answer to the problem of evil, but there is a response. The incarnation is God's response to human suffering. Unable to stay at a distance from human suffering, like a mother whose child is sick, God took on our human nature to be with us. When you visit a friend in hospital you are not expected to bring answers with you, or explanations or theories; these in fact would infuriate a sick person. Instead you bring yourself, and that is your response to suffering. In Christ, God goes beyond this by plunging into human suffering and death. The Cross of Christ is the ultimate response to evil and suffering.

Sunday

Jesus didn't hesitate to throw around the word "hypocrite"—presumably because it was the right one! I counted fifteen times he used it in the gospels. "Woe to you, scribes and Pharisees, you hypocrites!" The scribes were the experts in the interpretation of religious law; the Pharisees, in close alliance with them, saw religion as observance of law. In the heat of controversy Jesus told them they were like "whited sepulchres, which look beautiful on the outside but on the inside are full of dead men's bones and everything unclean" (Mt 23:27). The stuff that went into the making of the Pharisees is still universally available! We have to say to ourselves, "Thou art that man!"

Sir 35:12-14,16-18

The Lord is judge and shows no partiality. He will not disadvantage the poor, he who hears the prayer of the oppressed. He does not disdain the plea of the orphan, nor the complaint of the widow. The one who serves God wholeheartedly will be heard; his petition will reach the clouds. The prayer of the humble person pierces the clouds, and he is not consoled until he has been heard. His prayer will not cease until the Most High has looked down, until justice has been done in favor of the righteous.

2Tim 4:6-8,16-18

As for me, I am already poured out as a libation, and the moment of my departure has come. I have fought the good fight, I have finished the race, I have kept the faith. Now there is laid up for me the crown of righteousness with which the Lord, the just judge, will reward me on that day; and not only me, but all those who have longed for his glorious coming. At my first hearing in court no one supported me; all deserted me. May the Lord not hold it against them. But the Lord was at my side, giving me strength to proclaim the Word fully, and let all the pagans hear it. So I was rescued from the lion's mouth. The Lord will save me from all evil, bringing me to his heavenly kingdom. Glory to him for ever and ever. Amen!

Lk 18:9-14

Jesus told another parable to some persons fully convinced of their own righteousness, who looked down on others, "Two men went up to the Temple to pray; one was a Pharisee and the other a tax collector. The Pharisee stood by himself and said: 'I thank you, God, that I am not like other people, grasping, crooked, adulterous, or even like this tax collector. I fast twice a week and give the tenth of all my income to the Temple.'

"In the meantime the tax collector, standing far off, would not even lift his eyes to heaven, but beat his breast saying: 'O God, be merciful to me, a sinner.' I tell you, when this man went down to his house, he had been set right with God, but not the other. For whoever makes himself out to be great will be humbled, and whoever humbles himself will be raised."

A crippled woman attended the synagogue. Let's watch people's eyes. Jesus "saw her." He had eyes for the poor, for suffering people. The Pharisees had eyes too: but only for their rules. The ruler of the synagogue was furious that Jesus had healed on the Sabbath. He couldn't look at Jesus, he couldn't meet his eyes; he addressed the people with words meant for Jesus, for he lacked courage to speak to him face to face. But Jesus certainly looked at him when he perhaps shouted, "You hypocrites!" The absence of compassion in their religion was never so clear. It's no wonder they came to fear and hate him. Violence is the reaction of people who can't look you in the eye.

Jesus was teaching in a synagogue on the Sabbath and a crippled woman was there. An evil spirit had kept her bent for eighteen years so that she could not straighten up at all. On seeing her, Jesus called her and said, "Woman, you are freed from your infirmity." Then he laid his hands upon her and immediately she was made straight and praised God.

But the ruler of the synagogue was indignant because Jesus had performed this healing on the Sabbath day and he said to the people, "There are six days in which to work; come on those days to be healed and not on the Sabbath."

But the Lord replied, "You hypocrites! Everyone of you unties his ox or his donkey on the Sabbath and leads it out of the barn to give it water. And here you have a daughter of Abraham whom Satan had bound for eighteen years. Should she not be freed from her bonds on the Sabbath?"

When Jesus said this, all his opponents felt ashamed. But the people rejoiced at the many wonders that happened through him.

Eph 5:21-33   Lk 13:18-21

The images (mustard seed, yeast) speak of littleness, and not of immensity. Everything has tiny beginnings—that is to say, everything real. In the world of advertising and entertainment, things have to create a big splash to get our attention. It's an indication of their unreality. We're all very weak, and big talk is a kind of protest at our condition; the ego talks big. But real things grow from tiny seeds. To be reconciled to tiny beginnings, small steps, unremarkable moments… that seems to be the way to go. "A day of little things, no doubt, but who would dare despise it?" (Zech 4:10).

Jesus continued speaking, "What is the kingdom of God like? What shall I compare it to? Imagine a person who has taken a mustard seed and planted it in the garden. The seed has grown and become like a small tree, so that the birds of the air shelter in its branches."

And Jesus said again, "What is the kingdom of God like? Imagine a woman who has taken yeast and hidden it in three measures of flour until it is all leavened."

Eph 6:1-9   Lk 13:22-30

No doubt curiosity is a good thing; sheep and pigs have hardly any. It makes us different from them. But we limit ourselves if we are never more than curious about anything. Then it is a refusal of "studiosity": depth and wisdom. It is better to curb it then: not in order to close that gap that separates us from the beasts, but in order to open our spirit in a still deeper way. Jesus ignored questions that came from mere curiosity. He responded to the question by saying what we should do to be saved. He said it is a narrow door. If he had said, "It's easy, don't worry" very few would consider it worth lifting a finger for. Anything cheap, must be worthless. Anything of real value requires everything of us.

Jesus went through towns and villages teaching and making his way to Jerusalem. Someone asked him, "Lord, is it true that few people will be saved?"

And Jesus answered, "Do your best to enter by the narrow door, for many, I tell you, will try to enter and will not be able. When once the master of the house has got up and locked the door, you will stand outside; then you will knock at the door calling: 'Lord, open to us.' But he will say to you: 'I do not know where you come from.'

"Then you will say: We ate and drank with you and you taught in our streets! But he will reply: 'I don't know where you come from. Away from me all you workers of evil.'

"You will weep and grind your teeth when you see Abraham and Jacob and all the prophets in the kingdom of God, and you yourselves left outside. Others will sit at table in the kingdom of God, people coming from east and west, from north and south. Some who are among the last will be the first, and others who were first will be last!"

Eph 2:19-22   Lk 6:12-16

They can be the patrons of all anonymous people. Both have difficulty even in getting their names remembered! Simon is known as not Simon Peter! Jude is likewise almost anonymous. There is difficulty about his name too: John calls him "Judas, not the Iscariot!" Luke says Jude the brother of James, and for Matthew he is "Thaddeus." Their egos left no trace. They are the patrons of the vast majority of the Christians who have ever lived. There is a lot to be said for silence and anonymity: they can give depth. Without Simon and Jude the New Testament would be poorer; it would be all light and little shade. We might not so easily see ourselves in it.

Jesus went out into the hills to pray, spending the whole night in prayer with God. When day came, he called his disciples to him and chose twelve of them whom he called apostles: Simon, whom he named Peter, and his brother Andrew, James and John; Philip and Bartholomew; Matthew and Thomas; James son of Alpheus and Simon called the Zealot; Judas son of James, and Judas Iscariot, who would be the traitor.

Here we are once again in the Valley of the Squinting Windows. The Pharisees are watching him closely. In the way he describes things Luke sometimes shows he's an outsider, a Gentile. In today's reading he mentions "a leading Pharisee." In fact, the scholars tell us, the Pharisees were not a sect with rulers or leaders and disciples. Still, he knew as much as he needed to know about them. Probably one malicious stare from a Pharisee was a full education on the whole brood! In a history of malicious looking the Pharisees would represent the golden age.

One Sabbath Jesus had gone to eat a meal in the house of a leading Pharisee, and he was carefully watched. In front of him was a man suffering from dropsy; so Jesus asked the teachers of the Law and the Pharisees, "Is it lawful to heal on the Sabbath or not?" But no one answered. Jesus then took the man, healed him and sent him away. And he addressed them, "If your lamb or your ox falls into a well on a Sabbath day, who among you doesn't hurry to pull it out?" And they could not answer.

Phil 1:18-26   Lk 14:1, 7-11

Still "looking!" But then Jesus didn't have his eyes closed either: he noticed how the Pharisees competed for the places of honor. But unlike them he was not motivated by malice. From this small incident at table he drew a parable of the Kingdom. (The "Kingdom" is the Presence of God.) God is visible everywhere and in everything to eyes that see. The 'take-away saying' is, "Those who exalt themselves will be humbled, and those who humble themselves will be exalted." In a way, those who humble themselves are already exalted. Self-exaltation isn't worthy of a human being; it's a betrayal of our true dignity.

One Sabbath Jesus had gone to eat a meal in the house of a leading Pharisee, and he was carefully watched.

Jesus then told a parable to the guests, for he had noticed how they tried to take the places of honor. And he said, "When you are invited to a wedding party, do not choose the best seat. It may happen that someone more important than you has been invited, and your host, who invited both of you, will come and say to you: 'Please give this person your place.' What shame is yours when you take the lowest seat!

"Whenever you are invited, go rather to the lowest seat, so that your host may come and say to you: 'Friend, you must come up higher.' And this will be a great honor for you in the presence of all the other guests. For whoever makes himself out to be great will be humbled, and whoever humbles himself will be raised."

Sunday

Jesus was never impressed by figures. In the story of the two men who went up to the Temple to pray, the Pharisee had all his figures ready, "I fast twice a week, I give 10% of all I possess." But it got him nowhere. Meanwhile the tax-collector "went home at rights with God" without figures. But in today's story we have a tax-collector giving his figures! "I give half of my goods to the poor and if I have cheated anyone I repay him fourfold." He didn't realize how unnecessary it was. Jesus just ignored these figures and said, "Today salvation has come to this house." The Son of Man did not come looking for good bargains, but for people who were lost.

Wis 11:22-12:2

For the entire world lies before you, just enough to tip the scales, a drop of morning dew falling on the ground. But because you are almighty, you are merciful to all; you overlook sins and give your children time to repent. You love everything that exists and hate nothing that you have made; had you hated anything, you would not have formed it. How could anything endure if you did not will it? And how could anything last that you had not willed? You have compassion on all because all is yours, O Lord, lover of life. In fact your immortal spirit is in all. And so by degrees you correct those who sin, you admonish them, reminding them how they have strayed so that turning away from evil they may trust in you, Lord.

2Thes 1:11-2:2

We constantly pray for you; may our God make you worthy of his calling. May he, by his power, fulfill your good purposes and your work prompted by faith. In that way, the name of Jesus our Lord will be glorified through you, and you through him, according to the loving plan of God and of Christ Jesus the Lord. Do not be easily unsettled. Do not be alarmed by what a prophet says or by any report, or by some letter said to be ours, saying the day of the Lord is at hand.

Lk 19:1-10

When Jesus entered Jericho and was going through the city, a man named Zaccheus was there. He was a tax collector and a wealthy man. He wanted to see what Jesus was like, but he was a short man and could not see because of the crowd. So he ran ahead and climbed up a sycamore tree. From there he would be able to see Jesus who had to pass that way. When Jesus came to the place, he looked up and said to him, "Zaccheus, come down quickly for I must stay at your house today." So Zaccheus hurried down and received him joyfully. All the people who saw it began to grumble and said, "He has gone to the house of a sinner as a guest." But Zaccheus spoke to Jesus, "The half of my goods, Lord, I give to the poor, and if I have cheated anyone, I will pay him back four times as much." Looking at him Jesus said, "Salvation has come to this house today, for he is also a true son of Abraham. The Son of Man has come to seek and to save the lost."

Rev 7:2-4,9-14   1Jn 3:1-3   Mt 5:1-12

Today we are celebrating the billions of nameless saints who have lived since the time of Jesus and who have never been beatified or canonized. I think more often of them than of the 'official' saints. They are not lesser beings, they are just less known. "Those whose law is within themselves walk in hiddenness…" wrote an ancient Chinese sage. The Christ-nature is our law within. The poor in spirit, the meek— all who lived by the Beatitudes—express it in countless different ways.

When Jesus saw the crowds, he went up the mountain. He sat down and his disciples gathered around him. Then he spoke and began to teach them:

"Fortunate are those who are poor in spirit, for theirs is the kingdom of heaven.

"Fortunate are those who mourn, they shall be comforted.

"Fortunate are the gentle, they shall possess the land.

"Fortunate are those who hunger and thirst for justice, for they shall be satisfied.

"Fortunate are the merciful, for they shall find mercy.

"Fortunate are those with a pure heart, for they shall see God.

"Fortunate are those who work for peace, they shall be called children of God.

"Fortunate are those who are persecuted for the cause of justice, for theirs is the kingdom of heaven.

"Fortunate are you, when people insult you and persecute you and speak all kinds of evil against you because you are my followers. Be glad and joyful, for a great reward is kept for you in God. This is how this people persecuted the prophets who lived before you."

2 Tuesday

NOVEMBER

Is 25:6,7-9   1Cor 15:20-28   Lk 14:15-24

Upon hearing these words, one of those at the table said to Jesus, "Happy are those who eat at the banquet in the kingdom of God!"

Jesus replied, "A man once gave a feast and invited many guests. When it was time for the feast he sent his servant to tell those he had invited to come, for everything was ready. But all alike began to make excuses. The first said: 'Please excuse me. I must go and see the piece of land I have just bought.' Another said: 'I am sorry, but I am on my way to try out the five yoke of oxen I have just bought.' Still another said, 'How can I come when I have just married?'

"The servant returned alone and reported this to his master. Upon hearing the account, the master of the house flew into a rage and ordered his servant: 'Go out quickly into the streets and alleys of the town and bring in the poor, the crippled, the blind and the lame.'

"The servant reported after a while: 'Sir, your orders have been carried out, but there is still room.' The master said: 'Go out to the highways and country lanes and force people to come in, to make sure my house is full. I tell you, none of those invited will have a morsel of my feast.'"

In today's reading we hear Jesus using this metaphor of a banquet once again. We are brother and sister to all the dead. We are seated around the table of God the Father of us all. We are not a perfect house of sweet children, we are a bedraggled family, "the poor, the crippled, the blind and the lame." But there is love: more of it, perhaps, than if we were all able to meet our own expectations. Those who went before us were not perfect, but how heartless it would be to demand that your brother or sister should be perfect! Something perfect would stand apart, but the dead are bound to us with love, around the noisy table of the Body of Christ.

Wednesday 3

NOVEMBER

**ORDINARY TIME
31st Week**

St. Martin de Porres

Phil 2:12-18   Lk 14:25-33

When we were little children we lived fully! We didn't think about ourselves. But soon the fatal limiting began. We began to be self-conscious and to worry about ourselves, we began to have a distinctive character. It is a kind of armor around one; the more character you have, the more you are limited. There's a kind of infinity about a small child—everything is welcome, everything is possible. So when we meet someone like Jesus who is like a child (and who said we should be like children) we think he's an extremist. No, he's just alive! That's what makes him different from me!

One day, when large crowds were walking along with Jesus, he turned and said to them, "If you come to me, without being ready to give up your love for your father and mother, your spouse and children, your brothers and sisters, and indeed yourself, you cannot be my disciple. Whoever does not follow me carrying his own cross cannot be my disciple.

"Do you build a house without first sitting down to count the cost to see whether you have enough to complete it? Otherwise, if you have laid the foundation and are not able to finish it, everyone will make fun of you: 'This fellow began to build and was not able to finish.'

"And when a king wages war against another king, does he go to fight without first sitting down to consider whether his ten thousand can stand against the twenty thousand of his opponent? And if not, while the other is still a long way off he sends messengers for peace talks. In the same way, none of you may become my disciple if he doesn't give up everything he has."

Phil 3:3-8   Lk 15:1-10

It's rare for a sheep to do anything by itself. How did that one sheep get lost? It's not that they choose to get lost; rather they discover that they are lost. We human beings are more complicated: we sometimes deliberately strike out on our own; we even think at times that it's our very nature to be alone. And that kind of thinking even becomes fashionable in some periods of history! If "man" is essentially alone, then belonging to another human being must be a denial of his essence. We get lost when we think we're essentially alone. More than ever we need a Good Shepherd who can recall us to our true nature.

Tax collectors and sinners were seeking the company of Jesus, all of them eager to hear what he had to say. But the Pharisees and the scribes frowned at this, muttering. "This man welcomes sinners and eats with them."

So Jesus told them this parable:

"Who among you, having a hundred sheep and losing one of them, will not leave the ninety-nine in the wilderness and seek out the lost one till he finds it? And finding it, will he not joyfully carry it home on his shoulders? Then he will call his friends and neighbors together and say: 'Celebrate with me for I have found my lost sheep.' I tell you, just so, there will be more rejoicing in heaven over one repentant sinner than over ninety-nine upright who do not need to repent.

"What woman, if she has ten silver coins and loses one, will not light a lamp and sweep the house in a thorough search till she finds the lost coin? And finding it, she will call her friends and neighbors and say: 'Celebrate with me for I have found the silver coin I lost!' I tell you, in the same way there is rejoicing among the angels of God over one repentant sinner."

Phil 3:17–4:1   Lk 16:1-8

Astuteness only barely makes it as a virtue; one may wonder if it's a virtue at all. It consorts with words like shrewd and crafty, wily and cunning. It's concerned mainly with one's own interests, as the story in today's gospel well illustrates. It's a virtue that suits "the people of this world," but what are "the people of light" to find in it? How are we to be "astute" in our Christian life? Something is always growing in my life. Life doesn't come to a stop. I may give up the practice of my faith, but then my land is thrown open to everything that the wind blows over the fence.

At another time Jesus told his disciples, "There was a rich man whose steward was reported to him for fraudulent service. He summoned the steward and asked him: 'What is this I hear about you? I want you to render an account of your service for it is about to be terminated.'

"The steward thought to himself: 'What am I to do now? My master will surely dismiss me. I am not strong enough to do hard work, and I am ashamed to beg. I know what I will do: I must make sure that when I am dismissed, there will be some people to welcome me into their house.'

"So he called his master's debtors one by one. He asked the first who came: 'How much do you owe my master?' The reply was: 'A hundred jars of oil.' The steward said: 'Here is your bill. Sit down quickly and write there fifty.' To the second he put the same question: 'How much do you owe?' The answer was: 'A thousand measures of wheat.' Then he said: 'Take your bill and write eight hundred.'

"The master commended the dishonest steward for his astuteness. For the people of this world are more astute in dealing with their own kind than are the people of light."

Phil 4:10-19   Lk 16:9-15

This reading is a collection of attempts to raise the tone of the parable of the unjust steward. Everything back in its right place. Critics are sometimes far too clever. But we can still take the messages of these early Christians, even if they have little to do with the parable. Take this one, "You cannot serve God and wealth." It is common experience that those who have most want most. This must be because they don't really have what they have: it doesn't fulfill them, it only baits them into further accumulation. Greed is a bottomless pit and nothing will ever fill it. Whatever oversees your whole life, right into the arms of death, must be a religion. It's the other religion, God's main rival.

Jesus said to his disciples, "And so I tell you: use filthy money to make friends for yourselves, so that when it fails, these people may welcome you into the eternal homes.

"Whoever can be trusted in little things can also be trusted in great ones; whoever is dishonest in slight matters will also be dishonest in greater ones. So if you have not been trustworthy in handling filthy money, who could entrust you with true wealth? And if you have not been trustworthy with things which are not really yours, who will give you the wealth which is your own?

"No servant can serve two masters. Either he does not like the one and is fond of the other, or he regards one highly and the other with contempt. You cannot give yourself both to God and to Money."

"The Pharisees, who loved money, heard all this and sneered at Jesus. He said to them, "You do your best to be considered righteous by people. But God knows the heart, and what rises high among humans is loathed by God."

Sunday

How does one hold belief in the resurrection? With the mind alone? If so, then it would be no more than what Pascal called "the big bet." It goes as follows: You can't really lose by believing in it, for if there is life after death, you will not be disappointed; but if there is not, again you will not be disappointed—because to experience disappointment you would have to exist! But Jesus did not come to proclaim the Safe Bet; he came to proclaim the Good News. When he said as he died on the cross, "Father, into your hands I commit my spirit," he was not taking a bet on the resurrection; he was entrusting his whole being, body and soul, to the Father.

2Mac 7:1-2,9-14
2Thes 2:16—3:5

May Christ Jesus our Lord who has loved us, may God our Father, who in his mercy gives us everlasting comfort and true hope, strengthen you. May he encourage your hearts and make you steadfast in every good work and word. Finally, brothers and sisters, pray for us that the Word of God may spread rapidly and be glorified everywhere as it was with you. May God guard us from wicked and evil people, since not everyone has faith. The Lord is faithful; he will strengthen you and keep you safe from the Evil One. Besides, we have in the Lord this confidence that you are doing and will continue to do what we order you. May the Lord direct your hearts to the love of God and to the steadfastness of Christ.

Lk 20:27-38

Some Sadducees arrived. These people claim that there is no resurrection and they asked Jesus this question, "Master, in the Scripture Moses told us: 'If anyone dies leaving a wife but no children, his brother must take the wife, and the child to be born will be regarded as the child of the deceased man.' Now, there were seven brothers; the first married a wife, but he died without children; and the second and the third took the wife; in fact all seven died leaving no children. Last of all the woman died. On the day of the resurrection, to which of them will the woman be wife? For the seven had her as wife."

And Jesus replied, "Taking husband or wife is proper to people of this world, but for those who are considered worthy of the world to come and of resurrection from the dead, there is no more marriage. Besides, they cannot die for they are like the angels. They too are sons and daughters of God because they are born of the resurrection.

"Yes, the dead will be raised, and even Moses implied it in the passage about the burning bush, where he calls the Lord the God of Abraham, the God of Isaac and the God of Jacob. For he is God of the living andnot of the dead, and for him all are alive."

NOVEMBER

Tit 1:1-9   Lk 17:1-6

The millstones in this passage, then, are for Church leaders, if they fail those in their charge! They are not to scandalize their flock. They are to have the courage to point out wrongdoing, but at the same time they are to be ready to forgive wrongdoing against themselves—even to forgive the same person "seven times" a day. That means endlessly. "How could we ever live up to that?" they seem to ask, "Lord increase our faith!" And when the leaders have done all that, they are to say, "We are merely servants; we have done no more than our duty" (verse 10).

Jesus said to his disciples, "Scandals will necessarily come and cause people to fall; but woe to the one who has brought it about. It would be better for that one to be thrown into the sea with a millstone around the neck. Truly this would be better for that person than to cause one of these little ones to fall.

"Be careful. If your brother offends you, rebuke him and if he is sorry, forgive him. And if he offends you seven times in a day but says to you seven times: 'I'm sorry,' forgive him."

The apostles said to the Lord, "Increase our faith."

And the Lord said, "If you have faith even the size of a mustard seed, you may say to this tree: 'Be uprooted and plant yourself in the sea,' and it will obey you."

Ezk 47:1-12   1Cor 3:9-11,16-17   Jn 2:13-22

'St. John Lateran' is a church in Rome, not a person. In the words carved in front, it's the "mother of all churches." It was the first Christian church building. The ground for it was donated by the Emperor Constantine early in the 4th century. It was rebuilt four or five times! The statues that line the center isle are so massive in scale that you feel like Zacchaeus as you walk there. That's the first connection I see between today's reading and the Lateran basilica! The intended connection probably was "I must stay at your house today." A church is a symbol of a believing community, just as a house is a symbol of the self.

As the Passover of the Jews was at hand, Jesus went up to Jerusalem. In the Temple court he found merchants selling oxen, sheep and doves, and money-changers seated at their tables. Making a whip of cords, he drove them all out of the Temple court, together with the oxen and sheep. He knocked over the tables of the money-changers, scattering the coins, and ordered the people selling doves, "Take all this away and stop turning my Father's house into a marketplace!"

His disciples recalled the words of Scripture: Zeal for your House devours me as a fire. The Jews then questioned Jesus, "Where are the miraculous signs which give you the right to do this?" And Jesus said, "Destroy this temple and in three days I will raise it up."

The Jews then replied, "The building of this temple has already taken forty-six years, and you will raise it up in three days?"

Actually, Jesus was referring to the temple of his body. Only when he had risen from the dead did his disciples remember these words; then they believed both the Scripture and the words Jesus had spoken.

Tit 3:1-7   Lk 17:11-19

In today's reading Jesus did not complain that the other nine lepers had failed to return to thank him. He said, "No one has come back to give praise to God, except this foreigner." The first bit of trouble that Jesus drew on himself was in his home town, and he did it by praising foreigners. In the present case the praise of God came once again from a foreigner, a Samaritan leper. If praise of God does not come from expected quarters it begins to come from unexpected ones. We just have to do our work humbly, in the knowledge that if we don't do it the very stones will.

On the way to Jerusalem, Jesus was passing along the border between Samaria and Galilee, and as he entered a village, ten lepers came to meet him. Keeping their distance, they called to him, "Jesus, Master, have pity on us!" Then Jesus said to them, "Go and show yourselves to the priests." Now, as they went their way, they found they were cured. One of them, as soon as he saw he was cleansed, turned back praising God in a loud voice, and throwing himself on his face before Jesus, he gave him thanks. This man was a Samaritan.

Was no one found to return and give praise to God but this alien?" And Jesus said to him, "Stand up and go your way; your faith has saved you."

Phlm 7-20   Lk 17:20-25

You can say of a church —or of any and every Church organization— "Look, here it is! There it is!" But the Kingdom, to which they are meant to guide us, is always more. We can never say, "This is it!"—if by that we mean, "This is all there is." The whole Church itself is "a pilgrim now on earth" (Lumen Gentium); we are on the way, we have not yet arrived. Yet the Kingdom of God is not far away; it is "among you." The Kingdom (the Presence) is not only within the individual; it is within the great assembly of God's people; it is the presence of Christ in the Church. The Kingdom of God embraces us as individuals and as community. In the way that a meal does both things, the Eucharist feeds us as individuals and as community.

The Pharisees asked Jesus when the kingdom of God was to come. He answered, "The kingdom of God is not like something you can observe and say of it: 'Look, here it is! There it is!' See, the kingdom of God is among you."

And Jesus said to his disciples, "The time is at hand when you will long to see one of the glorious days of the Son of Man, but you will not see it. Then people will tell you: 'Look there! Look here!' Do not go, do not follow them. As lightning flashes from one end of the sky to the other, so will it be with the Son of Man. But first he must suffer many things and be rejected by this people."

NOVEMBER

Friday

12

ORDINARY TIME
32nd Week
St. Josaphat

2Jn 4-9   Lk 17:26-37

It is hard to know what Jesus is saying, except that we cannot tell when "the day of the Son of Man" will come. The imagery is drawn from Old Testament prophecy; all the cosmic convulsions are there, as in Amos and Isaiah. That day seems to mean the day on which he will return in glory. The emphasis is on the suddenness and the newness of it. It will disrupt the normal routines. It will even make your most familiar companions look like strangers. When there is a cataclysm of some kind, people remember vividly what they were doing just as it struck. Those normal routines are seen now from a different perspective: from high in the air, as it were, rather than from the familiar ground.

Jesus said to his disciples, "As it was in the days of Noah, so will it be on the day the Son of Man comes. Then people ate and drank; they took husbands and wives. But on the day Noah entered the ark, the flood came and destroyed them all. Just as it was in the days of Lot: people ate and drank, they bought and sold, planted and built. But on the day Lot left Sodom, God made fire and sulfur rain down from heaven which destroyed them all. So will it be on the day the Son of Man is revealed.

"On that day, if you are on the rooftop, don't go down into the house to get your belongings, and if you happen to be in the fields, do not turn back. Remember Lot's wife. Whoever tries to save his life will lose himself, but whoever gives his life will be born again.

"I tell you, though two men are sharing the same bed, it may be that one will be taken and the other left. Though two women are grinding corn together, one may be taken and the other left."

Then they asked Jesus, "Where will this take place, Lord?" And he answered, "Where the body is, there too will the vultures gather."

3Jn 5-8   **Lk 18:1-8**

"There was a corrupt judge...there was a widow." She kept pestering the judge until she got justice. Widows were always penniless, and therefore of slight interest to a corrupt judge. But this one was persistent. "She will wear me out!" said the judge. Sometimes our prayer becomes so polite and tame that we can hardly believe in it ourselves. Prayer has been called "an hour of truth", but it can become the place where we tell big lies even to ourselves! A good test of the truthfulness of your prayer is to put it in one word. We are too clever by half, too rational and too evasive. Would to God our prayer could always be so simple and truthful!

Jesus told his disciples a parable to show them that they should pray continually and not lose heart. He said, "In a certain town there was a judge who neither feared God nor people. In the same town was a widow who kept coming to him, saying: 'Defend my rights against my opponent.' For a time he refused, but finally he thought: 'Even though I neither fear God nor care about people, this widow bothers me so much I will see that she gets justice; then she will stop coming and wearing me out."

And Jesus explained, "Listen to what the evil judge says. Will God not do justice for his chosen ones who cry to him day and night even if he delays in answering them? I tell you, he will speedily do them justice. Yet, when the Son of Man comes, will he find faith on earth?"

I once caught myself thinking, "I really must live in the Now—but not now!" Apparently it's an old trick the mind plays on us. St. Augustine prayed, "Lord, make me chaste—but not yet!" We would like to do things "gradually," but that's self-deception; it's a way of not doing anything, because anything that's done is done now. When we really want something there's no tomorrow. When there's danger, waiting disappears, time disappears. We invent time when we want to get out of something. When we have problems we don't want to face we put them in the recycle bin called "tomorrow." Nobody ever changed his or her life tomorrow.

Mal 3:19-20
2Thes 3:7-12

You know how you ought to follow our example: we worked while we were with you. Day and night we labored and toiled so as not to be a burden to any of you. We had the right to act otherwise, but we wanted to give you an example. Besides, while we were with you, we said clearly: If anyone is not willing to work, neither should that one eat. However we heard that some among you live in idleness—busybodies, doing no work. In the name of Christ Jesus our Lord we command these people to work and earn their own living.

Lk 21:5-19

While some people were talking about the Temple, remarking that it was adorned with fine stonework and rich gifts, Jesus said to them, "The days will come when there shall not be left one stone upon another of all that you now admire; all will be torn down." And they asked him, "Master, when will this be, and what will be the sign that this is about to take place?" Jesus then said, "Take care not to be deceived, for many will come claiming my title and saying: 'I am he, the Messiah; the time is at hand.' Do not follow them. When you hear of wars and troubled times, don't be frightened; for all this must happen first, even though the end is not so soon." And Jesus said, "Nations will fight each other and kingdom will oppose kingdom. There will be great earthquakes, famines and plagues; in many places strange and terrifying signs from heaven will be seen. Before all this happens, people will lay their hands on you and persecute you; you will be delivered to the Jewish courts and put in prison, and for my sake you will be brought before kings and governors. This will be your opportunity to bear witness. So keep this in mind: do not worry in advance about what to answer, for I will give you words and wisdom that none of your opponents will be able to withstand or contradict. You will be betrayed even by parents, and brothers, by relatives and friends, and some of you will be put to death. But even though you are hated by all for my name's sake, not a hair of your head will perish. Through perseverance you will possess your own selves."

Monday

15

N O V E M B E R

ORDINARY TIME
33rd Week
St. Albert the Great

Rev 1:1-4;2:1-5   Lk 18:35-43

A blind man is one who sees nobody, and a beggar is one whom nobody sees. This man was both, a blind beggar: he should not have been part of any story, he should have fallen clean through the net. There is a haunting poem, Egyptian beggar by Terence Tiller: "...his crushed hand, as inexpressive as a bird's face, held / out like an offering, symbol of the blind, / he gropes our noise for charity.... / Soul's and body's terrible humility, / stripped year by year a little barer, wills / nothing: he claims no selfhood in his cry.... / his eyes white pebbles blind with deserts...." Terrible metaphor for spiritual blindness: when I read it again I had to go back to Luke's story, though I wanted to push on to tomorrow....

When Jesus drew near to Jericho, a blind man was sitting by the road, begging. As he heard the crowd passing by, he inquired what it was, and they told him that Jesus of Nazareth was going by. Then he cried out, "Jesus, Son of David, have mercy on me!" The people in front scolded him, "Be quiet!" but he cried out all the more, "Jesus, Son of David, have mercy on me!"

Jesus stopped and ordered the blind man to be brought to him, and when he came near, he asked him, "What do you want me to do for you?" And the man said, "Lord, that I may see!" Jesus said, "Receive your sight, your faith has saved you." At once the blind man was able to see, and he followed Jesus, giving praise to God. And all the people who were there also praised God.

Rev 3:1-6,14-22   Lk 19:1-10

When Jesus entered Jericho and was going through the city, a man named Zaccheus was there. He was a tax collector and a wealthy man. He wanted to see what Jesus was like, but he was a short man and could not see because of the crowd. So he ran ahead and climbed up a sycamore tree. From there he would be able to see Jesus who had to pass that way. When Jesus came to the place, he looked up and said to him, "Zaccheus, come down quickly for I must stay at your house today." So Zaccheus hurried down and received him joyfully.

All the people who saw it began to grumble and said, "He has gone to the house of a sinner as a guest." But Zaccheus spoke to Jesus, "The half of my goods, Lord, I give to the poor, and if I have cheated anyone, I will pay him back four times as much." Looking at him Jesus said, "Salvation has come to this house today, for he is also a true son of Abraham. The Son of Man has come to seek and to save the lost."

People generally make the harshest judgments on themselves. If you are such a person, it will do you good to read this from a mystic, Julian of Norwich: "Human judging is mixed because of the different things we see—sometimes it is good and understanding, sometimes harsh and distressing. Where our judgment is good and understanding it belongs to God's justice; where it is harsh and distressing our good Lord Jesus corrects it by his mercy and grace through the power of his holy Passion, and so makes it conform to his true justice.... Sinners sometimes deserve God's blame and wrath— yet I could see neither of these in God. So my longing was greater than I can express."

Rev 4:1-11   Lk 19:11-28

Imagine a mountain stream, dancing down between the stones, full of freshness and music and light. But a small volume of it begins to think, "Why am I constantly losing my boundaries? Let me claim my rightful boundaries and not mix with all this flood!" It pours itself out, forming a small pool by itself; suddenly there is great peace and quiet for it. But after some days the algae begin to grow and the water slowly becomes clouded and dirty. Things get worse and one day it thinks about pouring itself back into the stream, sure in its mind that it is losing everything. But... suddenly all the light and movement begin for it again! There is no life without risking oneself, giving oneself away.

Jesus (...) said, "A man of noble birth went to a distant place to have himself appointed king of his own people, after which he would return. Before he left, he summoned ten of his servants and gave them ten pounds. He said: 'Put this money to work until I get back.' But his compatriots who disliked him sent a delegation after him with this message: 'We do not want this man to be our king.' He returned, however, appointed as king. At once he sent for the servants to whom he had given the money, to find out what profit each had made. The first came in and reported: 'Sir, your pound has earned ten more.' The master replied: 'Well done, my good servant. Since you have proved yourself capable in a small matter, I can trust you to take charge of ten cities.' The second reported: 'Sir, your pound earned five more pounds.' The master replied: 'Right, take charge of five cities.' The third came in and said: 'Sir, here is your money which I hid for safekeeping. I was afraid of you for you are an exacting person; you take up what you did not lay down and reap what you did not sow.' The master replied: 'You worthless servant, I will judge you by your own words. So you knew I was an exacting person, (...) Why, then, did you not put my money on loan so that when I got back I could have collected it with interest?' Then the master said to those standing by: 'Take from him that pound, and give it to the one with ten pounds.' They objected: 'But, sir, he already has ten!' 'I tell you: everyone who has will be given more; but from those who have nothing, even what they have will be taken away. As for my enemies who did not want me to be king, bring them in and execute them right here in my presence.'" (...)

Rev 5:1-10   Lk 19:41-44

We speak of two kinds of depression: endogenous and reactive. The first is born inside you, and is therefore very hard to be rid of. The second is a reaction to something sad that happens, and as the cause passes away so will the depression. We should speak of two corresponding kinds of joy. Real joy is endogenous; it's the natural state (and also the supernatural). The other is superficial and passing, it depends on things and events that you can't really control. I feel sure that the joy of Jesus was endogenous, and his sadness reactive! His was the fundamental kind of joy that didn't need to be constantly fuelled by happy events. What freedom!

When Jesus had come in sight of the city, he wept over it and said, "If only today you knew the ways of peace! But now your eyes are held from seeing. Yet days will come upon you when your enemies will surround you with barricades and shut you in and press on you from every side. And they will dash you to the ground and your children with you, and leave not a stone within you, for you did not recognize the time and the visitation of your God."

Rev 10:8-11   **Lk 19:45-48**

Today's reading begins, "Jesus entered the Temple." It has been a journey, and now he has arrived. Now begins his ministry in Jerusalem, which will lead to his death. That Temple was leveled by the Romans in the year 70 AD. So does it matter to us? Yes. The Temple, Eckhart said in a well-know passage, is now the human soul. "So like Himself has God made the human soul that nothing else in heaven or on earth, of all the splendid creatures that God has so joyously created, resembles God so much as the human soul. For this reason God wants this temple cleared, that He may dwell there."

Jesus entered the Temple area and began to drive out the merchants. And he said to them, "God says in the Scriptures: My house shall be a house of prayer: but you have turned it into a den of robbers."

Jesus was teaching every day in the Temple. The chief priests and teachers of the Law wanted to kill him and the elders of the Jews as well, but they were unable to do anything, for all the people were listening to him and hanging on his words.

Rev 11:4-12   Lk 20:27-40

There are two main approaches to the question of life beyond death: the philosophical and the religious. In philosophical reflection the question is about the immortality of the soul. The Scriptures speak of the resurrection of the dead, not the immortality of the soul. In the world of the Scriptures the whole person falls into the power of death; and if there is any possibility of deliverance from this power, it is not established by arguments about the immortality of the soul but rather through belief that God will raise us up, as he raised Jesus. In this matter, then, we Christians are not invited to rake through the ashes for a spark of hope, but to look up at the slopes where the sun is rising!

Some Sadducees arrived. These people claim that there is no resurrection and they asked Jesus this question, "Master, in the Scripture Moses told us: 'If anyone dies leaving a wife but no children, his brother must take the wife, and the child to be born will be regarded as the child of the deceased man.' Now, there were seven brothers; the first married a wife, but he died without children; and the second and the third took the wife; in fact all seven died leaving no children. Last of all the woman died. On the day of the resurrection, to which of them will the woman be wife? For the seven had her as wife."

And Jesus replied, "Taking husband or wife is proper to people of this world, but for those who are considered worthy of the world to come and of resurrection from the dead, there is no more marriage. Besides, they cannot die for they are like the angels. They too are sons and daughters of God because they are born of the resurrection.

"Yes, the dead will be raised, and even Moses implied it in the passage about the burning bush, where he calls the Lord the God of Abraham, the God of Isaac and the God of Jacob. For he is God of the living and not of the dead, and for him all are alive."

Some teachers of the Law then agreed with Jesus, "Master, you have spoken well." They didn't dare to ask him anything else.

Sunday

The gospels tell us that "the kingdom of God is among you" (Lk 17:21). They also say that it is still to come, "May your kingdom come!" (Mt 6:10). The kingdom of God is already here in the sense that Jesus lives within and among us now. But we know also that his presence is obscured by the continued presence of evil in the world. Individuals and institutions are very far from being aligned on the will of God, and so the kingdom is incomplete. St. Paul imagines Christ eventually handing over a perfect kingdom to God his Father (1Corinthians 15:24), but since it is not yet perfect, his ultimate triumph is delayed.

2S 5:1-3

All the tribes of Israel came to David at Hebron and said, "We are your bone and flesh. In the past, when Saul was king over us, it was you who led Israel. And Yahweh said to you, 'You shall be the shepherd of my people Israel and you shall be commander over Israel." Before Yahweh, King David made an agreement with the elders of Israel who came to him at Hebron, and they anointed him king of Israel.

Col 1:12-20

Constantly give thanks to the Father who has empowered us to receive our share in the inheritance of the saints in his kingdom of light. He rescued us from the power of darkness and transferred us to the kingdom of his beloved Son. In him we are redeemed and forgiven. Christ is the beginning of everything. He is the image of the unseen God, and for all creation he is the firstborn, for in him all things were created, in heaven and on earth, visible and invisible: thrones, rulers, authorities, powers… All was made through him and for him. He is before all and all things hold together in him. And he is the head of the body, that is the Church, for he is the first, the first raised from the dead that he may be the first in everything, for God was pleased to let fullness dwell in him. Through him God willed to reconcile all things to himself, and through him, through his blood shed on the cross, God establishes peace, on earth as in heaven.

Lk 23:35-43

The people stood by watching. As for the rulers, they jeered at him, saying to one another, "Let the man who saved others now save himself, for he is the Messiah, the chosen one of God!" The soldiers also mocked him and when they drew near to offer him bitter wine, they said, "So you are the king of the Jews? Free yourself!" For above him was an inscription which read, "This is the King of the Jews." One of the criminals hanging with Jesus insulted him, "So you are the Messiah? Save yourself and us as well!" But the other rebuked him, saying, "Have you no fear of God, you who received the same sentence as he did? For us it is just: this is payment for what we have done. But this man has done nothing wrong." And he said, "Jesus, remember me when you come into your kingdom." Jesus replied, "Truly, you will be with me today in paradise."

NOVEMBER

Monday

22

ORDINARY TIME
34th Week

St. Cecilia

Rev 14:1-3,4-5   Lk 21:1-4

Common sense would tell us that this passage is first and foremost a criticism of the Temple system and its wealth, but mostly it is given a pious interpretation, as if Jesus saw nothing but the widow's generosity. Piety can be highly ambiguous. One of most pious men I ever met ruined the lives of several members of his family. One of the bitterest women I ever met is a daily Mass-goer. Instead of facing the evil that I do, I indulge in a life of piety to prove to myself and the world that I'm a good person. But first comes justice, then piety. As Dr Johnson famously said, "A scoundrel will beat you all in piety."

Jesus looked up and saw rich people putting their gifts into the treasure box; he also saw a poor widow dropping in two small coins. And he said, "Truly, I tell you, this poor widow put in more than all of them. For all gave an offering from their plenty, but she, out of her poverty, gave all she had to live on."

Rev 14:14-19   Lk 21:5-11

The destruction of the Temple in Jerusalem was not like the destruction of a church building. To destroy that Temple was to destroy the identity of the Jewish people. So when Jesus said, "The day is coming when there shall not be left one stone upon another of all that you now admire; all will be torn down," he was saying the unthinkable. The end is always unthinkable—for while you are still there to think about it, it's not yet the end. Death is unthinkable. I don't mean that it's terrible, but only that it's unthinkable. We can say we are thinking about "it," but that's not the real thing. That's why we tend to see others as mortal, but not ourselves really....

While some people were talking about the Temple, remarking that it was adorned with fine stonework and rich gifts, Jesus said to them, "The days will come when there shall not be left one stone upon another of all that you now admire; all will be torn down." And they asked him, "Master, when will this be, and what will be the sign that this is about to take place?"

Jesus then said, "Take care not to be deceived, for many will come claiming my title and saying: 'I am he, the Messiah; the time is at hand.' Do not follow them. When you hear of wars and troubled times, don't be frightened; for all this must happen first, even though the end is not so soon."

And Jesus said, "Nations will fight each other and kingdom will oppose kingdom. There will be great earthquakes, famines and plagues; in many places strange and terrifying signs from heaven will be seen."

N O V E M B E R

Wednesday

24

ORDINARY TIME
34th Week

St. Andrew Dung-Lac & Companions

Rev 15:1-4   **Lk 21:12-19**

Death, when it comes, is bound to be a new experience! We only die once, and no one can do it for us. "Don't worry in advance about what to answer," Jesus said. When a world is ending or when your own world is ending, how could you know in advance what to say? Death is unthinkable. What is thought-over is second-hand. Death will be new. Let's see what the wise Francis Bacon (1561–1626) has to say about death. "Men fear death, as children fear to go in the dark; and as that natural fear in children is increased with tales, so is the other."

Jesus said to his disciples, "People will lay their hands on you and persecute you; you will be delivered to the Jewish courts and put in prison, and for my sake you will be brought before kings and governors. This will be your opportunity to bear witness.

"So keep this in mind: do not worry in advance about what to answer, for I will give you words and wisdom that none of your opponents will be able to withstand or contradict.

"You will be betrayed even by parents, and brothers, by relatives and friends, and some of you will be put to death. But even though you are hated by all for my name's sake, not a hair of your head will perish. Through perseverance you will possess your own selves."

Rev 18:1-2,21-23;19:1-3,9   Lk 21:20-28

Jesus said to his disciples, "When you see Jerusalem surrounded by armies, then you must know that the time has come when it will be reduced to a wasteland. Then, if you are in Judea, flee to the mountains; if you are in the city, leave it; and let those who are in the fields not return to the city.

For these will be the days of its punishment and all that was announced in the Scripture will be fulfilled. How hard will it be for pregnant women and for mothers with babies at the breast! For a great calamity will come upon the land, and divine justice upon this people. They will be put to death by the sword or taken as slaves to other nations; and Jerusalem will be trampled upon by the pagans until the time of the pagans is fulfilled.

Then there will be signs in sun and moon and stars, and on the earth anguish of perplexed nations when they hear the roaring of the sea and its waves. People will faint with fear at the mere thought of what is to come upon the world, for the forces of the universe will be shaken. And at this time they will see the Son of Man coming in a cloud with power and great glory.

Now, when you see the first events, stand erect and lift up your heads, for your deliverance is drawing near."

Here is a poem by W.B. Yeats, The Second Coming, written in 1919. Yeats was filled with foreboding by the Russian Revolution, believing it to be the end of civilization. The 'Second Coming' would not be the return of Christ, but the birth of the totally sinister. Perhaps we have to feel the evil of the world before we have a right to proclaim Christian hope. "Turning and turning in the widening gyre / Things fall apart; the centre cannot hold; / Mere anarchy is loosed upon the world, / The blood-dimmed tide is loosed, and everywhere / The best lack all conviction, while the worst / Are full of passionate intensity. / Surely the Second Coming is at hand. "

Rev 20:1-4,11—21:2   Lk 21:29-33

"The Kingdom of heaven is near." Eckhart comments, "When I think about God's kingdom, I am often dumbfounded at its greatness: for God's kingdom is God Himself in all His richness. It is no small thing, God's kingdom. If one were to consider all possible worlds God might make, that constitutes God's kingdom. Sometimes I declare that in whatever soul God's kingdom dawns, which knows God's kingdom to be near her, is in no need of sermons or teaching: she is instructed by it and assured of eternal life for she knows and is aware how near God's kingdom is, and she can say with Jacob, 'God is in this place, and I knew it not—but now I know it....'

Jesus said to his disciples, "Look at the fig tree and all the trees. As soon as their buds sprout, you know that summer is already near. In the same way, as soon as you see these things happening, you know that the kingdom of God is near. Truly, I tell you, this generation will not pass away, until all this has happened: heaven and earth will pass away, but my words will not pass away."

Rev 22:1-7   Lk 21:34-36

The past is somewhat limited by reality, but the future is limited only by imagination. Everything we can't face, everything we want to postpone, we send there. Everything we want to change the easy way, we send there. Everything we want to have without doing anything to have it, we send there. The past can keep Button B, because the future has every Button in the alphabet! It's a comfortable place, full of easy promise....Unless, that is, it isn't! Today's reading puts it in a different light. It can "catch you suddenly like a trap." "Watch!" Jesus said. That doesn't mean, "Be a spectator." It means "Be awake!" What he called "that day" will not come as a future day but as Today.

Jesus said to his disciples, "Be on your guard; let not your hearts be weighed down with a life of pleasure, drunkenness and worldly cares, lest that day catch you suddenly as a trap. For it will come upon all the inhabitants of the whole earth. But watch at all times and pray, that you may be able to escape all that is bound to happen and to stand before the Son of Man."

Sunday

Welcome to a new Liturgical year! The Lord is here and not here: how can we make sense of that, without going into make-believe? Think of it this way. Imagine someone whose only musical interest was rock. He is in a room with others where they are playing, let's say, the Ode to Joy from Beethoven's Pastoral symphony. The music fills the room, it fills the ears of every person there; it holds nothing back, it gives itself completely. He has perfect hearing in the physical sense, but he is deaf to this music. The music is present to him and not present. In some such way, the Lord is present to us and not present.

Is 2:1-5

The vision of Isaiah, son of Amoz, concerning Judah and Jerusalem. In the last days, the mountain of Yahweh's house shall be set over the highest mountains and shall tower over the hills. All the nations shall stream to it, saying, "Come, let us go to the mountain of the Lord, to the house of the God of Jacob, that he may teach us his ways and we may walk in his paths. For the Teaching comes from Zion, and from Jerusalem the word of Yahweh. He will rule over the nations and settle disputes for many peoples. They will beat their swords into plowshares and their spears into pruning hooks. Nation will not raise sword against nation; they will train for war no more. O nation of Jacob, come, let us walk in the light of the Lord!"

Rom 13:11-14

You know what hour it is. This is the time to awake, for our salvation is now nearer than when we first believed; the night is almost over and day is at hand. Let us discard, therefore, everything that belongs to darkness, and let us put on the armor of light. As we live in the full light of day, let us behave with decency; no banquets with drunkenness, no promiscuity or licentiousness, no fighting or jealousy. Put on, rather, the Lord Jesus Christ, and do not be led by the will of the flesh nor follow its desires.

Mt 24:37-44

Jesus said to his disciples, "At the coming of the Son of Man it will be just as it was in the time of Noah. In those days before the Flood, people were eating and drinking, and marrying, until the day when Noah went into the ark. Yet they did not know what would happen until the flood came and swept them away. So will it be at the coming of the Son of Man. Of two men in the field, one will be taken and the other left. Of two women grinding wheat together at the mill, one will be taken and the other left. Stay awake, then, for you do not know on what day your Lord will come. Just think about this: if the owner of the house knew that the thief would come by night around a certain hour, he would stay awake to prevent his house to be broken into. So be alert, for the Son of Man will come at the hour you least expect."

29

Is 4:2-6   Mt 8:5-11

St. Augustine had a keener eye than anyone for paradox. Even if he had never written another word he would be remembered for saying that we could not seek God unless we had already found God: for how would you know it was God we found unless we already knew God? Augustine himself had been lost for many years, and he understood the mind and heart of the seeker. Then he came to understand the deepest thing about searching for God: that in our very searching, God is searching for us. This is the theme of Advent. We wait for God, knowing that God is waiting for us. We long for God, knowing that God is longing for us. We say, "Come, Lord Jesus," and he says, "Come!"

When Jesus entered Capernaum, an army captain approached him to ask his help, "Sir, my servant lies sick at home. He is paralyzed and suffers terribly." Jesus said to him, "I will come and heal him."

The captain answered, "I am not worthy to have you under my roof. Just give an order and my boy will be healed. For I myself, a junior officer, give orders to my soldiers. And if I say to one: 'Go,' he goes, and if I say to another: 'Come,' he comes, and to my servant: 'Do this,' he does it."

When Jesus heard this he was astonished and said to those who were following him, "I tell you, I have not found such faith in Israel. I say to you, many will come from east and west and sit down with Abraham, Isaac and Jacob at the feast in the kingdom of heaven."

Rom 10:9-18   Mt 4:18-22

In the first three gospels Andrew is not mentioned except in lists of the Twelve. But in John's gospel he appears three times, and in each case he is introducing other people to Jesus! He is regularly described as "the brother of Simon Peter" (Mt 10:2; Lk 6:14). Yet nowhere does he show any resentment about this. It is rare enough to find people who are willing to take the second place, to play second fiddle. How good it would be if the only thing that people could remember about you is that you brought people to Jesus!

As Jesus walked by the lake of Galilee, he saw two brothers, Simon called Peter, and Andrew his brother, casting a net into the lake, for they were fishermen. He said to them, "Come, follow me, and I will make you fish for people." At once they left their nets and followed him.

He went on from there and saw two other brothers, James, the son of Zebedee, and his brother John in a boat with their father Zebedee, mending their nets. Jesus called them. At once they left the boat and their father and followed him.

Is 25:6-10   Mt 15:29-37

It's easy to imagine this story being told over and over again to a great variety of congregations from the earliest times, as they celebrated the Eucharist. They are our ancestors in the faith. Each time they heard the story (in the version we are reading today) they heard also that the disciples came "bringing the lame, the crippled, the blind, the dumb and many others." Those early Mass-goers could identify themselves with that. To disabilities previously mentioned Matthew adds a category, "the lame." God's ragged family: that's who we are.

Jesus went to the shore of Lake Galilee, and then went up into the hills where he sat down. Great crowds came to him, bringing the dumb, the blind, the lame, the crippled, and many with other infirmities. The people carried them to the feet of Jesus, and he healed them. All were astonished when they saw the dumb speaking, the lame walking, the crippled healed and the blind able to see; so they glorified the God of Israel.

Jesus called his disciples and said to them, "I am filled with compassion for these people; they have already followed me for three days and now have nothing to eat. I do not want to send them away fasting, or they may faint on the way." His disciples said to him, "And where shall we find enough bread in this wilderness to feed such a crowd?" Jesus said to them, "How many loaves do you have?" They answered, "Seven, and a few small fish."

So Jesus ordered the people to sit on the ground. Then he took the seven loaves and the small fish and gave thanks to God. He broke them and gave them to his disciples, who distributed them to the people.

They all ate and were satisfied, and the leftover broken pieces filled seven wicker baskets.

Is 26:1-6   Mt 7:21, 24-27

Saying the right thing is not enough. There's obviously a difference between "just saying" and "really saying." What does really saying add to just saying? It adds you! —your real mind, your will, yourself. It's very hard, as we know, to put ourselves fully behind everything we say. For a start, we say so much! There's often less in our account than the sum total of the words we utter. They use that word in banking too: "to utter a check." The consequences of uttering a false check are soon felt, but there are so many false words in circulation that it's often hard to tell true from false.

Jesus said to his disciples, "Not everyone who says to me: Lord! Lord! will enter the kingdom of heaven, but the one who does the will of my heavenly Father.

"So, then, anyone who hears these words of mine and acts accordingly is like a wise man, who built his house on rock. The rain poured, the rivers flooded, and the wind blew and struck that house, but it did not collapse because it was built on rock. But anyone who hears these words of mine and does not act accordingly, is like a fool who built his house on sand. The rain poured, the rivers flooded, and the wind blew and struck that house; it collapsed, and what a terrible fall that was!"

Is 29:17-24   Mt 9:27-31

It seems to say that the word of God is able to penetrate all our barriers. St. Augustine wrote, "You called me; you cried aloud to me; you broke through my barrier of deafness. You shone upon me; your radiance enveloped me; you put my blindness to flight. You shed your fragrance about me; I drew breath and now I gasp for you. I tasted you, and now I hunger and thirst for you. You touched me and I burned for your peace." Notice that he uses all five senses. He is like an organist who uses the full range of the instrument. We are God's imperfect instruments; many of the reeds and pipes and pallets are broken or missing. But the Lord is working on us: one day, we hope, we will fill the world with God's praise.

As Jesus moved on from Capernaum, two blind men followed him, shouting, "Son of David, help us!" When he was about to enter the house, the blind men caught up with him, and Jesus said to them, "Do you believe that I am able to do what you want?" They answered, "Yes, sir!" Then Jesus touched their eyes and said, "As you have believed, so let it be." And their eyes were opened. Then Jesus gave them a stern warning, "Be careful and let no one know about this." But as soon as they went away, they spread the news about him through the whole area.

Is 30:19-21,23-26   Mt 9:35–10:1,6-8

It's not that we have no shepherds to direct us; it's that we have millions of them who don't care what happens to us. We are "harassed and helpless like sheep without a shepherd." What is surprising, when you think about it, is that these words were first used to describe a tiny 1st-century population, hardly more than a tribe. If they were to see the confusion we are in today! It's intriguing to think that nearly all the change we see in time is just on the surface, and that human nature doesn't change very much. It may be our only hope.

Jesus went around all the towns and villages, teaching in their synagogues and proclaiming the good news of the Kingdom, and he cured every sickness and disease. When he saw the crowds he was moved with pity, for they were harassed and helpless like sheep without a shepherd. Then he said to his disciples, "The harvest is abundant but the workers are only few. Ask the master of the harvest to send workers to gather his harvest."

Then he called his twelve disciples to him and gave them authority over the unclean spirits to drive them out and to heal every disease and sickness.

Go instead to the lost sheep of the people of Israel.

Go and proclaim this message: The kingdom of heaven is near. Heal the sick, bring the dead back to life, cleanse the lepers, and drive out demons. You received this as a gift, so give it as a gift.

Sunday

Everyone has a little pride in their own ancestry. It's probably a good thing when it's not carried too far. John the Baptist said the most awful things to his own people: he called them "a brood of vipers," and he said they deserved nothing but destruction. And the people flocked to hear him! Jesus was much friendlier. He sat down to table with all kinds of people that the locals would call scum. He spoke of mercy and forgiveness and hope. Jesus came in; he saw them from the inside; he didn't "play the prophet," as he was challenged to do. He got into their minds; he saw what they were made of. He knew them too well; if their illusions were to live on, he had to die.

Is 11:1-10

From the stump of Jesse a shoot will come forth; from his roots a branch will grow and bear fruit. The Spirit of the Lord will rest upon him—a Spirit of wisdom and understanding, a Spirit of counsel and power, a Spirit of knowledge and fear of the Lord. Not by appearances will he judge, nor by what is said must he decide, but with justice he will judge the poor and with righteousness decide for the meek. (...)

Rom 15:4-9

We know that whatever was written in the past was written for our instruction, for both perseverance and comfort given us by the Scripture sustain our hope. May God, the source of all perseverance and comfort, give to all of you to live in peace in Christ Jesus, that you may be able to praise in one voice God, Father of Christ Jesus, our Lord. Welcome, then, one another, as Christ welcomed you for the glory of God. (...)

Mt 3:1-12

In the course of time John the Baptist appeared in the desert of Judea and began to proclaim his message, "Change your ways, the Kingdom of heaven is now at hand!" It was about him that the prophet Isaiah had spoken when he said, A voice is shouting in the desert: prepare a way for the Lord; make his paths straight. John had a leather garment around his waist and wore a cloak of camel's hair; his food was locusts and wild honey. People came to him from Jerusalem, from all Judea and from the whole Jordan valley, and they were baptized by him in the Jordan as they confessed their sins.

When he saw several Pharisees and Sadducees coming to where he baptized, he said to them, "Brood of vipers! Who told you that you could escape the punishment that is to come? Let it be seen that you are serious in your conversion, and do not think: We have Abraham for our father. I tell you that God can raise children for Abraham from these stones! The axe is already laid to the roots of the trees; any tree that does not produce good fruit will be cut down and thrown in the fire. I baptize you in water for a change of heart, but the one who is coming after me is more powerful than me; indeed I am not worthy to carry his sandals. He will baptize you in the Holy Spirit and fire. He has the winnowing fan in his hand and he will clear out his threshing floor. He will gather his wheat into the barn, but the chaff he will burn in everlasting fire."

The Pharisees and teachers of the Law were "sitting there" and the paralyzed man was lying on his mat. They were as paralyzed as he: they in their "seat of learning," he in his bed of pain. Jesus said to him, "Get up!" and he got up and walked. But by the end of the story the Pharisees and teachers of the Law are still seated. Their religion wasn't such as to enable, or even to allow, anyone to get up and move. The effect of religious teaching, too often, is to keep people seated. The effect of real religion is to give us "the mind of Christ": his life's work was "to bring good news to the poor... to proclaim release to captives and recovery of sight to the blind, to let the oppressed go free..." (Lk 4:18).

One day Jesus was teaching and many Pharisees and teachers of the Law had come from every part of Galilee and Judea and even from Jerusalem. They were sitting there while the power of the Lord was at work to heal the ssick. Then some men brought a paralyzed man who lay on his mat. They tried to enter the house to place him before Jesus, but they couldn't find a way through the crowd. So they went up on the roof and, removing the tiles, tey lowered him on his mat into the middle of the crowd, in front of Jesus.

When Jesus saw their faith, he said to the man, "My friend, your sins are forgiven." At once the teachers of the Law and the Pharisees began to wonder, "This man insults God! Who can forgive sins but only God?

But Jesus knew their thoughts and asked them, "Why are you reacting like this? Which is easier to say: 'Your sins are forgiven,' or: 'Get up and walk'? Now you shall know that the Son of Man has authority on earth to forgive sins." And Jesus said to the paralyzed man, "Get up, take your mat and go home." At once the man stood before them. He took up the mat he had been lying on and went home praising God.

Amazement seized the people and they praised God. They were filled with a holy fear and said, "What wonderful things we have seen today!"

Is 40:1-11   Mt 18:12-14

This story shows that God doesn't think in percentages (see June 18). Compare it with the following, "Caiaphas, who was high priest that year, said [to the Sanhedrin], 'You know nothing at all! You do not understand that it is better for you to have one man die for the people than to have the whole nation destroyed'" (Jn 11:49-50). In other words, since it was politically expedient it was all right to put an innocent man to death. Caiaphas was the high priest, but he thought like a politician, an unscrupulous one at that. It should serve for all time as a warning to all priests, high and low.

Jesus said to his disciples, "What do you think of this? If someone has a hundred sheep and one of them strays, won't he leave the ninety-nine on the hillside, and go to look for the stray one? And I tell you: when he finally finds it, he is more pleased about it than about the ninety-nine that did not get lost. It is the same with your Father in heaven: there they don't want even one of these little ones to be lost."

Gen 3:9-15,20   Eph 1:3-6,11-12   Lk 1:26-38

Christian artists through the centuries have represented the Annunciation more often perhaps than any other theme in the gospels, except the crucifixion of Christ. Today's feast however (as distinct from the reading) is not about the conception of Jesus in his mother's womb, but about Mary's own conception - her having been conceived and born free of original sin. Of course there is no Scriptural text to support this specific doctrine, so the Liturgy uses Luke's account of the conception of Jesus. This makes sense, because it is only because of Jesus that we say the things we say about Mary. Mary—and all women with her—still has much work to do.

In the sixth month, the angel Gabriel was sent from God to a town of Galilee called Nazareth. He was sent to a young virgin who was betrothed to a man named Joseph, of the family of David; and the virgin's name was Mary.

The angel came to her and said, "Rejoice, full of grace, the Lord is with you." Mary was troubled at these words, wondering what this greeting could mean.

But the angel said, "Do not fear, Mary, for God has looked kindly on you. You shall conceive and bear a son and you shall call him Jesus. He will be great and shall rightly be called Son of the Most High. The Lord God will give him the kingdom of David, his ancestor; he will rule over the people of Jacob forever and his reign shall have no end."

Then Mary said to the angel, "How can this be if I am a virgin?" And the angel said to her, "The Holy Spirit will come upon you and the power of the Most High will overshadow you; therefore, the holy child to be born shall be called Son of God. Even your relative Elizabeth is expecting a son in her old age, although she was unable to have a child, and she is now in her sixth month. With God nothing is impossible." Then Mary said, "I am the handmaid of the Lord, let it be done to me as you have said." And the angel left her.

ADVENT
2nd Week
St. Juan Diego

Is 41:13-20   Mt 11:11-15

Jesus said, equivalently, that John the Baptist was the greatest man (or among the greatest) who ever lived. Yet, he added, "the least in the Kingdom of heaven is greater than he." The expression "the least" is the superlative form of the expression "little one." "Little ones" is the term used for disciples; so "the least" is the least disciple. The greatest man who ever lived thundered judgment, but even the least disciple knows the greater depth and the superior power of love. Let us meditate on the strange paradox that power is ultimately weak, and weakness ultimately powerful. "When I am weak, then I am strong," wrote St. Paul (2Cor 12:10). Expand it from your own experience.

Jesus said to the crowds, "No one greater than John the Baptist has come forward among the sons of women, and yet the least in the kingdom of heaven is greater than he. From the days of John the Baptist until now the kingdom of heaven is something to be conquered and the unyielding seize it.

"Up to the time of John, there was only prophesy: all the prophets and the Law; and if you believe me, John is this Elijah, whose coming was predicted. Let anyone with ears listen!"

Today's reading indicates that the message of Jesus was not getting through. There was widespread disaffection. The people rejected John because he was too different from them and Jesus because he was too like them. Jesus rejected the temptation to fame. He rejected theatre. And so he was not a success. Yes, the triumphal entry into Jerusalem (Mt 21:6-11) had a touch of theatre about it; and inevitably the crowd that shouted "Hosanna!" were soon shouting "Crucify him!" But the modern interpretation of Jesus as a superstar misses every point that believing Christians know in their very bones. Jesus had no illusions. That's who he is: the one who has no illusions.

Jesus said to the crowds, "Now, to what can I compare the people of this day? They are like children sitting in the marketplace, about whom their companions complain: 'We played the flute for you but you would not dance. We sang a funeral-song but you would not cry!'

"For John came fasting and people said: 'He is possessed.' Then the Son of Man came, he ate and drank, and people said: 'Look at this man! A glutton and drunkard, a friend of tax collectors and sinners!' Yet the outcome will prove Wisdom to be right."

Sir 48:1-4,9-11   Mt 17:10-13

Jesus predicted his suffering, to prepare his disciples for the shock. But otherwise he never talked or complained about it. When you talk about your suffering, people are usually too polite to change the subject. How boring a subject it is! People have too much suffering of their own, they don't know what to do with yours. If you said you had a leaking roof they could offer to fix it for you, but what can they do about your suffering if all you can do about it yourself is talk? And behind the talk they can often sense a plea for pity and sympathy; they sense that you are trying to make capital out of it. Instead we have to make a life out of it.

As they were coming down the mountainside, the disciples then asked Jesus, "Why do the teachers of the Law say that Elijah must come first?" And Jesus answered, "So it is: first comes Elijah to set everything as it has to be. But I tell you, Elijah has already come and they did not recognize him, but treated him as they pleased. And they will also make the Son of Man suffer."

Then the disciples understood that Jesus was referring to John the Baptist.

Sunday

The Christian is sometimes described as "one who is open to the absolute future." This is good of course—better than when the Church thought it had everything packaged already. There's a necessary openness to the future: the final description of God in the Bible is "the One who makes all things new" (Rev 21:5). Yet sometimes you wonder if we aren't being put back into the Old Testament time of waiting. There's a kind of "futurism" abroad now. Isn't there any fulfillment already? Hasn't anything taken place already in Christ?

Is 35:1-6,10

Let the wilderness and the arid land rejoice, the desert be glad and blossom. Covered with flowers, it sings and shouts with joy, adorned with the splendor of Lebanon, the magnificence of Carmel and Sharon. They, my people, see the glory of Yahweh, the majesty of our God. Give vigor to weary hands and strength to enfeebled knees. Say to those who are afraid: "Have courage, do not fear. See, your God comes, demanding justice. He is the God who rewards, the God who comes to save you." (...)

Jas 5:7-10

Be patient then, beloved, until the coming of the Lord. See how the sower waits for the precious fruits of the earth, looking forward patiently to the autumn and spring rains. You also be patient and do not lose heart, because the Lord's coming is near. Beloved, do not fight among yourselves and you will not be judged. See, the judge is already at the door. Take for yourselves, as an example of patience, the suffering of the prophets who spoke in the Lord's name.

Mt 11:2-11

When John the Baptist heard in prison about the activities of Christ, he sent a message by his disciples, asking him: "Are you the one who is to come or should we expect someone else?" Jesus answered them, "Go back and report to John what you hear and see: the blind see, the lame walk, the lepers are made clean, the deaf hear, the dead are brought back to life and good news is reaching the poor. And how fortunate is the one who does not take offense at me." As the messengers left, Jesus began to speak to the crowds about John, "When you went out to the desert, what did you expect to see? A reed swept by the wind? What did you go out to see? A man dressed in fine clothes? People who wear fine clothes live in palaces. What did you actually go out to see? A prophet? Yes, indeed, and even more than a prophet. He is the man of whom Scripture says: I send my messenger ahead of you to prepare the way before you. I tell you this: no one greater than John the Baptist has come forward among the sons of women, and yet the least in the kingdom of heaven is greater than he."

DECEMBER

Monday

13

**ADVENT
3rd Week**
St. Lucy

Num 24:2-7,15-17   Mt 21:23-27

St. Jerome (c. 340–420) wrote, "The Lord could have confuted them…by a simple answer, but He put a question to them of such skilful contrivance, that they must be condemned either by their silence or their knowledge." And St. John Chrysostom (347–407) added, "Even if He had told them, it would have profited nothing, because the darkened will cannot perceive the things that are of the light. For we ought to instruct the one who inquires; but the one who is only testing we ought to overthrow by a stroke of reasoning, and not to reveal to him the power of the mystery."

Jesus had entered the Temple and was teaching when the chief priests, the teachers of the Law and the Jewish authorities came to him and asked, "What authority have you to act like this? Who gave you authority to do all this?"

Jesus answered them, "I will also ask you a question, only one. And if you give me an answer, then I will tell you by what authority I do these things. When John began to baptize, was it a work of God, or was it merely something human?"

They reasoned out among themselves, "If we reply that it was a work of God, he will say: Why, then, did you not believe him? And if we say: The baptism of John was merely something human, beware of the people: since all hold John as a prophet." So they answered Jesus, "We do not know."

And Jesus said to them, "Neither will I tell you by what right I do these things."

Zep 3:1-2,9-13   Mt 21:28-32

Jesus went on to say, "What do you think of this? A man had two sons. He went to the first and said to him: 'Son, today go and work in my vineyard.' And the son answered: 'I don't want to.' But later he thought better of it and went. Then the father went to the second and gave him the same command. This son replied: 'I will go, sir,' but he did not go.

"Which of the two did what the father wanted?" They answered, "The first." And Jesus said to them, "Truly, I say to you: the publicans and the prostitutes are ahead of you on the way to the kingdom of heaven. For John came to show you the way of goodness but you did not believe him, yet the publicans and the prostitutes did. You were witnesses of this, but you neither repented nor believed him."

There's something worse than No. That's a pretended Yes. No goes so far that it can't live with itself anymore, and it becomes capable of turning into a real Yes. But a pretended Yes only blocks the path. A nominal believer is in a worse position than an unbeliever. When you say a real Yes you are moving towards people, towards God, towards things; you are expanding. This may sound too easy, but there is nothing easy about Yes. "I thank You God for most this amazing / day: for the leaping greenly spirits of trees / and a blue true dream of sky; and for everything / which is natural which is infinite which is yes" (E.E. Cummings)

Is 45:6-8,18,21-25   Lk 7:18-23

In the days before
microphones, preachers
had to project their
voices very great force,
and pause every few
words for the echo to
subside. It's impossible
to sound other than
dogmatic when you talk
like that. But perhaps the
more telling proclamation
of the word was quietly
in the ear of prisoners
and penitents, the lonely
and discouraged, the
overworked, the fearful
and the dying. If John
had had an opportunity
to preach again, there
would have been a
different quality, I think.
His presence would
have been much more
like that of Jesus.

The disciples of John gave him all this news. So he
called two of them and sent them to the Lord with this
message, "Are you the one we are expecting, or should
we wait for another?" These men came to Jesus and said,
"John the Baptist sent us to ask you: Are you the one we
are to expect, or should we wait for another?"

At that time Jesus healed many people of their sick-
nesses or diseases; he freed them from evil spirits and
he gave sight to the blind. Then he answered the messengers, "Go back and tell John what you have seen
and heard: the blind see again, the lame walk, lepers
are made clean, the deaf hear, the dead are raised to
life, and the poor are given good news. Now, listen: Fortunate are those who encounter me, but not for their downfall."

16 Thursday

DECEMBER

Johann Tauler (1300–1361) wrote, "St. John wrote of [John the Baptist] that he was a witness to the light.... What higher praise could we give to this Saint than to call him 'a witness to the light'? This light sheds its rays into the innermost and furthest depths of our souls, teaching us stability and strength. When we have received this witness we become immovable, like a mountain of iron, instead of being swayed to and fro like a reed.... Our Lord also said, 'He is more than a prophet,' that is, there are depths in us which reason cannot touch, where in the light we see light— that is, in an inward light, the light of grace...."

When John's messengers had gone, Jesus began speaking to the people about John. And he said, "What did you want to see when you went to the desert? A tall reed blowing in the wind? What was there to see? A man dressed in fine clothes? But people who wear fine clothes and enjoy delicate food are found in palaces. What did you go out to see? A prophet? Yes, I tell you, and more than a prophet. For John is the one foretold in Scripture in these words: I am sending my messenger ahead of you to prepare your ways. No one may be found greater than John among those born of women but, I tell you, the least in the kingdom of God is greater than he."

All the people listening to him, even the tax collectors, had acknowledged the will of God in receiving the baptism of John, whereas the Pharisees and the teachers of the Law, in not letting themselves be baptized by him, ignored the will of God.

Gen 49:2,8-10   Mt 1:1-17

One of my early memories is of my parents endlessly "tracing relations" in the long winter evenings around the fire. I ought to know the genealogy of every family for twenty miles around. No subject carries more interest for the insider, nor more boredom for the outsider. That shows that it's an intimate subject. Today's reading is a genealogy. The strangeness of the names and the people in it should put it well beyond our interest. But in the end it is about Jesus, and that makes it an intimate subject somehow.

This is the account of the genealogy of Jesus Christ, son of David, son of Abraham.

Abraham was the father of Isaac, Isaac the father of Jacob, Jacob the father of Judah and his brothers. Judah was the father of Perez and Zerah (their mother was Tamar), Perez was the father of Hezron, and Hezron of Aram. Aram was the father of Aminadab, Aminadab of Nahshon, Nahshon of Salmon. Salmon was the father of Boaz. His mother was Rahab. Boaz was the father of Obed. His mother was Ruth. Obed was the father of Jesse. Jesse was the father of David, the king. David was the father of Solomon. His mother had been Uriah's wife. Solomon was the father of Rehoboam. Then came the kings: Abijah, Asaph, Jehoshaphat, Joram, Uzziah, Jotham, Ahaz, Hezekiah, Manasseh, Amon, Josiah. Josiah was the father of Jechoniah and his brothers at the time of the deportation to Babylon. After the deportation to Babylon Jechoniah was the father of Salathiel and Salathiel of Zerubbabel. Zerubbabel was the father of Abiud, Abiud of Eliakim, and Eliakim of Azor. Azor was the father of Zadok, Zadok the father of Akim, and Akim the father of Eliud. Eliud was the father of Eleazar, Eleazar of Matthan, and Matthan of Jacob. Jacob was the father of Joseph, the husband of Mary, and from her came Jesus who is called the Christ—the Messiah.

There were then fourteen generations in all from Abraham to David, and fourteen generations from David to the deportation to Babylon, and fourteen generations from the deportation to Babylon to the birth of Christ.

18

Saturday

DECEMBER

Jer 23:5-8   Mt 1:18-25

This is how Jesus Christ was born. Mary his mother had been given to Joseph in marriage but before they lived together, she was found to be pregnant through the Holy Spirit.

Then Joseph, her husband, made plans to divorce her in all secrecy. He was an upright man, and in no way did he want to discredit her.

While he was pondering over this, an angel of the Lord appeared to him in a dream and said, "Joseph, descendant of David, do not be afraid to take Mary as your wife. She has conceived by the Holy Spirit, and now she will bear a son. You shall call him 'Jesus' for he will save his people from their sins."

All this happened in order to fulfill what the Lord had said through the prophet: The virgin will conceive and bear a son, and he will be called Emmanuel which means: God-with-us. When Joseph woke up, he did what the angel of the Lord had told him to do and he took his wife to his home.

Christmas is now upon us—the season in which we celebrate the Savior's birth. But December 25th was almost certainly not the date of his birth! That date was not fixed on till the year 440. Would it affect your faith if you heard that Jesus was born in the middle of August, for instance, or at the end of February…? Would it at least ruin your Christmas? Of course symbolically it was a wonderful choice of date: at the dead of the year when days are shortest and the sun seems to be abandoning the world, we celebrate the feast of the Unconquered Sun, the new Light, Christ, born into a despairing world. Our poor world offers him whatever it has. No problem!

Sunday

Celebrating the birth of Jesus at the winter solstice has immense symbolic meaning, however, as I mentioned yesterday; and that is why the date was chosen in the first place. The Sun is returning to us!—the surprise of Newgrange, experienced there since 3,200 B.C. But symbolically it is the surprise of the Incarnation: the Light has come into a dark world…. "The Word was made flesh, he lived among us, and we saw his glory, the glory that is his as the only Son of the Father, full of grace and truth" (Jn 1:14).

Is 7:10-14 Once again Yahweh addressed Ahaz, "Ask for a sign from Yahweh your God, let it come either from the deepest depths or from the heights of heaven." But Ahaz answered, "I will not ask, I will not put Yahweh to the test." Then Isaiah said, "Now listen, descendants of David. Have you not been satisfied trying the patience of people, that you also try the patience of my God? Therefore the Lord himself will give you a sign: The Virgin is with child and bears a son and calls his name Immanuel."

Rom 1:1-7 From Paul, a servant of Jesus Christ, an apostle called and set apart for God's Good News, the very promises he foretold through his prophets in the sacred Scriptures, regarding his Son, who was born in the flesh a descendant of David, and has been recognized as the Son of God endowed with Power, upon rising from the dead through the Holy Spirit. Through him, Jesus Christ, our Lord, and for the sake of his Name, we received grace and mission in all the nations, for them to accept the faith. All of you, the elected of Christ, are part of them, you, the beloved of God in Rome, called to be holy: May God our Father, and the Lord Jesus Christ, give you grace and peace.

Mt 1:18-24 This is how Jesus Christ was born. Mary his mother had been given to Joseph in marriage but before they lived together, she was found to be pregnant through the Holy Spirit. Then Joseph, her husband, made plans to divorce her in all secrecy. He was an upright man, and in no way did he want to discredit her. While he was pondering over this, an angel of the Lord appeared to him in a dream and said, "Joseph, descendant of David, do not be afraid to take Mary as your wife. She has conceived by the Holy Spirit, and now she will bear a son. You shall call him 'Jesus' for he will save his people from their sins." All this happened in order to fulfill what the Lord had said through the prophet: The virgin will conceive and bear a son, and he will be called Emmanuel which means: God-with-us. angel of the Lord had told him to do and he took his wife to his home. So she gave birth to a son and he had not had marital relations with her. Joseph gave him the name of Jesus.

Is 7:10-14   Lk 1:26-38

Meister Eckhart had a great gift of removing names and labels from familiar things and allowing them to be mysterious again. The soul, too, has no name. Just as no one can find a true name for God, so none can find the soul's true name, although mighty tomes have been written about this. But she is given a name according as she has a regard to her activity. In this birth God works powerfully or exerts power.... In God there is plenitude of power, therefore in his birth he produces his like. All that God is in power, truth and wisdom, he bears altogether in the soul."

In the sixth month, the angel Gabriel was sent from God to a town of Galilee called Nazareth. He was sent to a young virgin who was betrothed to a man named Joseph, of the family of David; and the virgin's name was Mary.

The angel came to her and said, 'Rejoice full of grace, the Lord is with you." Mary was troubled at these words, wondering what this greeting could mean.

But the angel said, "Do not fear, Mary, for God has looked kindly on you. You shall conceive and bear a son and you shall call him Jesus. He will be great and shall rightly be called Son of the Most High. The Lord God will give him the kingdom of David, his ancestor; he will rule over the people of Jacob forever and his reign shall have no end.

Then Mary said to the angel, "How can this be if I am a virgin?" And the angel said to her, "The Holy Spirit will come upon you and the power of the Most High will overshadow you; therefore, the holy child to be born shall be called Son of God. Even your relative Elizabeth is expecting a son in her old age, although she was unable to have a child, and she is now in her sixth month. With God nothing is impossible." Then Mary said, "I am the handmaid of the Lord, let it be done to me as you have said." And the angel left her.

ADVENT
4th Week

St. Peter Canisius

21 Tuesday

DECEMBER

Zep 3:14-18   Lk 1:39-45

A previous commentator remarked that it was a woman, Elizabeth, who gave Jesus this first public recognition; as later it was to be a woman, Mary Magdalene, who would bring first news of his resurrection. The scene is the Visitation. Two women, one young and one old, sharing the inexpressible knowledge of new life within them.... "The birth of a child is an uncontrollable glory; cat's cradle of hopes will hold no living baby. Long though it lay quietly. And when our baby stirs and struggles to be born, it compels humility: what we began is now its own" (Ann Ridler). They were the mothers of John the Baptist and Jesus. One was too old for much turmoil, the other too young. But what a revolution they harbored!

Mary then set out for a town in the Hills of Judah. She entered the house of Zechariah and greeted Elizabeth. When Elizabeth heard Mary's greeting, the baby leapt in her womb. Elizabeth was filled with holy spirit, and giving a loud cry, said, "You are most blessed among women and blessed is the fruit of your womb! How is it that the mother of my Lord comes to me? The moment your greeting sounded in my ears, the baby within me suddenly leapt for joy. Blessed are you who believed that the Lord's word would come true!"

1S 1:24-28　**Lk 1:46-56**

What have those two gentle women, Mary and Elizabeth, in common with Mao Tse-tung, one of the world's most heartless dictators? Revolution! But surely not violence? Yes, violence too; that's the most obvious thing in both revolutions. The difference is that Mao inflicted violence on hundreds of millions of people, while John the Baptist and Jesus endured violence. And countless Christians have endured it through the centuries. Strangely, this kind of revolution goes on forever, while the other burns itself out in a few generations, or even sooner. The most radical revolutionary becomes a conservative on the day after the revolution—and more than a conservative, a dictator.

And Mary said: "My soul proclaims the greatness of the Lord, my spirit exults in God my savior! He has looked upon his servant in her lowliness, and people forever will call me blessed. The Mighty One has done great things for me, Holy is his Name! From age to age his mercy extends to those who live in his presence. He has acted with power and done wonders, and scattered the proud with their plans. He has put down the mighty from their thrones and lifted up those who are downtrodden. He has filled the hungry with good things but has sent the rich away empty. He held out his hand to Israel, his servant, for he remembered his mercy, even as he promised our fathers, Abraham and his descendants forever."

Mary remained with Elizabeth about three months and then returned home.

Mal 3:1-4,23-24   Lk 1:57-66

Someone said that the statistical chances of being born a human being are about the same as the chances of a single grain of sand on the shore being picked up. Our birth in human form is a mystery that surpasses all calculations of chance. John the Baptist's birth was just a little different from others, but no different in respect of the call to life itself. The people were gripped by "a holy fear." This was not a craven fear but a deep reverence in face of the sacred. The child born in today's reading was, in Jesus' judgment, the greatest man who ever lived. I want to say something strange now: isn't everyone? If you keep your eye on one person that person is the greatest who ever lived.

When the time came for Elizabeth, she gave birth to a son. Her neighbors and relatives heard that the merciful Lord had done a wonderful thing for her and they rejoiced with her.

When on the eighth day they came to attend the circumcision of the child, they wanted to name him Zechariah after his father. But his mother said, "Not so; he shall be called John." They said to her, "No one in your family has that name"; and they asked the father by means of signs for the name he wanted to give. Zechariah asked for a writing tablet and wrote on it, "His name is John," and they were very surprised. Immediately Zechariah could speak again and his first words were in praise of God.

A holy fear came on all in the neighborhood, and throughout the Hills of Judea the people talked about these events. All who heard of it pondered in their minds and wondered, "What will this child be?" For they understood that the hand of the Lord was with him.

2S 7:1-5,8-11,16   Lk 1:67-79

Zechariah's great canticle is a song of praise. How refreshing an atmosphere praise creates! And there is no violence just behind his praise, as there often is in the Psalms: the Psalm that begins so beautifully, "Sing a new song to the Lord," says, ten lines later, "Let the praise of God be on their lips and a two-edged sword in their hand to deal out vengeance to the nations...." But in Zechariah there is none of this. There's no second side to him. He's the right one to lead us to the crib of the Prince of Peace.

Zechariah, filled with holy spirit, sang this canticle,
 "Blessed be the Lord God of Israel,
for he has come and redeemed his people.
He has raised up for us a victorious Savior
in the house of David his servant,
as he promised through his prophets of old,
salvation from our enemies
and from the hand of our foes.
He has shown mercy to our fathers
and remembered his holy covenant,
the oath he swore to Abraham, our father,
to deliver us from the enemy,
that we might serve him fearlessly
as a holy and righteous people
all the days of our lives.
And you, my child,
shall be called prophet of the Most High,
for you shall go before the Lord
to prepare the way for him
and enable his people to know of their salvation
when he comes to forgive their sins.
This is the work of the mercy of our God,
who comes from on high as a rising sun
shining on those who live in darkness
and in the shadow of death,
and guiding our feet into the way of peace."

25 Saturday

Is 52:7-10   Heb 1:1-6   Jn 1:1-18

In the beginning was the Word. And the Word was with God and the Word was God; he was in the beginning with God.

All things were made through him and without him nothing came to be. Whatever has come to be, found life in him, life which for humans was also light. Light that shines in the dark: light that darkness could not overcome. A man came, sent by God; his name was John. He came to bear witness, as a witness to introduce the Light so that all might believe through him. He was not the Light but a witness to introduce the Light.

For the Light was coming into the world, the true Light that enlightens everyone. He was already in the world and through him the world was made, the very world that did not know him. He came to his own, yet his own people did not receive him; but all who have received him he empowers to become children of God for they believe in his Name.

These are born, but without seed or carnal desire or will of man: they are born of God. And the Word was made flesh; he had his tent pitched among us, and we have seen his Glory, the Glory of the only Son coming from the Father: fullness of truth and loving-kindness.

John bore witness to him openly, saying: This is the one who comes after me, but he is already ahead of me for he was before me.

From his fullness we have all received, favor upon favor. For God had given us the Law through Moses, but Truth and Loving-kindness came through Jesus Christ. No one has ever seen God, but God-the-Only-Son made him known: the one who is in and with the Father.

My friends' little daughter said to me, "You're the only priest we know by heart." I walked a little above the ground for the rest of the day! Children are poets, and it reminded me of a poem by Alice Meynell. The connection is in the last line. "Given, not lent, / And not withdrawn—once sent, / This Infant of mankind, this One, / Is still the little welcome Son. / New every year, / New born and newly dear, / He comes with tidings and a song, / The ages long, the ages long; / Even as the cold / Keen winter grows not old, / As childhood is so fresh, foreseen, / And spring in the familiar green. / Sudden as sweet / Come the unexpected feet. / All joy is young, and new all art, / And He, too, whom we have by heart."

Sunday

François Mauriac is back to us for a Christmas visit. "The open door through which, on the paternal side, a torrent of heredities submerges us, opens for this child upon infinite Being: upon the Father. From this source he inherits an ocean of divinity while we sinners reap the hidden passions of the dead of our race: a sinister torchlight procession in which each man leaves after him the torches that will consume his descendants and whose flames will end by setting fire to a world vowed to murder and to abominable vices."

HOLY FAMILY 26

Sir 3:2-6,12-14

For the Lord established that children should respect their father; he confirmed the right of the mother over her sons. Whoever honors his father atones for his sins; he who gives glory to his mother prepares a treasure for himself. Whoever honors his father will receive joy from his own children and will be heard when he prays. Whoever glorifies his father will have a long life. Whoever obeys the Lord gives comfort to his mother. My son, take care of your father in his old age, do not cause him sorrow as long as he lives. Even if he has lost his mind, have patience; do not be disrespectful to him while you are in full health. For kindness done to one's father will never be forgotten, it will serve as reparation for your sins.

Col 3:12-21

Clothe yourselves, then, as is fitting for God's chosen people, holy and beloved of him. Put on compassion, kindness, humility, meekness and patience to bear with one another and forgive whenever there is any occasion to do so. As the Lord has forgiven you, forgive one another. Above all, clothe yourselves with love which binds everything together in perfect harmony. May the peace of Christ overflow in your hearts (...)

Mt 2:13-15,19-23

After the wise men had left, an angel of the Lord appeared in a dream to Joseph and said, "Get up, take the child and his mother and flee to Egypt, and stay there until I tell you for Herod will soon be looking for the child in order to kill him." Joseph got up, took the child and his mother, and left that night for Egypt, where he stayed until the death of Herod. In this way, what the Lord had said through the prophet was fulfilled: I called my son out of Egypt. After Herod's death, an angel of the Lord appeared in a dream to Joseph and said, "Get up, take the child and his mother and go back to the land of Israel, because those who tried to kill the child are dead." So Joseph got up, took the child and his mother and went to the land of Israel. But when Joseph heard that Archilaus had succeeded his father Herod as king of Judea, he was afraid to go there. He was given further instructions in a dream, and went to the region of Galilee. There he settled in a town called Nazareth. In this way what was said by the prophets was fulfilled: He shall be called a Nazorean.

In art St. John is represented by an eagle, because no one soared so near heaven as he did. Still, he had his feet on the ground too. It was he who showed us, rather than the institution of the Eucharist, Jesus washing the disciples' feet at the Last Supper and saying (equivalently), "Do this in memory of me." The most down-to-earth service of one another, it seems, is like another Eucharist—certainly a communion. As Eckhart put it, "Heaven can only work in the ground of the earth." The prologue to that gospel begins with the language of sublimity, but soon we hear the heart-swelling words, "The Word was made flesh and lived among us, and we saw his glory...."

On the first day of the week, Mary of Magdala ran to Peter and the other disciple whom Jesus loved. And she said to them, "They have taken the Lord out of the tomb and we don't know where they have laid him."

Peter then set out with the other disciple to go to the tomb. They ran together but the other disciple outran Peter and reached the tomb first. He bent down and saw the linen cloths lying flat, but he did not enter.

Then Simon Peter came following him and entered the tomb; he, too, saw the linen cloths lying flat. The napkin, which had been around his head was not lying flat like the other linen cloths but lay rolled up in its place. Then the other disciple who had reached the tomb first also went in; he saw and believed.

1Jn 1:5–2:2   Mt 2:13-18

This reading is a series of echoes of earlier events in Jewish history and echoes of Jewish Scriptures. Jesus is represented as re-enacting in his own life the career of Israel, for he is the new Israel. The mention of Bethlehem suggests messiahship, the mention of Ramah recalls the Babylonian exile, and the mention of Egypt recalls the Exodus. When we lose sight of the symbolic background of a passage in the Scriptures we are bound to falsify it. The New Testament is a love story, and everything in it is about Jesus—even when it appears to be about others.

After the wise men had left, an angel of the Lord appeared in a dream to Joseph and said, "Get up, take the child and his mother and flee to Egypt, and stay there until I tell you for Herod will soon be looking for the child in order to kill him."

Joseph got up, took the child and his mother, and left that night for Egypt, where he stayed until the death of Herod. In this way, what the Lord had said through the prophet was fulfilled: I called my son out of Egypt.

When Herod found out that he had been tricked by the wise men, he was furious. He gave orders to kill all the boys in Bethlehem and its neighborhood who were two years old or under. This was done in line with what he had learned from the wise men about the time when the star appeared.

In this way, what the prophet Jeremiah had said was fulfilled: A cry is heard in Ramah, wailing and loud lamentation: Rachel weeps for her children. She refuses to be comforted, for they are no more.

Wednesday 29

Today's reading shows us Mary and Joseph following this prescription of the Law. Many commentators, ancient and modern, remark how humbly they submitted to this. But it would have been unthinkable for them not to do so; nor would they have thought of it as humility. The sign of their humble status is the offering they brought. The Book of Leviticus prescribed a lamb and a pigeon or turtledove, or "if she cannot afford a lamb, she is to take two turtledoves or two young pigeons" (12:8). The offering brought by Mary and Joseph was the offering of the poor.

When the day came for the purification according to the law of Moses, they brought the baby up to Jerusalem to present him to the Lord, as it is written in the law of the Lord: Every firstborn male shall be consecrated to God. And they offered a sacrifice as ordered in the law of the Lord: a pair of turtledoves or two young pigeons.

There lived in Jerusalem at this time a very upright and devout man named Simeon; the Holy Spirit was in him. He looked forward to the time when the Lord would comfort Israel, and he had been assured by the Holy Spirit that he would not die before seeing the Messiah of the Lord. So he was led into the Temple by the Holy Spirit at the time the parents brought the child Jesus, to do for him according to the custom of the Law.

Simeon took the child in his arms and blessed God, saying,

"Now, O Lord, you can dismiss
your servant in peace,
for you have fulfilled your word
and my eyes have seen your salvation,
which you display for all the people to see.
Here is the light you will reveal to the nations
and the glory of your people Israel."

His father and mother wondered at what was said about the child. Simeon blessed them and said to Mary, his mother, "See him; he will be for the rise or fall of the multitudes of Israel. He shall stand as a sign of contradiction, while a sword will pierce your own soul. Then the secret thoughts of many may be brought to light."

30 Thursday

1Jn 2:12-17   Lk 2:36-40

There was also a prophetess named Anna, daughter of Phanuel, of the tribe of Asher. After leaving her father's home, she had been seven years with her husband, and since then she had been continually about the Temple, serving God as a widow night and day in fasting and prayer. She was now eighty-four. Coming up at that time, she gave praise to God and spoke of the child to all who looked forward to the deliverance of Jerusalem.

When the parents had fulfilled all that was required by the law of the Lord, they returned to their town, Nazareth in Galilee. There the child grew in stature and strength and was filled with wisdom: the grace of God was upon him.

Simeon and Anna are the two beautiful old people we meet every year at this time. How peaceful their presence is! We need them. They are grandparent figures. There's an extraordinary poverty of wisdom on the subject of old age now. Simeon and Anna were among those known as "the Quiet of the Land." These were people who had no big dream of victories for Israel, but who lived in quietness and prayer, waiting for God; Anna was eighty-four years old, the account says; yet her spirit seems bright and fresh. Far from being out of touch, she seems more in touch than anyone. "She came up to them at that very moment…." She lived in the Now, not in the past.

1Jn 2:18-21   Jn 1:1-18

It's the last day of the year, but the gospel reading begins "In the beginning...." Yesterday, Anna, though she was at the end of her life, was "looking forward," not back. In the life of faith it is always the beginning. There are no dead ends for a Christian; the end is always the beginning of something immense. The Scriptures are deep beyond words, and I pray that I haven't misused or trivialized them, or mangled them too badly. I feel nothing but gratitude for having been allowed to accompany you: we were like the disciples on the road to Emmaus, as he walked with us. "For all that has been, thanks; to all that will be, yes!" Happy New Year!

In the beginning was the Word. And the Word was with God and the Word was God; he was in the beginning with God.

All things were made through him and without him nothing came to be. Whatever has come to be, found life in him, life which for humans was also light. Light that shines in the dark: light that darkness could not overcome. A man came, sent by God; his name was John. He came to bear witness, as a witness to introduce the Light so that all might believe through him. He was not the Light but a witness to introduce the Light.

For the Light was coming into the world, the true Light that enlightens everyone. He was already in the world and through him the world was made, the very world that did not know him. He came to his own, yet his own people did not receive him; but all who have received him he empowers to become children of God for they believe in his Name.

These are born, but without seed or carnal desire or will of man: they are born of God. And the Word was made flesh; he had his tent pitched among us, and we have seen his Glory, the Glory of the only Son coming from the Father: fullness of truth and loving-kindness.

John bore witness to him openly, saying: This is the one who comes after me, but he is already ahead of me for he was before me.

From his fullness we have all received, favor upon favor. For God had given us the Law through Moses, but Truth and Loving-kindness came through Jesus Christ. No one has ever seen God, but God-the-Only-Son made him known: the one who is in and with the Father.

PRAYERS

SIGN OF THE CROSS

In the name of the Father,
and of the Son,
and of the Holy Spirit. Amen.

DOXOLOGY

Glory be to the Father,
and to the Son, and to the Holy Spirit;
as it was in the beginning,
is now, and ever shall be,
world without end. Amen.

THE LORD'S PRAYER

Our Father, who art in heaven,
hallowed be your name;
your Kingdom come;
your will be done on earth
as it is in heaven.
Give us this day our daily bread;
and forgive us our trespasses
as we forgive those
who trespass against us;
and lead us not into temptation,
but deliver us from evil. Amen.

HAIL MARY

Hail Mary, full of grace,
the Lord is with you.
Blessed are you among women,
and blessed is the fruit
of your womb, Jesus.
Holy Mary, Mother of God,
pray for us sinners, now,
and at the hour of our death.
Amen.

COME HOLY SPIRIT

Come, Holy Spirit,
fill the hearts of your faithful
and enkindle in them
the fire of your love.
Send forth your spirit
and they shall be created
and you will renew
the face of the earth.
Lord, by the light of the Holy Spirit,
you have taught
the hearts of your faithful.
In the same Spirit help us
to relish what is right
and always rejoice in your consolation.
We ask this through Christ our Lord.
Amen.

THE BENEDICTUS

Blessed be the Lord,
the God of Israel!
He has visited his people
and redeemed them.
He has raised up for us
a mighty savior in the house of David
his servant,
as he promised by the lips
of holy men those who were
his prophets from of old.
A savior who would free us
from our foes, from the hands
of all who hate us.
So his love for our fathers is fulfilled
and his holy covenant remembered.
He swore to Abraham our father
to grant us, that free from fear,

PRAYERS

and saved from the hands of our foes,
we might serve him in holiness
and justice all the days
of our life in his presence.
As for you, little child,
you shall be called a prophet
of God, the Most High.
You shall go ahead of the Lord
to prepare his way before him.
To make known to his people
their salvation through forgiveness
of all their sins,
the loving-kindness
of the heart of our God
who visits us
like the dawn from on high.
He will give light
to those in darkness,
those who dwell
in the shadow of death,
and guide us into the way of peace.

THE MAGNIFICAT

My soul magnifies the Lord,
and my spirit rejoices
in God, my Savior;
because he has regarded
the lowliness of his handmaid;
for behold henceforth
all ages shall call me blessed.
Because he who is mighty
has done great things for me,
and holy is his name;
and his mercy is from generation
to generation on those who fear him.
He has shown might with his arm,

he has scattered the proud
in the conceit of their heart.
He has put down the mighty
from their thrones
and has exalted the lowly.
He has filled the hungry
with good things,
and the rich he has sent away empty.
He has given help
to Israel, his servant,
mindful of his mercy
–even as he spoke to our fathers–
to Abraham and to his posterity forever.
Amen.

HAIL HOLY QUEEN

Hail Holy Queen,
Mother of mercy, hail,
our life, our sweetness, and our hope.
To you do we cry,
poor banished children of Eve;
to you do we send up our sighs,
mourning and weeping
in this vale of tears.
Turn, then, most gracious advocate,
your eyes of mercy toward us;
and after this, our exile,
show us the blessed fruit
of your womb, Jesus;
O clement, O loving,
O sweet Virgin Mary.

MEMORARE

Remember,
O most gracious Virgin Mary,
that never was it known

that anyone who fled
to your protection,
implored your help,
or sought your intercession
was left unaided.
Inspired by this confidence,
I fly to you,
O Virgin of Virgins, my Mother.
To you I come, before you I stand,
sinful and sorrowful.
O Mother of the Word Incarnate,
despise not my petitions
but in your mercy,
hear and answer me. Amen.

THE ANGELUS

V. The angel of the Lord declared
   to Mary.
R. And she conceived by the Holy Spirit.
   Hail Mary
V. Behold the handmaid of the Lord.
R. Be it done to me according
   to your Word.
   Hail Mary
V. And the Word was made flesh.
R. And dwelt among us.
   Hail Mary
V. Pray for us, holy Mother of God
R. That we may be made worthy of the
promises of Christ

Let us pray. Pour forth, we beseech you,
O Lord, your grace into our hearts, that
we to whom the Incarnation of Christ your
Son was made known by the message
of an angel, may, by his passion and cross

be brought to the glory of his resurrection, Through Christ our Lord. Amen.

QUEEN OF HEAVEN

Queen of heaven, rejoice, alleluia!
For Christ, your Son and Son of God,
has risen as he said, alleluia!
Pray to God for us, alleluia!

V. Rejoice and be glad, O Virgin Mary,
   alleluia.
R. For the Lord has truly risen, alleluia.

Let us pray. God of life, you have given
joy to the world by the resurrection of your
Son, our Lord Jesus Christ. Through the
prayers of his mother, the Virgin Mary, bring
us to the happiness of eternal life. We
ask this through Christ our Lord. Amen.

APOSTLES' CREED

I believe in God,
the Father almighty,
creator of heaven and earth.
I believe in Jesus Christ,
his only son, our Lord.
He was conceived
by the power of the Holy Spirit
and born of the Virgin Mary.
He suffered under Pontius Pilate,
was crucified, died,
and was buried.
He descended to the dead.
On the third day he rose again.
He ascended into heaven,
and is seated
at the right hand of the Father.

PRAYERS

He will come again
to judge the living and the dead.
I believe in the Holy Spirit,
the holy Catholic Church,
the communion of saints,
the forgiveness of sins,
the resurrection of the body,
and the life everlasting. Amen.

MORNING OFFERING

O Jesus,
through the Immaculate Heart of Mary,
I offer you all of my prayers,
works, joys, and
sufferings of this day
in union with the Holy Sacrifice
of the Mass throughout the world.
I offer them
for all the intentions
of your Sacred Heart:
the salvation of souls,
reparation for sin,
the reunion of all Christians.
I offer them for the intentions
of our bishops,
and of all Apostles of Prayer,
and in particular
for those recommended
by our Holy Father this month. Amen.

GRACE BEFORE MEALS

Bless us, O Lord,
and these your gifts
which we are about to receive
from your bounty,
through Christ our Lord. Amen.

GRACE AFTER MEALS

We give you thanks almighty God,
for all your gifts,
through Christ our Lord,
who live and reign,
now and forever. Amen.

ACT OF CONTRITION

My God, I am sorry for my sins
with all my heart.
In choosing to do wrong
and failing to do good,
I have sinned against you
whom I should love above all things.
I firmly intend, with your help,
to do penance,
to sin no more,
and to avoid
whatever leads me to sin.
Our Savior Jesus Christ
suffered and died for us.
In his name, my God, have mercy.

PRAYER FOR PEACE
(ST. FRANCIS OF ASSISI)

Lord, make me
an instrument of your peace.
Where there is hatred, let me sow love;
Where there is injury, pardon;
Where there is doubt, faith;
Where there is despair, hope;
Where there is darkness, light;
Where there is sadness, joy.
O Divine Master,
grant that I may not so much
seek to be consoled, as to console;

to be understood, as to understand;
to be loved, as to love.
For it is in giving
that we receive;
it is in pardoning
that we are pardoned;
and it is in dying
that we are born
to eternal life.

PRAYER FOR GENEROSITY

O Lord, teach me
to be generous.
Teach me to serve you
as you deserve;
To give and not to count the cost;
To fight and not to heed the wounds;
To toil and not to seek for rest;
To labor and not to ask for reward
Save that of knowing that I am doing
your holy will. Amen.

SOUL OF CHRIST

Soul of Christ, sanctify me.
Body of Christ, save me.
Blood of Christ, inebriate me.
Water from the side of Christ, wash me.
Passion of Christ, strengthen me.

O GOOD JESUS, HEAR ME.

Within your wounds, shelter me.
Permit me not to be
separated from you.
From the evil one protect me.
At the hour of my death
call me and bid me

Come to you,
that I may praise you
with all your saints
for ever and ever. Amen.

THE BEAUTITIDES

Fortunate are those who have the spirit
of the poor, for theirs is the kingdom of
heaven.
Fortunate are those who mourn, they
shall be comforted.
Fortunate are the gentle, they shall
possess the land.
Fortunate are those who hunger and thirst
for justice, for they shall be satisfied.
Fortunate are the merciful, for they
shall find mercy.
Fortunate are those with a pure heart,
for they shall see God.
Fortunate are those who work for peace,
they shall be called children of God.
Fortunate are those who are persecuted for the cause of justice, for theirs is
the kingdom of heaven.
Fortunate are you, when people insult
you and persecute you and speak all
kinds of evil against you because you
are my followers. Be glad and joyful,
for a great reward is kept for you in
God.

PRAYING THE ROSARY

The Holy Rosary is a Prayer recited aloud
or in silence. On the beads are prayed
the ten Hail Marys called decades. Each
decade is framed by an Our Father, and

a Doxology. While praying these prayers, we recall twenty mysteries or events in the life of Jesus, a different mystery for each decade. The Mysteries of the Rosary are as follows:

- Joyful Mysteries (Mondays and Saturdays)
  1. The Annunciation
  2. The Visitation
  3. The Birth of Our Lord
  4. The Presentation of the Child Jesus
  5. The Finding of Jesus in the Temple
- Sorrowful Mysteries (Tuesdays and Fridays)
  1. The Agony in the Garden
  2. The Scourging at the Pillar
  3. The Crowning with Thorns
  4. The Carrying of the Cross
  5. The Crucifixion and Death of Jesus
- Glorious Mysteries (Wednesdays and Sundays)
  1. The Resurrection
  2. The Ascension
  3. The Descent of the Holy Spirit
  4. The Assumption of Mary into Heaven
  5. The Crowning of Mary as Queen of Heaven and Earth
- Light Mysteries (Thursdays)
  1. The Baptism of Jesus
  2. The Wedding of Cana
  3. The Proclamation of the Kingdom of God
  4. The Transfiguration
  5. The Institution of the Eucharist

THE WAY OF THE CROSS

In the church or at home, this prayer will help you to meditate on the last moments of Jesus' life. To begin each one of the stations pray:

V. We adore Thee, O Christ, and we bless Thee.
R. Because by Thy holy cross Thou hast redeemed the world.

Then, you make a minute or two of silence meditating on the content of the station. You can end praying Our Father.

1. The Last Supper
2. Jesus in the Garden of Gethsemane
3. Jesus Before the Sanhedrin
4. Jesus Before Pontius Pilate
5. The Whipping and Crowning of Thorns
6. The Carrying of the Cross
7. Simon of Cyrene Helps Jesus Carry His Cross
8. Jesus Comforts the Women of Jerusalem
9. The Stripping and Crucifixion of Jesus
10. The Repentant Thief
11. Mary and John Before the Cross of Jesus
12. The Death of Jesus on the Cross
13. The New Sepulchre
14. The Resurrection of Jesus

PRAYING THE BIBLE IN GROUPS

First Step. We invite the Lord and his Spirit. The coordinator asks a member of the group to invoke the presence of the Lord and his Spirit. The rest of the group may complete the prayer and share their prayer alone.

Second Step. To read the text. The coordinator points our the chapter and versicles to be read. One member of the group reads the text aloud. After the reading, all observe a moment of silence.

Third Step. Abiding with the text. Let each participant say aloud a word or a sentence that is of special importance to him or her. After each participant says the word or sentence, there is a short moment of silence. Each one can repeat interiorly two or three times the words that were spoken allowing them to sink in. Once all have spoken, the whole text is read again, aloud and slowly.

Fourth Step. Silence. After a second reading of the text, the coordinator invites everybody to keep silent letting them know how long the silence will be (3 to 5 minutes). This silence prepares the participants to reflect together on the text and to pray the text.

Fifth Step. Sharing what has touched their life. Participants are invited to share spontaneously from their hearts what has touched them. This is the time to put together the words reflected upon from Scripture and the individual feelings and experiences of each participant.

Sixth Step. Praying together. The coordinator invites the group to pray. Participants respond with spontaneous prayers to God who has spoken to them through the text. The meeting may conclude with a song.

PRAYING THE BIBLE ALONE

Begin with this prayer:

Father, you created me
and put me on earth for a purpose.
Jesus, you died for me
and called me
to complete your work.
Holy Spirit, you help me
to carry out the work
for which I was created and called.
In your presence and name—
Father, Son, and Holy Spirit,
I begin my meditation.

Follow these steps:

1. Read the meditation prayerfully. (About one minute.)

2. Think about what struck you most as you read the meditation. Why this? (About four minutes.)

3. Speak to God about your thoughts. (About one minute.)

4. Listen to God's response. simply rest in God's presence with an open mind and an open heart. (About four minutes.)

5. End each meditation by praying the Lord's Prayer slowly and reverently.

Short List of Biblical Prayers that can be used at any time or according to your personal situation.

- Genesis 15:2-3. Supplication of Abraham for his son.
- Exodus 5:22-23. Moses complains to God about the situation of his People.
- Isaiah 12:1-6. Song of thanksgiving for the liberation of the People.
- Daniel 3:26-49. Prayer of the Three Youths condemned to the furnace.
- Luke 1:45-55. Song of Mary, the Magnificat, for what God has made in her and in history
- Luke 1:68-79. Zechariah's thanksgiving-ing song for what God has made for his people.
- Matthew 6:9-13. The Our Father
- John 11:41-42. Jesus' prayer of thanks-giving at Lazarus' resurrection.
- Acts 4:24-30. Communitarian prayer asking for interior fortitude to announce the Word of God

BIBLICAL PRAYERS FOR A PERSON IN DANGER OR VERY SICK

Read each supplication slowly, asking the sick person or the person in danger to repeat it, if possible, as a litany. Other supplications from the Bible can be added.

- The Lord is my light and my salvation. (Psalm 27:1)
- My soul thirsts for God, for the living God. (Psalm 42:3)
- Although I walk through the valley of the shadow of death, I fear no evil, for you are beside me. (Psalm 23:4)
- I stretch out my hands to you, and thirst for you like a parched land. (Psalm 143:6)
- To you, O Lord, I lift up my soul. (Psalm 25:1)
- My loving God will come to help me. (Psalm 59:11)
- Fill me with joy and gladness. (Psalm 51:10)
- Send forth your light and your truth; let them be my guide. (Psalm 43:3)
- Come, blessed of my Father! Take possession of the kingdom prepared for you. (Matthew 25:34)
- We will be with the Lord forever. (1 Thessalonians 4:17)
- Who shall separate us from the love of Christ? (Romans 8:35)
- We love our brothers and sisters, and with this we know that we have passed from death to life. (1 John 3:14)
- Now has salvation come, with the power and the kingdom of our God. (Revelation 12:10)
- Yes, I am coming soon. Amen. Come Lord Jesus! (Revelation 22:20)